6/95

3000 800024 41199
St. Louis Community College

WITHDRAWN

St. Louis Community College
at Meramec
Library

Wasting America's Future

The Children's Defense
Fund Report on the
Costs of Child Poverty

Beacon Press
Boston

by
Arloc Sherman

Introduction by
Marian Wright Edelman

Foreword by
Robert M. Solow

Beacon Press
25 Beacon Street
Boston, Massachusetts 02108-2892

Beacon Press Books
are published under the auspices of
the Unitarian Universalist Association of Congregations.

© 1994 by Children's Defense Fund

All rights reserved

Printed in the United States of America

99 98 97 96 95 94   8 7 6 5 4 3 2

Text design by John Kane
Typesetting by Robin Foster and Stephen Wilhite
Photos by Stephen Shames

Library of Congress Cataloging-in-Publication Data

Children's Defense Fund (U.S.)
    Wasting America's Future: The Children's Defense Fund
report on the costs of child poverty / Children's Defense Fund.
        p. cm.
    Includes bibliographical references and index.
    ISBN 0-8070-4106-8 (cloth). — ISBN: 0-8070-4107-6 (pbk.)
    1. Poor children — United States. I. Title.
HV741.C53771994
362.5'083—dc20   94-28889
                                                                CIP

About the Costs of
Child Poverty Research Project

The Children's Defense Fund began the Costs of Child Poverty Research Project in 1991, with generous support from The Prudential Foundation, in order to bring new attention to the growing but often ignored or misunderstood crisis of poverty among America's children. The project's mission is to compile the best evidence regarding the effects of poverty on children, and on the human and economic costs of these effects for the nation as a whole. To help guide our work, CDF assembled an Advisory Board composed of leading experts in economics, medicine, child psychology, business, and other fields. (See listing, next page.) Moreover, where necessary, we have performed new analyses of government data or commissioned new research by independent academic experts.

Members of the Advisory Board participated actively in the project, contributing invaluable guidance and oversight. Advisory Board members Robert Haveman and Barbara Wolfe contributed a major new quantitative analysis of child poverty and educational attainment, described in Chapter 4, and additional analyses shown in the Introduction to this report. Advisory Board Chair Robert M. Solow and Advisory Board member Donald Rubin spent additional time analyzing these data in different ways. Senior Project Advisor Martha Hill provided day-to-day guidance on demographic and economic questions. At several key junctures, when a range of methodological approaches was suggested by different members of the Advisory Board, Professor Solow obligingly chose which course we would follow.

In addition to the Advisory Board, many other individuals deserve thanks. Jim Weill, CDF's General Counsel, provided the initial inspiration for this project and a constant source of wisdom and guidance to bring it to fruition. Pediatricians Barry Zuckerman, Deborah Frank, Alan Meyers, and Suzanne Steinbach of Boston City Hospital helped fill in many details regarding poverty's medical consequences. Mary Corcoran, Terry Adams, Judith Kasper, and others conducted special quantitative analyses. Ellyn Cavanagh, Larry Brown, and many others were kind enough to share stories of individual children from low-income families. Associates of The Prudential Foundation helped to form the project at the outset. Hirokazu Yoshikawa, Gordon Fisher, Dahlia Remler, and many others read and helped improve key sections of the report. At CDF, thanks are owed to Cliff Johnson, Deborah Weinstein, Donna Jablonski, David Heffernan, Belva Finlay, MaryLee Allen, and Robin Scott for oversight and editing; to Sandra Adams and Christine Wood for entering many rounds of editorial changes and providing other assistance; to Paul Smith for extensive data analysis and other research guidance; to Martha Teitelbaum and Paula Franklin for their knowledge of medical and public health issues; and to Alice Yang for finding many of the children whose personal stories are told here. Thanks also go to Deanne Urmy, our editor at Beacon, for believing in this book. Research assistance was provided by Jodi Sandfort and by Dana Mitra, Karen Weiner, Stacey Klickstein, Traci Higgins, Laurie Summers, and Lori Leibovich. Gail Pearson volunteered her expertise as a pediatrician and an economist. Stephanie Arnold checked Chapters 2 and 3 for accuracy. Scott Blinder contributed the analysis of lead poisoning in Chapter 4. T'Wana Lucas helped with many logistical details. Anne Theisen provided priceless moral support.

Major background sources for the research in this report include *Alive and Well?*, written by Lorraine Klerman (New York: National Center for Children in Poverty, 1991); *Children in Poverty,* edited by Aletha Huston (New York: Cambridge University Press, 1991); "Double Jeopardy" by Steven Parker and others (*Pediatric Clinics of North America*, December 1989), and a number of papers and articles by Barbara Starfield, Naomi Goldstein, Vonnie McLoyd, and David R. Williams.

CDF is deeply grateful to The Prudential Foundation for its continuing interest in the well-being of children and its multi-year financial commitment to this project.

The opinions in this report are solely those of the Children's Defense Fund, as is responsibility for any research errors.

Children's Defense Fund
Costs of Child Poverty Research Project

Board of Advisors

Chairman
Robert M. Solow
Institute Professor
Department of Economics
Massachusetts Institute of Technology

J. Lawrence Aber
Co-Director
National Center for Children in Poverty

Rebecca M. Blank
Department of Economics
Northwestern University

Sheldon Danziger
Institute of Public Policy Research
University of Michigan

Ronald Ferguson
John F. Kennedy School of Government
Harvard University

Peter Gottschalk
Department of Economics
Boston College

Robert Haveman
Institute for Research on Poverty,
LaFollette Institute of Public Affairs,
and Department of Economics
University of Wisconsin, Madison

Lorraine V. Klerman
Director, Maternal and Child Health
University of Alabama, Birmingham

Sara S. McLanahan
Office of Population Research
Princeton University

Vonnie McLoyd
Center for Human Growth and
Development
University of Michigan, Ann Arbor

Donald Rubin
Chairman, Department of Statistics
Harvard University

Barbara Starfield
Director, Health Policy and Management
School of Hygiene and Public Health
Johns Hopkins University

Marta Tienda
Department of Sociology
University of Chicago

Barbara Wolfe
Institute for Research on Poverty,
Department of Preventive Medicine,
and Department of Economics
University of Wisconsin, Madison

Project Staff

Arloc Sherman
Senior Program Associate
Children's Defense Fund

Senior Project Advisor

Martha S. Hill
Institute for Social Research
University of Michigan, Ann Arbor

About CDF

The Children's Defense Fund (CDF) exists to provide a strong and effective voice for all the children of America who cannot vote, lobby, or speak for themselves. We pay particular attention to the needs of poor and minority children and those with disabilities. Our goal is to educate the nation about the needs of children and encourage preventive investment in children before they get sick, drop out of school, suffer family breakdown, or get into trouble.

CDF is a national organization with roots in communities across America. Although our main office is in Washington, D.C., we reach out to towns and cities across the country to monitor the effects of changes in national and state policies and to help people and organizations concerned with what happens to children. CDF maintains state offices in Minnesota, Ohio, and Texas, and local project offices in Marlboro County (South Carolina), the District of Columbia, Greater Cleveland, Greater Cincinnati, and New York City. CDF has developed cooperative projects with groups in many states.

CDF is a private, nonprofit organization supported by foundations, corporate grants, and individual donations.

Children's Defense Fund
25 E Street N.W.
Washington, D.C. 20001
(202) 628-8787

...Contents

Foreword   vii

Robert M. Solow

Introduction   xiii

Marian Wright Edelman

Chapter 1: Who Are Poor Children and How Poor Are They?   1

Chapter 2: What Money Buys for Children and Families   9

    Money Buys Good Food   13

    Money Buys Safe and Decent Shelter   18

    Money Buys Opportunities To Learn   23

    Money Reduces Family Stress and Conflict   29

    Money Buys a Decent Neighborhood   38

    Money Buys Health Care, Health Supplies, and Safety Devices   42

    Money Buys Healthy Recreation   46

    Money Buys Transportation, Communication, and Economic Opportunity 49

    Poverty's Effects Add Up and Interact   52

Chapter 3: Human Costs Linked to Child Poverty   59

    Health   64

    Education and Learning   78

    Other Problems Linked to Child Poverty   84

    Evidence from Randomized Experiments   93

Chapter 4: The Economic Costs of Child Poverty   97

    Child Poverty Reduces Lifetime Worker Output   101

    What We Have Left Out   113

    The Cost of *Ending* Child Poverty   116

    Comparison of Benefits and Costs of Ending Child Poverty   119

Endnotes   121

Index   149

Foreword

Robert M. Solow

This report tells us something that should, perhaps, be obvious: Allowing children to grow up in poverty can be expensive.

To some readers the details of this report may seem grim. Vast amounts of money and productive capacity (tens of billions of dollars by our best lower bound estimates) are being wasted for every year that we continue to neglect the poverty among America's children. The human costs are even worse; they are counted in young lives lost needlessly, in stunted growth and hunger, in illness, in family conflict and divorce, and in a terrible subversion of learning and opportunity.

For many years, Americans have allowed child poverty levels to remain astonishingly high — higher than for American adults; higher than for children in nations that are our competitors; higher than for the entire period of the late 1960s and 1970s, a period when we had less wealth as a nation than we do now; and far higher than one would think a rich and ethical society would tolerate. The justification, when one is offered at all, has often been that action is expensive: "We have more will than wallet." I suspect that in fact our wallets exceed our will, but in any event this concern for the drain on our resources completely misses the other side of the equation: Inaction has its costs, too.

This book is therefore cause for optimism. Now, possibly for the first time, we have evidence that we can save money by reducing children's poverty.

The evidence in this volume indicates that ending child poverty is, at the very least, highly affordable. More likely it is a gain to the economy, and to the businesses, taxpayers, and citizens within it. But that should be icing on the cake. Nobody in this age is so callous as to think of children foremost as a source of profit — at least I hope not. As an economist, I believe that good things are worth paying for, and that even if curing children's poverty were expensive in the long run, it would be hard to think of a better use in the world for money. If society cares about children, it should be willing to spend money on them.

The economic analysis here should reassure us that we may safely set aside the ledger books for a moment. By easing our fears about cost, the findings return us to the moral task; they remind us that society must choose what it wants for its children. And the findings should remind us that we can sometimes afford to be vigorous in pursuing what is right.

For many readers, the essence of this report may be found in the personal stories of children and families, many of whom endure unfair and damaging circumstances with grace. For readers of a scientific or scholarly bent, the strength of the report is the weight of the findings: not what they prove — proofs of anything are hard to come by, at least in the social sciences, and we have not broken that barrier here — but what they clarify and rule out. The report proceeds much the same way doctors go about establishing the existence and consequences of a new disease. Chapter 1 defines child poverty and shows it exists. Chapter 2 documents the existence of plausible biological and social pathways through which poverty can do lasting harm to children. Chapter 3 describes the outcomes and effects on children, and Chapter 4 offers estimates of just some of child poverty's effects on the economy.

There is always the possibility that the damage we associate with and attribute to the experience of poverty actually is caused by some other factor that also is responsible for the poverty. In that case, child poverty would be a symptom rather than an eradicable cause. Throughout Chapters 3 and 4 every reasonable test of this possibility is attempted. The consistent result is that poor children really do fare worse on average, even when they are compared with children of the same family structure, race, and parents' general level of education.

To our deepest fears that nothing works, Marian Wright Edelman and her staff continue to bring the refreshing news that many things do indeed work. Many problems have solutions: some solutions are new, others have been under-appreciated, still others have been lauded in election years and left to languish in between. CDF knows that money isn't the only thing families need; they need energetic parents, strong values, community support. Even when it comes to government policies, a fairer tax code, access to a job, or cash support isn't the only thing families need: They need health care, many need Head Start, and a few need counseling or more serious interventions. Marian and the Children's Defense Fund deserve our thanks for breaking down seemingly insurmountable problems into manageable pieces, for showing us that drastically reducing children's poverty is not a pipe dream but a practical, hardheaded, and — as this report shows — affordable possibility.

Introduction

Marian Wright Edelman

*The test of our progress is not whether we
add to the abundance of those who have
much. It is whether we provide enough to
those who have little.*

Franklin Delano Roosevelt

*If a free society cannot help the many who
are poor, it cannot save the few who are rich.*

John F. Kennedy

This book is about the ways poverty steals children's potential
and in doing so steals from all of us. It documents, for the first
time, the multiple, cumulative, and interactive toll of poverty
on children, regardless of race, family structure, or parental
educational attainment; the tens of billions of dollars it costs
our society every year we permit 14.6 million children to grow
up without the basic necessities of life; and the need to change
our assumptions that we cannot afford to eliminate child
poverty in light of the higher human and economic costs of
inaction.

Most importantly, this book challenges us to realize and act
urgently on the fact that child poverty is not an act of God but
a reflection of human political and value choices. It is inconsistent with our nation's pursuit of life, liberty, happiness, and fair
opportunity for every American.

America's dream is not just for rich and middle-class children, for children living in some states or racial groups or
types of families. And it is not just for elderly or middle-aged
adults who can vote and lobby and make campaign contribu-
tions and ensure that their suffering and needs are felt and
heard.

It is morally shameful as well as economically foolish for
our rich nation, blessed with one of the highest standards of
living in the world, to let children be the poorest group of

Americans. We are an under-developed nation when it comes to caring for our children and ensuring them the Healthy Start, the Head Start, the Fair Start, and the Safe Start the American dream envisages. I hope you find it as astonishing and unacceptable as I do that:

> • *Nearly one in every three American children will be poor for at least a year before turning 16.*
> • *One in five American children — 14.6 million — is poor.*
> • *More American children lived in poverty in 1992 than in any year since 1965, although our Gross National Product doubled during the same period.*
> • *The younger children are, the poorer they are. One in every four children under six is poor, as are 27 percent of children under three.*
> • *Nearly one in every two poor children lives in extreme poverty, in families whose incomes fall below half the federal poverty line. The average poor family with children in 1992 had a total income of $7,541 — or $5.40 per person a day, $37.80 per person a week.*

The High Cost of Poverty to Children

These statistics don't capture the minute-by-minute, hour-by-hour, day-by-day human costs poverty exacts that no child in a decent, moral nation should be asked to pay. As chapters 2 and 3 describe in excruciating detail, poverty stacks the odds against children before birth and decreases their chances of being born healthy and of normal birthweight or of surviving; it stunts their physical growth and slows their educational development; frays their family bonds and supports; and increases their chances of neglect or abuse. Poverty wears down

CHILDREN'S DEFENSE FUND

their resilience and emotional reserves; saps their spirits and sense of self; crushes their hopes; devalues their potential and aspirations; and subjects them over time to physical, mental, and emotional assault, injury, and indignity.

Poverty even kills. Low-income children are:

- *2 times more likely to die from birth defects.*
- *3 times more likely to die from all causes combined.*
- *4 times more likely to die in fires.*
- *5 times more likely to die from infectious diseases and parasites.*
- *6 times more likely to die from other diseases.*

Child poverty stalks its survivors down every avenue of their lives. It places them at greater risk of hunger, homelessness, sickness, physical or mental disability, violence, educational failure, teen parenthood, and family stress, and deprives them of positive early childhood experiences and the adolescent stimulation and creative outlets that help prepare more affluent children for school and then college and work.

The worst of it is, poverty doesn't trigger just one or two or even 10 discrete problems that can be easily isolated and addressed. Many poverty-related problems and deficits interact and combine with each other in a unique way for every child, so we cannot make real headway against the effects of poverty by tackling them one at a time.

In sum, poverty forces children to fight a many-front war simultaneously, often without the armors of stable families, adequate health care and schooling, or safe and nurturing communities. It is a miracle that the great majority of poor children stay in school, do not commit crimes, and strive to be productive citizens in a society that guarantees them a prison bed if they fail (for over $30,000 a year) but refuses to provide them a Head Start (for less than $3,800 a year) or a summer job (for less than $1,400) to help them succeed.

	Poor children younger than 18 in 1992	Percent poor
Total	14,617,000	21.9%
White	8,955,000	16.9
Non-Latino White	6,048,000	13.2
Black	4,938,000	46.6
Latino*	3,116,000	39.9
Asian/Pacific Islander	342,000	16.3
In young family (family head younger than 30)	4,355,000	42.3
In married-couple family	5,268,000	10.9
In female-headed family	8,032,000	54.3
In male-headed family	576,000	24.4
Not in a family	741,000	64.8
Central city	6,411,000	32.5
Suburb	4,568,000	14.4
Rural**	3,638,000	23.5
Northeast	2,395,000	19.6
Midwest	3,218,000	19.5
South	5,798,000	25.2
West	3,206,000	21.3
[Adults 18 to 64	18,281,000	11.7]

* The term Latino is used in this report as an alternative to the term Hispanic used by the federal government. It should be noted that aggregate Latino data presented throughout this book include persons with ancestral lines to Spain and other Spanish-speaking countries. The Census Bureau considers Hispanic (Latino) to be an ethnicity, not a race; persons of Hispanic (Latino) origin may be of any race.
** Outside metropolitan areas
Source: U.S. Census Bureau.

The High Costs of Poverty to Our Nation and Every American

If we do not care about the healthy development of other people's children because it is right or implicit in America's deepest professed values about ensuring a fair playing field for every citizen, then perhaps we will care because it is in our self-interest and our national interest to care.

With the guidance of a distinguished board of advisors chaired by Nobel Laureate economist Robert M. Solow, we conservatively estimate that future losses to the economy

Gauging the economic costs of child poverty

- Every year we tolerate the current child poverty level will cost the nation an estimated $36 billion to $177 billion in reduced future worker productivity and employment.

- Child poverty is likely responsible for tens of billions of dollars in additional education, special education, lifetime medical, and other costs that we have *not* counted here.

- One hypothetical mixture of policies (including public sector jobs combined with tax credits and direct income support and work incentive payments) to end one year of child poverty would cost taxpayers an estimated $62 billion.

- Long-term plus immediate gains to the economy are estimated at between $52 billion and $193 billion (including the elimination of costs associated with child poverty and the value of work performed through public job creation initiatives).

- The estimated bottom-line effect of ending one year of child poverty range from a net cost of $10 billion to a net gain of $131 billion.

For a detailed explanation of these data, see Chapter 4.

stemming from the effects *of just one year* of child poverty for 14.6 million children reach as high as $177 billion. Even if one ignores the costs associated with higher rates of future unemployment, poor worker health, and inadequate academic skills, the cost of child poverty still is estimated at between $36 billion and $99 billion.

These staggering annual costs of continuing child poverty for 14.6 million children do not include the hundreds of millions of dollars spent on children who repeat grades or require special education; the tens of billions of dollars in health costs projected to come from our failure to prevent long-term disabilities; and the costs of teen pregnancy and parenthood, violence, and future welfare dependency that poverty leaves in its wake.

It does not have to be this way in our nation. It is not this way in other industrialized nations. And it is not this way for millions of adult Americans.

High Child Poverty Rates Are Not Inevitable, Necessary, or Defensible

Our extraordinarily high child poverty rates are not some unavoidable attribute of modern, urbanized societies that we cannot change. They are highly unusual and represent unconscionable choices we have made and misguided priorities we have set. Other industrialized nations with fewer resources and similar economic and social problems have placed a higher priority on protecting and investing in their children. American children are twice as likely to be poor as Canadian children, 3 times as likely to be poor as British children, 4 times as likely to be poor as French children, and 7 to 13 times more likely to be poor than German, Dutch, and Swedish children. Isn't it ironic that a nation that mouths family values does so much less than its industrialized peers to protect families against poverty and its consequences?

Even within America our failure to cushion children against poverty stands out. Families with children are nearly 3 times more likely to be poor than families without children. And young families with children — those headed by someone younger than 30 — are nearly 6 times more likely to be poor than childless families overall. More than two in five children (42 percent) in young families lived in poverty in 1992.

Our child poverty rate is twice that of adults ages 18 to 64 (11.7 percent). Child poverty has grown by one-half since 1969, while the poverty rate among Americans 65 and older dropped by one-half (from 25.3 percent to 12.9 percent), due in large part to Social Security and Supplemental Security Income.

Why Does the United States Have Such High Child Poverty?

Because we cling to a number of myths, stereotypes, and false assumptions to avoid confronting our selfishness and shortsightedness and hypocrisy as a nation.

 Myth 1: Poor children are "other people's children," Black and Brown children who live in inner cities and whose parents simply are lazy or want to live on welfare.

This racial intolerance virus embedded in our American psyche overruns our conscience and moral sense and national interest. In fact:

The toll of inequality

Ever since slavery ended, the U.S. has at least partly lived up to the ideal that eveyone should have an equal opportunity to prosper. Now, heightened inequality is undermining this concept. The U.S. will continue to suffer socially if the trend continues. And it's likely to suffer economically, too.

Business Week, August 15, 1994

CHILDREN'S DEFENSE FUND

- *More White than Black children are poor.*
- *More poor children live outside central cities than in them.*
- *Rural children are slightly more likely to be poor than children overall.*
- *Poor children's families earn twice as much money from work as they receive from welfare.*
- *Most poor families that turn to welfare for help move off the rolls within two years.*

Many Americans would rather judge or punish parents than protect children, as so much of our debate on welfare reform shows. Americans have a deep belief in hard work and personal responsibility — values I share. But sometimes the correct value of self-sufficiency clouds the harsh realities faced by millions of families struggling to make ends meet without success. Although they are doing the very best they can with what they have in a changing economy, trapped in a vise between declining wages and inadequate support in crucial areas like health care, child care, housing, and education, we persist in blaming poor parents and ignoring how poverty affects their ability to meet their children's needs.

Myth 2: If these poor parents were more responsible they could provide the important things for their children.

Many of the most important things a child needs while growing up have little to do with the family budget. A child needs love and encouragement. Parents who listen, teach strong values by example, and are patient. A nurturing community that offers safe housing in safe neighborhoods, good schools, and after-school and summer enrichment. And when parents and communities fail to provide these things, children suffer.

But raising a child also takes money. Children and parents do not live by bread alone and need food for their spirits as well as their bodies. At the same time, they cannot live without bread.

Poor parents constantly are forced to make impossible budget choices about which pressing family needs to address and which to risk ignoring. Should they pay the rent if it means running out of food for their growing children before the end of the month? Should they buy winter clothes for the school-age children if it means falling behind on the rent? Is it worth it to fix the lock on the front door if it means missing another utility bill and having the heat or electricity cut off?

In these circumstances, no matter what choices parents make, their children are at risk of harm. The longer a family is forced to take these kinds of chances, the greater the likelihood the children will suffer.

And that's only part of the struggle. There is powerful evidence that the burden of poverty also makes it much harder for parents to provide the intangible nurturing that children need to grow up strong, secure, and productive.

Financial distress strikes at the very heart of families, making parents short-tempered, damaging the nurturing relationship between parents and children, and draining away energy that might otherwise be put into constructive family activities. Poverty also threatens the stability of marriages. Both poor White and poor Black couples with children break up at twice the rate of nonpoor parents, meaning that poor children — already deprived of so much — face a heightened risk of losing the security of a two-parent family.

Myth 3: Poverty is not really the problem. The problem is parents who haven't gotten themselves educated, have babies out of wedlock, and don't stay married.

The central point that emerges from all of the research on poverty's effects on children is this: When you strip everything else away, poverty matters, and matters a great deal. Family structure, parental educational attainment, race and ethnicity, and many other factors *do* affect outcomes for children. Yet study after study documents that poor children fare substantially worse than nonpoor children even *after* these effects are taken into account. For example, even among White families with two parents and a mother who finished high school, poor children are more than twice as likely not to finish high school as nonpoor children.

A large body of research that "holds constant" many other attributes of parents and families shows that poverty's effects on

Poverty matters for all types of children

Percentage of children who never finish high school, by poverty experience during childhood

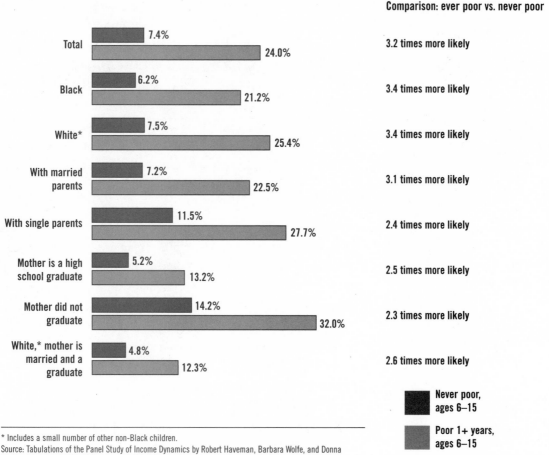

Comparison: ever poor vs. never poor

	Never poor, ages 6–15	Poor 1+ years, ages 6–15	Comparison
Total	7.4%	24.0%	3.2 times more likely
Black	6.2%	21.2%	3.4 times more likely
White*	7.5%	25.4%	3.4 times more likely
With married parents	7.2%	22.5%	3.1 times more likely
With single parents	11.5%	27.7%	2.4 times more likely
Mother is a high school graduate	5.2%	13.2%	2.5 times more likely
Mother did not graduate	14.2%	32.0%	2.3 times more likely
White,* mother is married and a graduate	4.8%	12.3%	2.6 times more likely

* Includes a small number of other non-Black children.

Source: Tabulations of the Panel Study of Income Dynamics by Robert Haveman, Barbara Wolfe, and Donna Ginther. Based on 1,705 children ages 0-6 in 1968; outcomes measured at ages 21-27.

children cannot be dismissed or explained away. *Lack of adequate income itself is central to the reason poor children suffer.*

I am aware that some skeptics, confronted with such evidence, say quietly to themselves — even if they won't say it to others — that none of this accounts for poor parents' "character flaws." But here, too, research has shown that, by and large, the outcomes for the very same poor children and the behavior of the very same poor parents do indeed change in response to rising economic fortunes. In some "real-world" experiments, when researchers took "before" and "after" looks at the same groups of families as their economic circumstances changed, they found that:

> • *The incidence of child abuse tended to increase with growing economic hardship and decline as economic prospects improved (see page 86).*
>
> • *Infant mortality rates across the nation tended to rise during periods of high joblessness and fall as employment improved (see page 65).*
>
> • *Children were better nourished, performed better in school, and finished more education when their families were more secure financially (see pages 93-96).*

Although gaps remain in research about the effects of poverty on children, the overwhelming preponderance of available evidence reinforces what we already know from personal experience and common sense: adequate family income opens doors that many poor children never know are there; an adequate income provides a shield from risks that poor children cannot escape; an adequate income offers buffers against adversity that all children desperately need but poor children rarely find. The things you and I take for granted and would never allow our own children to do without are precisely the things that all children need to put them firmly on the road to success.

CHILDREN'S DEFENSE FUND

What America Can Do To End Child Poverty

The most important step each of us can take is to believe that child poverty can and must be eliminated in our rich, democratic society. If there is anything I believe in the depths of my heart, it is that Americans have the means to prevent child deprivation with strong leadership, moral commitment, a re-ordering of national investment priorities, and a transformation of our values.

We have been preparing for and waging the wrong wars over the last three decades and still are. When 1.3 million Americans, including at least 50,000 children, lost their lives to guns at home between 1968 and 1991 in a period when 31,000 American soldiers died in wars abroad, does it make sense that we spend $767 million a day, or $23 billion a month, on our defense budget while we ignore needed investments in Head Start, child health, and nutrition? Where are the greatest threats to America's children? Are they outside our borders? Or are they within our homes and deteriorating schools and neighborhoods plagued by violence and drugs and guns and greed and family and community breakdown? How can we claim to be fighting these threats when real per-capita federal outlays on discretionary programs for education, employment, and social services (a category that includes Head Start, Job Corps, summer jobs, and child abuse prevention) have fallen by 27 percent since FY 1980? How can we maintain that we can't afford to combat child poverty when we gave away $39 billion in 1990 alone to the richest 1 percent of Americans in new tax breaks enacted since 1977? Has America reached a depth of purpose no bigger than our individual wants? Is our legacy to the world the Marlboro Man, Rambo, and an overwhelming nuclear weapons stockpile that now serves little conceivable constructive purpose? Or is there the opportunity for new vision and moral and economic leadership?

The second most important step we can take to end child poverty is to begin strengthening parents, who are the most important influences in their children's lives, and communities so that they reinforce rather than undermine parents' efforts.

Pay now or pay later

There are no easy solutions, but if we don't tackle [poverty] now, we'll sure pay later with more violent crime and with drugs, AIDS, teen pregnancies, more welfare families and more homeless.

75-year-old retired social worker. Copyright © 1993. The [Louisville, Kentucky] *Courier Journal.* Reprinted with permission

Parents need work and to be able to work without sacrificing their children's safety. Both parents should be held accountable for supporting their children through stronger child support measures. Young people, boys and girls, should be counseled not to have children until they are economically and emotionally ready to support them for a lifetime. Comprehensive efforts to prevent teen pregnancy by providing positive life options — including education and jobs — must be a top priority. All employers need to examine whether their policies help or hinder parents' ability to raise children. They need to acknowledge their self-interest in a well-prepared future work force and share a fairer proportion of responsibility for ensuring health care and child care and decent wages for their employees and jobs for young people and parents.

Children and youths need to be connected to caring adults 24 hours a day, seven days a week, 365 days a year. Religious

---

Preventing teen pregnancy and other adolescent problems

Six factors are extremely important in bolstering the motivation and capacity of teens to make wise choices about their futures and to prevent too-early pregnancy, substance abuse, crime, and violence:

• **Education and strong basic skills.** Youths who are behind a grade or have poor basic skills or poor attendance are at high risk of early parenthood. Low-income and minority teens have higher rates of school failure.

• **A range of non-academic opportunities for success.** Children and teens need to feel good about themselves. They need strong self-esteem and a clear vision of a successful and self-sufficient future. For youths who are not doing well in school, non-academic avenues for success are crucial.

• **Links to caring adults who provide positive role models, values, and support for teens.** Parents are the most important sources of guidance and nurturing for children of all ages, and our society needs to support parents in this role. In addition, a relationship with a caring adult outside the family can have an extraordinary impact on a teenager.

• **Family life education and life planning.** All teens need sexuality and parenting education as well as help in understanding the impact of present choices in planning their futures. Parents, schools, and religious institutions need to communicate more effectively with the young about sexuality.

• **Comprehensive adolescent health services.** A range of preventive, comprehensive, and convenient services are needed for teens in a range of settings.

• **A basic standard of living for all teens and their families,** including access to jobs, nutrition, housing, income, and services to meet special needs. Teens growing up in poverty face greater risks of a variety of problems. And as teens grow up and start their own families, jobs, work-related skills training, and adequate food and shelter for these young families are crucial to the healthy development of the next generation of youngsters.

CHILDREN'S DEFENSE FUND

congregations, schools, community centers, and parks and recreation departments need to offer exciting, inviting alternatives to the gangs and drug dealers who have filled voids in lonely child lives. And children need to be exposed to and socialized by adults in their family, community, and school life who teach work and service ethics by example and who speak and struggle on their behalf for a fair investment from the private sector and government at all levels.

Parents, with help from communities, employers, schools, and service providers, can make an enormous difference in the lives of their children. But they cannot do the job alone. As child development expert Urie Bronfenbrenner correctly wrote: "A child requires public policies and practices that provide opportunity, status, example, encouragement, stability, and above all, time for parenthood....And unless you have those external supports, the internal systems [in a family] can't work. They fail."

While it is fashionable to assert that government can't solve anything — and it certainly cannot and should not be asked to solve everything — government has made an extraordinary and positive difference in the life chances of millions of Americans. The only way we have ever broken the back of any major social problem in this country has been to bring individuals, families, communities, the private sector, and government together to work toward lasting change.

As a nation we did exactly that when we took deliberate steps to reduce poverty among older Americans, combining key changes in Social Security and the Supplemental Security Income (SSI) program with an explosion of community efforts to help the elderly. And we virtually eliminated child hunger in the late 1960s. When Sen. Robert Kennedy traveled with me in the Mississippi Delta in 1967, seeing homes with empty pantries and malnourished children with bloated bellies, the television cameras carried these shocking pictures into America's living rooms. Elected officials and ordinary citizens reacted by pulling together to combat childhood hunger, and we made great strides in wiping out gross malnutrition in a few short years.

An agenda for governments at all levels

Governments at all levels must be strong and active partners in the fight to end child poverty in America. Here are some immediate steps that federal, state, county, and local community leaders can take to move us toward a day when no child is forced to grow up poor:

Create private and public sector job opportunities. Government can create real jobs in the public sector, doing urgently needed work in human services, education, or the environment. Public strategies also can encourage private sector job creation through community development loan funds or narrowly targeted tax credits.

Reform the welfare system. Real reform must leave children better rather than worse off. It must reward work by allowing parents with low earnings to receive partial cash assistance payments. The state pays less, but the family's overall income is higher. To make parents competitive for better jobs, welfare reform must bolster their academic and job skills. No welfare program should drive two-parent families apart, but should offer help to both one- and two-parent families. Families that now have no option but welfare should be assured a decent standard of assistance that protects the health and development of children.

Strengthen child support. Enforcement efforts must be improved, preferably by federalizing them. States should seek authority to implement demonstrations of child support assurance guaranteeing all children in single-parent families a minimum amount of support each month.

Increase the minimum wage. The federal minimum wage is $4.25 an hour. Full-time, year-round work at this wage brings in a gross income of only 72 percent of the federal poverty level for a family of three. The minimum wage should be raised so that it is sufficient to lift a small family above poverty, and then should be adjusted regularly so that it keeps pace with inflation. If it had been increased with inflation since 1978, the minimum wage would now be $5.54 an hour.

Expand child care and Head Start assistance. Without quality child care and Head Start, parents cannot find and keep stable jobs and children will not be prepared for school.

Continue to improve the Earned Income Credit. Now virtually always paid on an annual basis, the Earned Income Credit should be distributed to low-wage workers through advance payments made regularly throughout the year to be available to meet day-to-day expenses.

Replace the current personal exemption for children with a fairer refundable tax credit. The refundable credit would be available to every family with children in America, but would offer more assistance than under current tax laws to low- and moderate-income families.

Prevent teen pregnancy. Aggressive new efforts to prevent pregnancy and too-early childbearing are desperately needed, emphasizing efforts that encourage responsible behavior while building opportunities and supports for teens (see box, page xxvi).

Ensure adequate housing for poor families with children. In even the lowest cost state, fair market rents take more than 40 percent of a full-time minimum wage income. In most states, the lowest fair market rent consumes more than half of minimum wage earnings. Subsidies that reduce the percentage of income families must spend on housing would prevent homelessness and ease economic pressures on low-wage families.

Mount strong parenting education, family support, and family preservation initiatives. Such programs, if implemented effectively, can help struggling parents raise and nurture their children in their own homes, avoiding unnecessary separation of children from their families.

Establish after-school and summer programs. Children in every community need effective programs that focus on academic improvement, cultural enrichment, and recreation.

Provide and coordinate emergency services for poor families. Soup kitchens, housing shelters, and assistance in finding permanent housing, employment, or essential social services can make an enormous difference for families in crisis.

That same kind of pulling together is the means by which we can eliminate child poverty in the 1990s.

All that we have learned about poverty's effect on children leads to one inescapable conclusion: it is essential to our nation's moral health and economic future that we eliminate child poverty. Ending child poverty will not be cheap. But I believe poverty is a lot more expensive in the long run.

The United States must finally become a developed nation in the care and protection of our children. Our high rates of child poverty, with all the related health, education, and social costs you will read about in the following chapters, threaten not only our national economic security and ability to compete, but also make a mockery of our pretension to be a moral, democratic, family-oriented society worthy of emulation by others.

A great nation faces up to its shortcomings and acts to remedy them. American history is full of examples of our doing that. We ended the evil of slavery, outlawed child labor, created Social Security and Medicare to give older Americans a measure of security, guaranteed voting rights for women and African Americans and ended legal racial segregation.

Now our task and opportunity is to save our children, families, communities, and nation by ending child poverty. Let us keep our eyes on what children need to grow up healthy and productive, and not allow ourselves to be sidetracked by ever-shifting political winds or be deterred by the endless stream of excuses attempting to justify national indifference and neglect to children who are our growing edge. It will cost money to end child poverty, but I know without a doubt that individually and collectively we will be richer for having done so. The great undertaking of saving America's children will save America's soul and our future.

Marian Wright Edelman

Marian Wright Edelman
President, Children's Defense Fund

Chapter 1

Who Are Poor Children and How Poor Are They?

Imagine that you support yourself and two children on a yearly income of $12,000. Each month you pay $541 for rent and utilities — an amount that was fairly typical for a modest two-bedroom apartment in the United States in 1992[1] — and you spend $340 on food,[2] or about $1.24 per family member per meal. After paying for these necessities you have $119 left. To keep your job, you also must spend $175 each month on child care and $40 per month for bus fare.[3] If you get food stamps, they save you about $150 on food, leaving you a total of $54 per month for everything else. This $54 must cover all clothes, repairs for broken appliances, cleaning supplies, medical checkups, braces, prescription medicines, school supplies and school fees, a children's toy or book, entertainment, furniture, and even the newspaper and telephone you need to look for a better job. Every time you pay a bill, you think about something important your family must do without. Every day you face impossible choices about cutting back on food, housing quality, and your children's other needs.

What is remarkable about your all-too-common situation is that by government standards your yearly income is *several hundred dollars above* the 1992 poverty line; you are not, in the eyes of the federal government, officially poor.

The government has an official definition of poverty, which the Census Bureau uses for tallying the number of poor Americans every year. These poverty thresholds take into account total family income, family size, and an adjustment each year for inflation in consumer prices. According to the latest poverty thresholds, families with less than the following amounts of annual cash income in 1992[4] were considered poor:

One person (not in a family)	$ 7,143
Family of two people	9,137
Family of three people	11,186
Family of four people	14,335
Family of five people	16,952

Poor families' incomes are usually far below these thresholds — an average of $6,289 below it in 1992. For example, only

One poor family

Consider the case of Cheryl, who lives in Kensington with her 5-year-old daughter. Their rent for a tiny four-room house is $400 a month — $116 more than the princely $316 a month they receive from AFDC. Cheryl cut a deal with the landlord to pay him $300 and for her [to] do chores to make up the difference. The remaining $16 goes to whichever utility is about to be cut off.... As for other necessities — such as clothes — her daughter never has worn anything new: all hand-me-downs, including the shoes she's wearing now, which are two sizes too big.

Editorial, "Hope and dignity on $316 a month," *Philadelphia Daily News*, December 6, 1993

one in six among poor children's families had incomes within even $2,000 of the poverty line. More than half of all poor families with children have incomes that are at least $5,700 below the poverty line. Given how meager these annual incomes are, the many consequences of child poverty described in this book become even easier to understand.

The official poverty definition is low by almost anyone's standard. When the Gallup polling organization asked Americans where they would draw the poverty line for a family of four, the average response was 24 percent higher than the government's poverty line — meaning that Americans believe a family of four would have needed more than an additional $3,000 (in 1992 dollars) in order not to be poor. In Idaho, a special commission established by state officials tallied up a minimal budget item by item. The commission found the bare minimum needed to get by, even in low-cost Idaho, was 17 percent higher than the federal poverty line.[5] A similar commission in New Hampshire concluded in 1991 that a four-person family needed $17,940 a year to get by — 29 percent more than the 1991 poverty line.[6]

Even by the government's low official standard, however, the number of American children whose families have such inadequate incomes is staggering.

More than 14 million children are living in poverty. In 1992 more than one out of every five American children younger than 18 (21.9 percent) lived in a family whose income was below the poverty line.[7] Among children younger than six, one in four (25.7 percent) lived in poverty, according to the latest Census Bureau figures.[8] These rates are nearly double those for adults ages 18 to 64 (11.7 percent in 1992). The number of poor children younger than 18 has increased by 5 million (from 9.6 million to 14.6 million since 1973), while the poverty rate of children has increased by one-half (from 14.4 to 21.9 percent).

Nearly one out of every three American children (32 percent) experiences at least one year of official poverty before turning 16.[9]

Children are falling deeper and deeper into poverty. There are disturbing signs that poor children are falling even further below the poverty line than before. Nearly one in two poor children (46 percent) lives in extreme poverty, in families with incomes below one-half of the poverty line. This proportion has risen steadily — from 31 percent in 1975 (the first year for which data on extreme poverty are available) to its present record-high level.

Poor children do not fit stereotypes. Although past and continuing racial discrimination in employment, housing, and education contribute to making Black and Latino children more likely to be poor than non-Latino White children — Black and Latino child poverty rates are about 3 times those of non-Latino White children — the *number* of poor non-Latino White children (6.0 million) is still considerably larger than the *number* of poor Black children (4.9 million) or poor Latino children (3.1 million).

Contrary to stereotypes, more poor children live outside cities — in suburban areas and nonmetropolitan smaller cities and rural areas — than in cities. Also, not all poor families are on welfare or out of work. Poor children's families receive about twice as much income from work as from welfare, and about two out of three poor families with children work at least part-time or part-year. Families in poverty no longer tend to be large families; the average poor family with children contains an average of only 2.2 children (only slightly larger than the average of 1.9 children in all families).

Reasons for the rise in child poverty. One major reason for the rise in child poverty in recent years is the failure of hourly wages to keep pace with inflation, particularly for young workers and those with less than a college education. A second major reason is the rising number of families headed by a single parent, usually the mother; mother-only families are at high risk of poverty due to the absence of a second adult earner, the historically lower earning power of women, and the failure of absent parents to provide financial support or of state child

---

Doing without 'the extras'

Sandy Wells told a *Time* magazine reporter in 1990 about how her family of five survives on her husband's $5.68 an hour job making respirators in a local factory. Almost half his take-home pay is spent renting the trailer they live in and the lot at the trailer park. With the help of food stamps, they have meals. But they do without the extras — like the 50-cents-a-meeting fee they couldn't pay to keep her daughter in the Brownies, the $20 a month they could not afford for a telephone, and the $1.50 they can't afford for skate rental to send the children on class skating trips.

"They know the value of money, my kids do," she told the reporter. "They get money, they don't spend it on candy or toys. They say, 'Mom, I want to buy shoes for school.'"

support enforcement agencies to ensure that payments are made. (However, the poverty caused by marital changes appears to be more than balanced by other changes in family characteristics that reduced poverty. These include a substantial decline in women's fertility and a large increase in the number of mothers who have completed a high school education.) A third reason for high and rising child poverty rates, and in particular for the greater depth of children's poverty, is a decline in the value of government assistance for poor families with children. The inflation-adjusted value of Aid to Families with Dependent Children (AFDC) plus food stamps declined by 26 percent between 1972 and 1992.[10] By comparison with other nations, the United States lifts a far smaller proportion of low-income families with children out of poverty. The relative importance of these three causes of rising child poverty has been described in other research reports.[11]

Why is the poverty line so low? One problem is that the poverty line originally was designed around the cost of a minimal diet (called the Economy Food Plan) that was unrealistically low from the start. The poverty line was set at 3 times the cost of the Economy Food Plan, to ensure that nonpoor families had enough income to purchase food and other items. Although families that bought the foods listed in the Economy Food Plan were supposed to get adequate amounts of most nutrients, even the U.S. Department of Agriculture (USDA), which designed the plan, warned at the time that it was meant only for "temporary or emergency use when funds are low."[12] (Later, USDA stressed that "the cost of this plan is not a reasonable measure of basic money needs for a good diet," and suggested that states designing assistance programs for families consider a food plan that cost "about 25 percent more than the Economy Plan."[13])

A second problem is that the poverty definition is based on outdated family spending and homemaking patterns from 1955. The Thrifty Food Plan (the successor to the Economy Food Plan) still assumes families will bake daily and cook all their food from scratch, never buy fast food or eat out, use dried beans and no canned food, be experts in nutrition, and

"Poor" and "low income"

In this report, we use the federal government's official poverty definition whenever possible. Families and children who fall within this definition are considered "poor." However, many useful studies and sources of information about children do not adhere to the federal definition. Instead, they may refer to children from families below other cutoffs (such as $10,000 a year) or families below some multiple of the poverty line. To describe these children we frequently use the looser term "low income."

Is the official poverty definition flawed?

The official poverty definition used by the Census Bureau is widely accepted by demographers, policymakers, and others as a useful measure of the economic status of America's children and families. Although a number of legitimate objections to the official poverty definition have been raised, there is little reason to doubt the basic message of the Census data: child poverty rates are high and rising.

Some of the legitimate objections to the official poverty definition are that it does not consider geographic variations in the cost of living; nor does it account for the value of food stamps or housing assistance ("in-kind" help) received by families, for the impact of federal taxes or tax refunds, or for incomes lost due to high medical bills, child care, or other expenses. It only considers annual income, not savings or assets. The poverty definition does not account for changing notions of what Americans need for a decent standard of living, or for changes in expenditure patterns since the 1950s.

Yet reasonable revisions to the poverty definition probably would not reduce the child poverty rate dramatically, if at all, or alter the basic finding that the child poverty rate has been much higher in the 1980s and early 1990s than it ever was in the 1970s. (For example, estimates that take into account the value of housing and food assistance benefits find that the proportion of children living in poverty are almost as high as under the official definition — about one in five in both cases — while the number of children below this experimental poverty line rises even faster since 1979 than under the official definition, presumably because declines in the value of housing assistance have contributed to the financial strains on families.) In fact, revising the poverty definition in a balanced way to address the full range of objections could result in many more children being counted as poor than are counted now.

Recently there have been scattered efforts to dismiss the extent or depth of poverty by attacking the definition, but those efforts do not stand up to scrutiny. For example, one conservative "think tank" claims that "The Census Bureau...omits all government welfare benefits poor families receive in counting income," and that "the missing funds amounted to $11,888 for every 'poor' household." In fact, much of this $11,888 in "missing funds" never is received by poor families at all, but rather includes the government's entire budget of many billions of dollars for programs such as Pell Grants (which serve many nonpoor students from families with modest incomes, as well as students from families below the poverty line) or reduced-price school lunches (which serve only nonpoor students) as well as Medicaid spending for individuals in nursing homes and other institutions (whom the Census Bureau for technical reasons omits entirely from its tally of the poor). These allegations of "missing funds" also count items that normally would not be considered "welfare benefits" — including such public services as teacher salaries for Head Start or compensatory education in the public schools, as well as the salaries of government administrators in programs such as Medicaid. The attacks on the poverty definition deceptively imply these are "welfare benefits poor families receive," while in fact such spending does nothing to help poor families pay their bills or purchase food for their children.

In short, while the official definition of poverty used by the Census Bureau is not perfect, it appears to be the best available indicator of what children and families need to get by. Moreover, it provides a reliable measure of changes in child and family poverty over short spans of time, such as decades.

**Signs of growing strains
on students**

[Eighth-grade dean of students Larry] Crain said students seem to bring more emotional and physical baggage to school these days. He sees regular signs of poor nutrition in their lank hair and reluctance to miss free meals at school.

"If a kid is going to be sent home sick or for discipline, the kid will almost always say, 'Can I eat lunch first?' That says something to me," he said.

Copyright © 1993. The [Louisville, Kentucky] *Courier-Journal.* Reprinted with permission

have a working refrigerator, freezer, and stove, and ample shelf space free from rodents and roaches. More importantly, no adjustments have been made for changes since 1955 in spending patterns for nonfood items — including the increase in such costly new necessities as child care for working mothers and heightened expectations that employees and job applicants should own an extensive store-bought wardrobe, have a car, and be reachable by telephone. All of these changes increase the amount of money families need to "get by." Updating the official poverty line with more up-to-date spending patterns would raise the poverty line by as much as two-thirds (to 1.68 times the value of the current official line).[14] Updating the poverty line would be consistent with the views of its original users, who stated that it should be revised periodically to account for changes in specific spending patterns and general standard of living.[15]

Chapter 2

What Money Buys for Children and Families

In this prosperous nation where so much is taken for granted, we sometimes forget just why a secure family income matters to children — what money buys to allow the typical American child to grow and develop, and what children in families with too little money must live without.

For most American children, the income their parents receive brings good food. Warm clothing. Safe shelter. A children's book and a quiet lighted room where they can learn to read it. Milk or juice or safe water to drink when they're thirsty. A functioning car that carries them, buckled into a safety seat if they're very young, to a dependable child care center or a doctor's office, or to a dance lesson or a sports practice if they're older.

Such children are sheltered from hunger. They do not live with falling plaster and rats in their bedrooms or their cribs, in small apartments crowded by people saving on rent. They do not skip breakfast from necessity or shirk English class because they cannot afford new notebooks. They do not fall hopelessly behind in high school for lack of new eyeglasses to see the blackboard or quit in order to earn a few extra dollars for their families. They do not give up on ever having careers because they see no hope of going to college.

For children who live in poverty many doors are closed, many horizons narrowed and many prospects dimmed. Although poor children can and often do succeed despite their poverty, researchers from a wide range of disciplines — including psychology, sociology, economics, and medicine — have documented a host of ways in which basic economic security helps children and poverty hurts them. Taken as a whole, the research shows that poverty leaves its mark in almost every part of a child's life. This chapter describes some of these "pathways" and mechanisms by which poverty causes its damage. Chapter 3 then provides a composite picture of the final results, or "outcomes," for children that are brought about by poverty's destructive force.

What are the most important things money buys? The answer is not clear. For some children, the answer may be bet-

Examples of "pathways" from poverty to adverse child outcomes

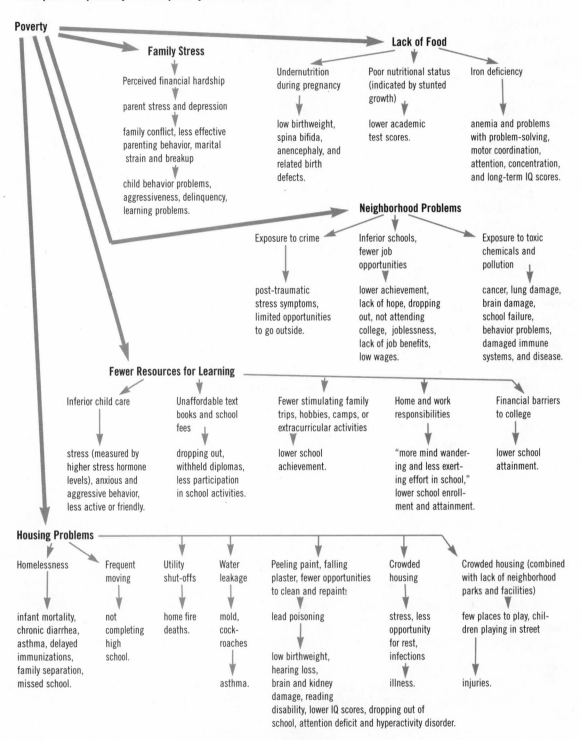

Poverty

Family Stress

Perceived financial hardship

parent stress and depression

family conflict, less effective parenting behavior, marital strain and breakup

child behavior problems, aggressiveness, delinquency, learning problems.

Lack of Food

Undernutrition during pregnancy

low birthweight, spina bifida, anencephaly, and related birth defects.

Poor nutritional status (indicated by stunted growth)

lower academic test scores.

Iron deficiency

anemia and problems with problem-solving, motor coordination, attention, concentration, and long-term IQ scores.

Neighborhood Problems

Exposure to crime

post-traumatic stress symptoms, limited opportunities to go outside.

Inferior schools, fewer job opportunities

lower achievement, lack of hope, dropping out, not attending college, joblessness, lack of job benefits, low wages.

Exposure to toxic chemicals and pollution

cancer, lung damage, brain damage, school failure, behavior problems, damaged immune systems, and disease.

Fewer Resources for Learning

Inferior child care

stress (measured by higher stress hormone levels), anxious and aggressive behavior, less active or friendly.

Unaffordable text books and school fees

dropping out, withheld diplomas, less participation in school activities.

Fewer stimulating family trips, hobbies, camps, or extracurricular activities

lower school achievement.

Home and work responsibilities

"more mind wandering and less exerting effort in school," lower school enrollment and attainment.

Financial barriers to college

lower school attainment.

Housing Problems

Homelessness

infant mortality, chronic diarrhea, asthma, delayed immunizations, family separation, missed school.

Frequent moving

not completing high school.

Utility shut-offs

home fire deaths.

Water leakage

mold, cock-roaches

asthma.

Peeling paint, falling plaster, fewer opportunities to clean and repaint

lead poisoning

low birthweight, hearing loss, brain and kidney damage, reading disability, lower IQ scores, dropping out of school, attention deficit and hyperactivity disorder.

Crowded housing

stress, less opportunity for rest, infections

illness.

Crowded housing (combined with lack of neighborhood parks and facilities)

few places to play, children playing in street

injuries.

ter nutrition and greater access to good quality child care and health care during their crucial early years of development. For many others, it may lie in the combination of decent, stable housing and a safe neighborhood that offers recreational opportunities and good schools. For older adolescents, the chance to stay in school rather than work to support the family may be critical. Yet in the most basic sense, adequate income simply may let parents focus more of their time and energies on parenting rather than on a constant struggle for survival.

In fact, searching for the most important things that money buys — and thereby attempting to identify the biggest "pathways" leading from inadequate income to bad outcomes for children — may cause us to miss a central fact about poverty. Poverty may affect children so profoundly because its consequences reach in so many directions simultaneously. Some consequences are large and immediately apparent, others small or slow to materialize. Over time, however, all of them add up and interact, compounding the problems of poor children in ways that we only are beginning to understand. It may be this cascade of countless small and large problems that makes poverty so dangerous to children.

Rather than examining all of the factors that shape children's vulnerabilities and resilience as other studies have done,[1] the discussion that follows summarizes current research on the role of poverty itself. The diverse array of "pathways" presented here shows how difficult it is to respond to the symptoms of child poverty one by one and how important it is to find direct ways of reducing tragically high and persistent rates of child poverty in America.

Money Buys Good Food

Poverty threatens good nutrition. Although poor American households appear to buy better foods than other Americans — they get more nutritional value out of each dollar they spend on food than do the nonpoor[2] and spend less on alcohol[3] — pro-

'Mom...I'm still hungry'

In 1983 Mary Tamper's middle-income world came tumbling down when her husband, William, died of leukemia, leaving Mary struggling to support her young son, Justin, on a meager salary from her job as a teacher's aide.

In the following months, Mary was sick frequently. In addition, she found out she was pregnant with twins. One of the twins died in the womb, a result of the strains on Mary, according to her doctors. The other contracted bacterial meningitis soon after birth. The medical bills for Mary's and the baby's illnesses and food and housing expenses soon depleted Mary and William's savings.

Desperate, Mary turned to public safety net programs to supplement her small earnings. She was approved for WIC (the federal Special Supplemental Food Program for Women, Infants, and Children), $770 a month in Social Security survivors' benefits, and a tiny $11 monthly food stamp allowance. But she was denied welfare and Medicaid because her income, low as it was, put her above the eligibility threshold. By early 1986, Mary's family was living on the edge, stretching to make ends meet on $165 a month after paying the rent.

"There were times when money ran short and we had no food," says Mary. WIC helped, but was not enough. "There were...times when my son would say, 'Mom, I know you just fed me, but I'm still hungry.' That hurt me more than any knife or sword could because there was no food in the cupboard to feed him."

By 1990 there was a little more money to go around. The family's survivors' benefit had been raised to about $900 a month, and its rent burden was lower, thanks to a government housing subsidy. Still, Mary and the boys are nowhere near having financial security. Looking back, Mary says, "Has hunger hurt my boys? Yes." Justin, the older son, is slower to learn in school and not as easy-going as most other children — a result, Mary feels, of inadequate nutrition and the strains of growing up poor.

From Tamper's testimony before the U.S. Senate Committee on the Budget, February 1990

viding adequate nutrition on a below-poverty budget is, almost by definition, difficult or impossible. The poverty line is built around a food budget that the federal government acknowledges is not appropriate for long-term use; moreover, poor children's families must make do with incomes not at this poverty line but usually far below it, as Chapter 1 describes.[4] Not surprisingly, low-income children are less likely than affluent children (those above 3 times the poverty line) to receive the recommended dietary allowance (RDA) of 12 out of 16 nutrients, according to a federal survey of one- to five-year-olds.[5] Poor children's nutrition problems may cause lasting damage to their health and learning.

Iron deficiency. Serious shortfalls in any one nutrient can have lasting effects on a child's growth and development. An example is iron deficiency. Poor young children were more than 3 times as likely to have low iron levels in their blood, according

to a nationwide survey taken from 1976 to 1980.[6] More recently, 28 percent of the mostly poor children seen at a Boston,
Massachusetts, clinic in 1989-1990 were iron deficient.[7] Iron
deficiency causes anemia, which interferes with the ability of
the red blood cells to carry enough oxygen from the lungs to
the body, and in severe cases can affect brain chemistry. (See
Chapter 3 for anemia rates and trends.) Low iron, with or
without anemia, has been shown to impair children's problem-
solving, motor coordination, attention, concentration, and long-
term IQ scores.[8]

Hunger. Hunger afflicted one-third of poor children (and no
children above 3 times the poverty level), according to a 1989
study in Pontiac, Michigan.[9] The Food Research and Action
Center, which sponsored the study, reported equally high or
higher rates of hunger among poor children in six other U.S.
cities and rural areas as well.[10] Hungry children were reported
by their parents to be between 2 and 11 times more likely to
experience fatigue, concentration problems, dizziness, irritability, frequent headaches and ear infections, unwanted
weight loss, and frequent colds.[11]

Stunted growth. Poor children are 2 to 3 times more likely to
have stunted growth (unusually low height for the child's age),
as Chapter 3 explains. The higher levels of stunting found in
poor children are indicators of poor nutritional status.

Poor nutritional status, in turn, causes learning problems.
Stunted children have been found to score lower than other
children on several tests of academic ability; these disadvantages remain even when researchers hold constant a long list
of other factors (including characteristics of the mother such as
marital status, academic test scores, formal education, smoking and drinking alcohol, and age at first birth; the child's race
and health and size at birth; and long-term family income).[12]

Clinical malnutrition and failure to thrive. Although starvation
and clinical malnutrition of the type seen in developing nations

are considered rare in the United States, doctors at one clinic in Boston report that they see malnourished children at a rate of two or three new cases every week.[13]

Undernutrition at younger ages contributes to "failure to thrive"[14] — a serious syndrome associated with "lasting deficits in growth, cognition, and socioemotional functioning"[15] and accounting for 1 to 5 percent of all hospitalizations of young children in the United States.[16] Poverty can lead directly to failure to thrive simply by making adequate food unaffordable. Frequently, however, poverty also contributes in other ways: by creating anxiety in the child or a distracting environment, or by triggering health problems, which in turn make it difficult for children to eat. According to doctors, "Poverty contributes to inadequate food intake...by increasing crowding, with its attendant disorganization and distractions; by limiting access to quality day care; and by increasing health risks such as low birthweight, lead toxicity, and reactive airway disease."[17] Parental stress and anxiety,[18] family conflict,[19] or, in a minority of cases, intentional maltreatment[20] also can explain why young children do not eat (links between family stress, conflict, or abuse and child poverty are described later in this chapter). Failure to thrive has been linked to "acute and long-term nutritional and psychological deficits that can seriously threaten children's physical health and psychological development."[21]

Moderate undernutrition. Undernutrition in the United States is frequently subtle. Rather than causing visible starvation in very young children, for example, it may quietly weaken their resistance to disease and make them sluggish or distracted at a time when they should be learning how to interact with the world around them. According to nutritionist Ernesto Pollitt:

> *Continuous infection and low energy intake may have systemic effects affecting psychological domains such as motivation or emotionality. This, in turn, could shape critical*

developmental processes such as parent-child interaction, attachment, or play behavior.[22]

In the short term, such subtle malnutrition can lead to a dynamic of limited communication between babies and their parents and interfere with young children learning how to observe the world and play well with other children, Pollitt and others observe. Longer term consequences may include learning problems and poor adaption to school.

Missed meals. Even relatively mild or brief lapses in good nutrition resulting from poverty may interfere with children's schooling. Tests show that merely missing breakfast may reduce children's attention[23] and ability to solve problems accurately (although it may sharpen short-term memory).[24] When an academic subject (such as math) is taught by building each lesson on top of the previous one, a child who fails to learn even a modest number of important lessons because of missed meals might find it difficult or impossible to catch up.

Undernutrition during pregnancy. Poor nutrition among low-income pregnant women has been implicated in low birth-weight[25] and other problems at birth. Poverty-related low birthweight has been identified as one statistically significant way in which poverty contributes to infant mortality.[26]

Specific types of maternal undernutrition are known to contribute to infant death or grave disability. For example, not getting enough folic acid during pregnancy causes spina bifida, anencephaly (being born with part of the brain missing), and related birth defects.[27] Low-income mothers are 22 percent more likely to receive less than half of the recommended daily allowance of folic acid.[28] One recommended source of folic acid is dark-green vegetables[29] such as lettuce and broccoli. Yet women with low incomes eat less of these vegetables,[30] probably in part because of their relatively high cost.

Money Buys Safe and Decent Shelter

Poverty limits a family's ability to pay for housing and utilities, with consequences for a child's health and learning.

Homelessness. At the harshest extreme of poverty, an estimated 100,000 American children are homeless each day, according to the National Academy of Sciences.[31] Children now make up an estimated 30 percent of all homeless persons seeking shelter.[32] Homeless children are exposed to the communicable diseases and chaos found in shelters and suffer increased infant mortality, chronic diarrhea, asthma, delayed immunizations, family separation, missed school, and other damage.[33]

Unaffordable, inadequate housing. Millions of other poor children live in fear of homelessness or do not have safe, healthy,

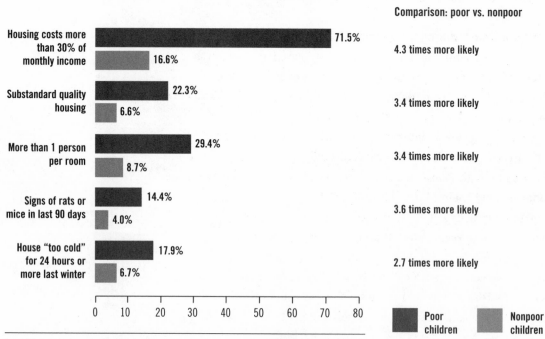

Percentage of children living in households with selected housing problems and characteristics, 1989

Comparison: poor vs. nonpoor

Housing problem	Poor children	Nonpoor children	Comparison
Housing costs more than 30% of monthly income	71.5%	16.6%	4.3 times more likely
Substandard quality housing	22.3%	6.6%	3.4 times more likely
More than 1 person per room	29.4%	8.7%	3.4 times more likely
Signs of rats or mice in last 90 days	14.4%	4.0%	3.6 times more likely
House "too cold" for 24 hours or more last winter	17.9%	6.7%	2.7 times more likely

Source: U.S. Census Bureau and U.S. Department of Housing and Urban Development, American Housing Survey data for 1989. Tabulations of public use files by the Children's Defense Fund.

Utility shut-offs and fires

In the winter in cold climates, daily newspaper readers find it hard to miss the stories about fire deaths resulting from makeshift heating and lighting arrangements. The *Washington Post* told of a February 1994 fire in Baltimore that killed nine, including seven children ages eight months to 11 years old. A mother there threw her two-year-old from a second-floor window to a neighbor below. The cause of the fire: overturned candles used because the electricity had been shut off.

The same newspaper reported in December 1993 that neighbors listened in horror as five- and six-year-old sisters trapped in their burning Washington, D.C., home screamed for help. Again, candles were being used because electricity had been shut off.

Fire deaths caused by "desperate substitutes" for heating and lighting caused 39 Pennsylvania deaths in the previous five years, the *Philadelphia Inquirer* quoted state Public Utility Commissioner John Hanger as saying in December 1993.

or decent homes. Rapid increases in the costs of homeownership, rent, and utilities left the families of 7 million poor children in 1989 (71.5 percent of all poor children)[34] housed but paying more than they can afford for housing according to federal affordability standards.[35] High housing costs mean that poor families have less money to purchase food and other necessities, and often compel poor families to accept substandard and inadequate housing. The resulting housing problems can trigger or exacerbate lasting educational and health problems. Overall, poor children are more than 3 times as likely to live in inadequate housing,[36] and they experience a host of specific housing problems.

Moving from house to house. Children in poverty move about twice as often as nonpoor children[37] due to families' inability to pay rent, tensions from living in crowded or doubled-up quarters, the need to search for another job, or other reasons. Effects of frequent moving on children are large and can include disruption of school and dropping out. Each time a family moves has been estimated to diminish a child's chances of finishing high school by more than 2 percentage points, holding other factors equal.[38]

Heating and electrical problems and utility shut-offs. Poor children are more likely to go without heat, either because of missing or broken equipment or because of utility shut-offs. In 1989 poor children were 2.7 times more likely to live in homes that parents or other survey respondents said were "too cold" for more than 24 hours the previous winter.[39] Exposure to cold can weaken children's health and may cause the dampness, mold, and allergies described below.

Occasionally, a family whose heat has been shut off or that cannot afford to repair or replace broken heating equipment may be driven to rely on portable electric "space heaters" to heat an entire home, which can strain the heater dangerously beyond its intended use. Poor children are nearly 3 times more likely to live in homes heated principally by such space heaters. And while they are not commonly used as a family's main source of heat — 1.4 percent of poor children and 0.5 percent of nonpoor children in 1989 lived in homes heated mainly by portable electric heaters[40] — they have become the leading cause of home fire deaths related to heating equipment.[41] Most of these fire deaths occur when the space heater ignites materials left too close to the hot unit, or because of short circuits and electrical failure.[42]

Leaks. A greater proportion of poor children (22.5 percent in 1989) than nonpoor children (14.5 percent) live in homes with internal water leakage, such as leaky pipes.[43]

Cold, dampness, mold, and allergies. Several British studies have uncovered a link between damp, moldy housing and child health problems, including wheezing, sore throat, runny nose, cough, headaches, and fever.[44] Damp housing conditions — often caused by water leaks, by lack of heat or uneven heating that encourages condensation of moisture, and by poor ventilation — encourage the growth of molds and fungi that cause asthma and other respiratory problems.[45] These problems are exacerbated by the lack of regular health care for many poor children. These health problems, in turn, pose a potentially serious threat to a child's health and schooling, as asthma and other respiratory conditions are the most common chronic illness among children and were the cause of an estimated 10 million missed school days in 1985.[46]

Sleeping on floors and in dresser drawers

"Judy" and her three young children live in a crowded, beat-up apartment in Dade County, Florida. In an effort to better herself and provide for her children, Judy is attending nursing school. For now, the family ekes out a living with welfare assistance. Their income is so low that Judy has not been able to afford beds. So she and the two older children sleep on the floor, and the youngest, a baby, sleeps in a dresser drawer. In the winter, Judy has to stuff clothes and rags into the gaps in the wall around the broken heater to keep the draft out.

Although no serious crisis has befallen the children yet, they suffer from frequent colds and viruses, a sign that the family's compromised living conditions and the constant stress of poverty are taking their toll.

Cockroaches and allergies. A related problem is cockroach infestation. Proteins found in decaying cockroaches and cockroach feces are considered an important cause of allergies and asthma for low-income children.[47] Cockroach infestations often are caused by dampness and can be avoided by maintaining a dry and clean environment, repairing cracked walls and leaky pipes, and exterminating regularly. Poverty makes all of these measures harder to accomplish.

Rats and mice. Poor children are more than 3 times as likely to live in homes with signs of rats or mice in the past 90 days.[48] In addition to the concern that rodents will bite young children, infestations of rats and mice can contribute to children's asthma and other respiratory problems by filling the indoor air with rodent urinary proteins.[49]

Peeling paint and falling plaster. Poor children are 3 times more likely to live in homes with peeling paint or falling plaster, which create a danger of lead poisoning if the house ever was painted with lead paint (13.1 percent of poor children, compared with 4.3 percent of nonpoor children, live in homes with substantial areas of peeling paint or falling plaster).[50]

Crowded housing. Poor children are more than 3 times as likely to live in crowded homes, with more than one person per room (29.4 percent versus 8.7 percent of nonpoor children).[51]

According to one literature review, "Research indicates that crowded housing leads to greater stress, less opportunity for rest and recuperation, and more susceptibility to infection, all of which may result in greater illness."[52] The overall health status of White children living in crowded housing is reported by their mothers to be lower than that of children in uncrowded housing, holding constant other factors (such as income, marital status, and mothers' education).[53] Crowding and stress, as well as any resulting illnesses, also can interfere with homework and other opportunities for learning.

Injuries may be another result of overcrowded housing. In neighborhoods with crowded housing, children are more likely to be hit by cars and trucks. As one study explains, "Crowding of individual housing units will result in more time spent outside. Crowding of large numbers of these housing units in a neighborhood increases the number of such children, at the same time providing less room for them to play. Areas with low-income populations are infrequently equipped with playgrounds and parks; the streets become the most accessible substitute."[54]

Growing up in overcrowded housing may have still other long-lasting impacts on health. For example, a British medical report notes that a bacterium strongly implicated in adult ulcers and stomach cancer *(Helicobacter pylori)* probably is acquired very early in life, in most cases in childhood through exposure in their own homes. Crowded housing, as well as inadequate hot-water plumbing, are "powerful independent risk factors" for the disease, the study finds,[55] possibly increasing risk of infection by making homes dirtier and less hygienic, as well as increasing the number of potentially infected people and their proximity. Crowded housing may therefore help explain why this infection is associated with socioeconomic deprivation in the United States.[56]

Cleaning and repainting problems. Poverty makes it harder for families to afford effective cleansers, vacuum cleaners, vacuum cleaner bags, mops, air filters, air conditioners, and water purifiers — household items that may reduce children's exposure to such hazards as asthma-causing dust, lead-based paint dust, and lead-contaminated drinking water. Lack of cleaning materials, lack of air conditioning, poor ventilation, inability to afford frequent laundering of bedclothes, and crowded, cluttered conditions that make meticulous dusting impossible may all lead to buildups of dust mites that can cause asthma.[57] Further, while frequent repainting inside the home can reduce the risk of a child being poisoned by lead from old paint dust, poor families are less able to afford frequent paint jobs.

Fire-prone mobile homes. Poor children are 1.5 times more likely than nonpoor children to live in mobile homes.[58] House fires involving young children are 3 times more likely to end in a death if they occur in a mobile home, according to one North Carolina study.[59] Cramped space and fewer exits may add to the dangers of a mobile home during a fire.

Overall housing quality, distractions, and distress. Overcrowding, utility shut-offs, inadequate heating, and other housing quality problems may disrupt a child's ability to rest and do homework, while the dissatisfaction with substandard housing may contribute to stress and depression in adults. (The effects of parental stress and depression on children are described later in this chapter.)

Money Buys Opportunities To Learn

Poverty directly limits children's resources for learning both at home and in school. Problems start with the inability of parents to afford stimulating toys, children's books, preschools, and good quality child care arrangements. The problems continue through the quality and quantity of schooling children receive, as well as the school supplies, eyeglasses, hearing aids, stimulating activities such as summer camp or family travel, and other activities and materials that encourage learning.

Inferior child care. Poverty drives many families to use cheaper, lower quality child care — ranging from an inexperienced babysitter to an overcrowded family day care home or a low-budget child care center. Although low-income parents stretch their budgets enormously to buy suitable care for their children (poor families that use paid child care devote more than one-fourth of their entire incomes to it on average, contrasted with 7 percent of income among nonpoor families),[60] this is still nowhere near enough to buy good quality care. Good quality child care centers charge an average of $4,800 a year for a four-year-old in full-time care, according to the U.S. General Accounting Office,[61] which is more than 60 percent of the income of the average poor family with children[62] and far above what poor families can afford to pay. The public programs to assist low-income parents (such as child care subsidies and Head Start) are funded inadequately; consequently, many eligible low-income families receive no assistance[63] and others may be forced into low quality care due to subsidized child care policies that restrict the quality of care families can use.[64]

The result for poor children is often worse care. A nationwide study of relative and family child care (care provided in the home of a relative or a nonrelative) notes that "children from lower income families are in poorer quality settings" on average, where providers charge less, are less well educated, are less likely to be regulated, are less sensitive and more restrictive in their dealings with children, and are more likely to engage in "inadequate" practices deemed "potentially harmful to a child's growth," such as rarely or never talking to infants and toddlers.[65] Cost was a major predictor of quality: low-cost providers were more likely to be inadequate. (In contrast to relative and family care, the situation for poor preschoolers who attend center-based child care is more favorable, probably because a substantial minority of them receive good quality care through Head Start.[66])

Child care quality, in turn, helps shape a child's development. The same study of relative and family care found that children in unresponsive and restrictive settings showed signs of being less emotionally secure with their providers and less likely to play complex games, compared with children from similar backgrounds who were enrolled in higher quality settings. Experiments confirm that differences in child care quality can have concrete and lasting impacts. For example, lowering the number of children per adult (which generally increases providers' costs and the fees they charge) significantly improves children's emotional state and behavior, according to one Swedish study. Affected children had less stress (measured by stress hormone levels), less anxious and aggressive behavior, and were more active and friendly with each other,[67] a finding consistent with data from the United States.[68] The benefits of allowing poor children to attend a high quality, enriched child care and development program have been found to stretch well into adulthood, and include more high school completion, higher earnings, and fewer arrests.[69]

Inferior schools. When poor children reach school age, they often must attend inferior schools. Because of where they are compelled to live, "students from poor families usually receive their education in the poorest schools," according to the National Academy of Sciences. "These schools have fewer financial and material resources, and they are often unable to retain the most skilled administrators and teachers. Student achievement levels in these schools are significantly lower on virtually all measures than for students in suburban schools."[70]

Students in high-poverty schools are more likely to have low achievement scores (regardless of their own poverty status)[71] and, in subjects such as mathematics, their teachers appear to place less emphasis on learning how to think, according to the U.S. Department of Education.[72] Nationwide, third-grade teachers in the poorest schools are 2 to 4 times more likely to report inadequate supplies of textbooks, workbooks, and audiovisual equipment, compared with teachers in schools with the least poverty.[73]

Unaffordable text books and school fees. Moreover, some schools make students pay for basic educational materials and activities. Thirty-four states allow schools to charge fees for academic or extracurricular activities. In 20 states schools may charge lab fees and fees for field trips, and in eight states schools may charge students for required textbooks. In 15 states, the chief school official said it was common practice to assess fees for academic texts and workbooks.[74] Although some states require schools to waive fees for poor students, a student's reluctance to admit to poverty, as well as noncompliance by school administrators, can mean that fees are charged anyway.

In Utah, state law requires schools to waive school fees for low-income families, but a court ordered an emergency injunction in 1992 after receiving evidence of widespread violations by schools across the state.[75] One parent recounted to a state children's advocacy organization:

> *My daughter was told that this year, fees couldn't be waived. They threatened to withhold her grades and diploma and they always hounded her for money. I didn't have a job and we didn't have any money, but every couple of weeks they would pressure my daughter for the money. She finally gave up and dropped out of school.*[76]

Even when low-income students are not driven to drop out, and when schools do not threaten to withhold grades or diplomas, school fees and expenses can interfere with their education. Difficulty paying fees can mean that low-income students do not participate fully in class, or do not sign up for classes that charge special fees for science labs, art supplies, or supplementary texts. Activities such as field trips, team sports, and clubs, which teach self-confidence and a variety of specific skills, may become inaccessible. In all of these situations, low-income students are denied an equal public education solely because their families are poor. Further, granting waivers may not render school fees entirely harmless. In Utah, where school fees sometimes mount into the hundreds of dollars per child each year, school fee opponents point to the humiliation involved in requesting waivers and the animosity they say breaks out between students who get waivers and those who do not.

Fewer educational materials in the home. Poverty also limits opportunities to learn outside the institutions of child care and school. Poor families cannot as easily afford learning materials such as exciting magazines and books, maps, and encyclopedias. In 1992 low-income households spent about half as much as those with middle incomes on reading materials,[77] and poor preschool children were significantly less likely than nonpoor children in 1986 to have 10 or more books.[78]

Fewer stimulating activities. Similarly, poor children are less likely to attend camp, go on family trips, or join in extracurricular activities. Such learning opportunities are associated with improved achievement in school. One study found that low socioeconomic status contributed to children's learning problems in Atlanta, in part because disadvantaged children had fewer stimulating activities during the summer: "Socioeconomic status predicted the number and quality of programs attended, the length of time and distance traveled on family vacations, and the number of hours spent reading, playing with friends, taking athletic or music classes, pursuing hobbies, or going to camp. Each of these activities in turn related to achievement growth."[79]

Less exposure to computers. Children from nonpoor backgrounds also have an enormous head start in practicing on computers at home. For example, fewer than 7 percent of high school students with family incomes below $10,000 (versus 21 percent of all high school students and 53 percent of those with income above $75,000) used computers at home in 1989.[80] At school, inequities in access to computers are shrinking, but wealthy seventh-graders (those in the top income quartile) are still one-third more likely to use computers than their low-income peers in the bottom quartile.[81] Children who become comfortable with computers appear to have a great advantage in later life; workers who use computers on the job have been found to earn 10 to 15 percent more than similar workers who do not.[82]

Greater home responsibilities that compete with school. The need to work long hours to bring in more income, as well as the need to care for sick relatives or take on other family responsibilities, can interfere with the quality of students' learning and keep them from finishing high school or college. A 1991 study found that on average, "students who work more than 20 hours per week have grade-point averages that are about one-third of a letter grade lower than those of their peers who work 10 hours a week or less." Students who worked long hours reported "more mind wandering and less exerting effort in school—even after taking into account their overall orientation toward school" and other background factors.[83] In 1992, 23 percent of all tenth- to twelfth-grade dropouts said they could not work and go to school at the same time, 12 percent said they had to care for a family member, and 11 percent said they had to support their families.[84] (These categories overlap: respondents were allowed to answer yes to more than one question.)

Barriers to college. Even when poor children finish high school and are academically prepared to attend college, poverty creates barriers to postsecondary education. One barrier is the cost of attendance. The inflation-adjusted costs of tuition, room, and board rose by one-third (32 percent) at public colleges and by more than one-half (55 percent) at private colleges between 1980 and 1991, while the incomes of poor and moderate-income families with children went down.[85] One year of public four-year college for an average full-time, low-income student cost $6,983 in 1989-1990, according to the U.S. Department of Education (counting tuition, fees, room and board, books, transportation, and miscellaneous expenses).[86] Although financial aid covered some of these students' costs, the remaining expenses (averaging $3,813) still were considered unaffordable by federal standards in 60 percent of cases — meaning that, for three out of five students from low-income families, too little money was left in the family budget for purchasing other necessities. The situation was no better in two-year (community) colleges, because lower average tuition and other costs in these schools were balanced by lower financial aid awards. Moreover, the Education Department findings paint an optimistic picture of college barriers because they only describe those low-income students who successfully enrolled in college — not the many students who were unable to enroll because they did not know about financial aid, could not obtain financial aid, or had families that could not afford to fill the gap left by an inadequate level of financial aid.

Money Reduces Family Stress and Conflict

One of the most disturbing recent findings about poverty is that it seems to strike at the heart of the American family by straining the capacity of parents to provide warmth, guidance, and steady discipline for their children. Poverty appears to create this effect by heightening parental stress and depression and by fueling conflict throughout the family.

As economic hardship increases or decreases, so do parents' signs of stress and depression. Ironically, while these responses may reflect deep concern for the well-being of their children, distressed parents sometimes act in ways that ultimately do great harm to children's learning and emotional development. Distressed parents tend to nurture their children less effectively and may be more likely to punish them harshly and without a clear reason. In extreme cases, poverty-related distress may trigger or exacerbate child abuse. If not addressed, parental distress may contribute to other problems, including family breakup and drug use by the parents, and later delinquency and crime among the children.

Parents' mental health. Adults who experience job loss or income loss show more signs of stress and depression.[87] (Moreover, the economic problems generally appear to happen first in these situations; the opposite relationship, where psychological problems trigger job loss, appears to be relatively rare.)[88] Low-income adults also manifest more medical symptoms thought to be related to stress, such as migraines and other severe headaches.[89] The impact of economic loss may be particularly strong for parents raising children.[90]

Low income and job loss can affect parents' mental health in many ways. Distress may be caused by the inability to pay bills and meet the family's basic needs. Hunger and the fear of hunger, imminent eviction and homelessness, mounting debt,

---

Shame, fear, and anger

"Susan" was raised in poverty and I am still learning the many ways it hurt her. I am her mother. Susan was born two weeks after my eighteenth birthday and by the time she was 12 we had moved more than 30 times, always one step ahead of or behind the eviction notices, gas and light disconnect notices, and various other bills haunting our mailbox. We laughed a lot and tried to make it an adventure, like the time she was six and the two of us had to move our bed across town on a bus.

But then I would cry and cry and cry for days at a time. Being poor made me crazy, and Susan learned to be my support, caretaker, and defender before she could read. She made herself into a model child so that people would say I was a good mother and let us stay together.

A few times I tried to kill myself out of fear and shame at not being able to keep a roof over our heads, out of anger over not being able to keep a job and needing to return over and over again to welfare, out of desperation whenever the welfare department would cut off my eligibility by mistake. When I would be put into a mental hospital, Susan would stay with my mother and father. What I didn't know until she was grown was that my brother was forcing sex upon her each time she stayed with them. She was so afraid of what would happen to our little family that she hid her pain.

Poverty was more than not having enough. It was about not having any control over the most intimate parts of

our lives, and, for me, about feeling shame, fear, and anger all the time. After more than 20 low-wage jobs, I enrolled in college when Susan was eight. A few years later we received a rent subsidy which allowed us to stay in one place. Things got a bit better. For the first time in either of our lives, we had community, permanent friends, and a sense of belonging. Today, Susan and I are successful professionals, and best friends. It didn't take much: a rent subsidy, a generous state university admissions policy, and access to mental health services. The rest we did on our own.

"Anne," an employment training program manager in Oregon

CHILDREN'S DEFENSE FUND

repossession, unattended health problems, and other tensions arising from managing a too-tight budget all take their psychological toll on poor parents each day. Crowded housing and unpleasant or dangerous surroundings may heighten distress. (Consider, for example, the stress of feeling unable to protect one's children from neighborhood violence.) So may living in isolation, without telephone service, social activities, or other supports. So may the shame or embarrassment of being unable to offer one's children the lifestyle other children take for granted. In non-financial ways, too, unemployment or low earnings may cause distress by taking away the dignity and self-worth that come from doing rewarding work and being a successful breadwinner. Unemployment also may cause distress by reducing social contact with co-workers.

Of all the facets of unemployment and low earnings, tangible financial strain seems to be among the most hazardous to adult mental health. Financial strain — defined as "constraints on buying food, medical care, and clothing, and on whether there is enough money to cover the basic bills each month" — was identified as "the only important" factor explaining why presently unemployed workers had worse mental and physical health, in a recent study of mostly blue-collar workers in southeastern Michigan.[91] (An earlier study had similar findings.[92])

Consequences of parental distress for child mental health. Parents experiencing poverty-related stress are less likely to respond positively to their children and are more likely to use harsh and inconsistent discipline. According to University of Michigan psychologist Vonnie McLoyd:

> *Because they are more emotionally distressed than their advantaged counterparts, it is not surprising that the capacity of poor parents for supportive, sensitive, and involved parenting is diminished. Numerous studies of both Black and White adults...report that mothers who are poor...are more likely to use power-*

assertive techniques in disciplinary encounters and are generally less supportive of their children. They value obedience more, are less likely to use reasoning, and more likely to use physical punishment....

Rewarding, explaining, consulting, and negotiating with the child require patience and concentration — qualities typically in short supply when parents feel harassed and overburdened.[93]

McLoyd adds that distressed low-income parents may use harsh or inconsistent discipline even when they are aware that this is not best for their child. "Thus," she says, "psychological overload, rather than ignorance of the principles of effective parenting...may explain differences between poor and nonpoor parents' style of interaction with their children."[94]

For children, the results of harsh and inconsistent discipline and unsupportive parenting include emotional and behavior problems. "Children whose parents are nonsupportive have lower self-esteem...and more psychological disorders, exhibit more antisocial aggression and behavioral problems...and are more likely to show arrested ego development," notes McLoyd. Children raised in these ways "may imitate the parent by handling interpersonal conflict with coercion rather than negotiation [and receive] fewer opportunities to learn and master verbal and instrumental strategies that help in initiating and maintaining positive peer interaction."[95]

Parental stress is linked to "poorer performance on developmental tests at eight months, lower IQ scores and impaired language development at four years, and poorer emotional adjustment and increased school problems at school age...", adds a literature review by a team of pediatricians. "The data suggest that stress causes negative outcomes by inhibiting positive interactions and the attachment between parent and child."

Depression in mothers also is linked to developmental and behavioral problems for children, the pediatricians found. Depressed mothers act unhappy around their children; they are less spontaneous, less vocal, and have less physical contact. This, in turn, affects the children. Even when mothers *pretend* to act depressed in clinical experiments, their three-month-old infants react negatively. Children of depressed mothers are more likely to suffer a variety of medical problems, and to have "sleep problems, depression, attention deficit disorder, socially isolating behaviors at school age, and withdrawn and defiant behaviors during adolescence."[96]

Family conflict and arguments about money. Economic stress can heighten family conflicts and irritability over many topics, including money itself. During the farm crisis of the 1980s, families stricken by economic troubles — such as having to give up medical insurance or to cut back on utilities — had more marital problems and argued more about "not having enough money," according to sociologist Rand D. Conger and others, who studied a group of White teenagers and their families from rural Iowa. Ominously, such "financial conflict affected problems in adolescent development" by apparently driving up "parent hostility which, in turn, directly increased the risk of adolescent symptoms" of a broad range of problems such as aggressive or antisocial behavior, depression, and anxiety.[97]

The initial shock of poverty. The duration of poverty may influence parent and child mental health in complicated ways. Nationwide, both *being* poor currently and *remaining* poor for a long time are linked to greater mental health problems among four- to eight-year-olds, according to sociologists Jane D. McLeod and Michael Shanahan.[98] However, only being currently poor appears to create parenting problems, they find. Currently poor parents tend to be less emotionally responsive and more punitive to their children. Their children, in turn, tend to act out (what the researchers call "externalizing symptoms" such as cheating, arguing, or bullying). This finding bolsters the view that being poor contributes to aggression in children, and does so entirely by making some parents less responsive and more punitive.

Surprisingly, *remaining* poor for long periods does not amplify these parenting problems, McLeod and Shanahan find. Instead, "Family interactions apparently stabilize as poverty persists and the family adapts."[99] One parenting problem (responsiveness) does not seem to get worse during long periods spent in poverty, while the other (punitiveness, measured by frequent spankings) actually recedes once families have time to adjust to the initial shock of poverty. Notably, mothers who recently have escaped poverty administer the fewest spankings of all.[100] (This finding dispels the notion that permanent — cultural or inborn — traits in poor parents make them more punitive toward their children.)

Nonetheless, remaining poor is linked significantly with other mental health problems in children ("internalizing symptoms" such as feeling unloved, fearful, or withdrawn). The authors speculate that longer term poverty could cause these problems through poor nutrition, exposure to violent crime, abuse, or other environmental hazards of poverty.[101] This study is noteworthy because, unlike most previous psychological studies, McLeod and Shanahan were able to use a large nationwide sample; to carefully measure children's experience with poverty over a period of several years; and to hold constant the effects of race, mothers' marital status, age, education, and other factors.

Parental distress and children's learning. In addition to its role in children's mental health problems, parental stress also may interfere with children's concentration and learning. In a study of Black single mothers, more frequent punishment by mothers was associated with greater difficulty in concentrating among children in the seventh and eighth grades (measured by how often the child was reported to have trouble with such tasks as making up his or her mind, remembering things, and keeping his or her mind on school work).[102]

Among Black two-parent families in a rural area, similarly, lack of financial resources was related to greater parental depression and a pessimistic outlook about life. These in turn were related to greater marital strain and more conflicts between parents about how to raise their children — problems that ultimately led to lower scores on reading and math tests and other mental health and behavior problems for the children.[103]

More generally, parental rejection and coercive discipline — patterns similar to those of highly stressed parents — may damage children's school performance. One style of parenting that appears to encourage school success for children across a variety of ages and racial and social lines, identified by Temple University psychologist Laurence Steinberg and others, combines three qualities: (1) *warmth,* measured in one study by students' responses to items such as "How often does your family do something fun together?" and "I can count on her to help me out if I have some kind of problem"; (2) *strict supervision,* measured by questions such as "How much do your parents try to know where you go at night?"; and (3) *allowing "psychological autonomy,"* which the researchers contrasted to coercive discipline, and which they measured with questions such as "How often do your parents tell you that their ideas are correct and that you should not question them?"[104] Stress seems to trigger some of the opposite qualities in parents (notably rejection and coercive discipline).

Child abuse and neglect. At the extremes of harsh discipline, parental stress may trigger or exacerbate physical abuse or neglect. (Poverty also may increase the risk of child abuse and neglect by individuals other than the parents, as described in Chapter 3.)

Child abuse and neglect are not only tragic in themselves; they also appear to contribute to juvenile delinquency, crime, and violence in later life. In a detailed study of intergenerational violence done for the National Institute of Justice, "being abused or neglected as a child increased the likelihood

---

'Poverty destroys families'

It's asking a great deal of schools to expect them to turn out uniformly bright, capable students when so large a proportion of their children live in homes where the income runs below the minimal requirements for housing and nutrition. Poverty destroys families, and in a vicious circle, the dissolution of families makes the poverty greater.

Copyright © 1993. *The Washington Post.* Reprinted with permission

of arrest as a juvenile by 53 percent, as an adult by 38 percent, and for a violent crime by 38 percent," although the study also cautions that "most members of both groups had no juvenile or adult criminal record."[105] The findings were based on a 20-year study, which followed more than 900 abused and neglected children and more than 600 comparison children who were matched by race, sex, age, and approximate family socioeconomic status.

The importance of social support. Stressful events may combine with other aspects of poverty — such as isolation and lack of support — to increase the risk of punitive treatment and abuse by parents. Conversely, parents may be protected from the stresses of poverty if they feel they can count on help from friends, relatives, publicly run family support programs, or other sources. In a recent nationwide study, "the negative effects of poverty [on self-reported parenting behavior] were only apparent for those parents with relatively little social support" (defined as having two or fewer people to call for help in an emotional or financial crisis, or if the parent needed help in the middle of the night). Nearly one in four parents who had *neither* adequate incomes *nor* adequate support reported being highly punitive toward their children (slapping or yelling at them "very often") — double the rate for parents with sufficient incomes, or sufficient support, or both.[106]

Divorce, separation, and unmarried childbearing. Poverty-related stress also may trigger a marital break-up, or stop two

---

Likelihood of punitive behavior by parents, by poverty
and level of support
(Percentage of parents who report slapping or yelling
at their children "very often")

	Poor	Not Poor
Low Level of Support	23%	12%
High Level of Support	11	10

Patricia Y. Hashima and Paul R. Amato, "Poverty, Social Support, and Parental Behavior," *Child Development* 65, no. 2 (April 1994):394–403.

CHILDREN'S DEFENSE FUND

parents from getting married. Donald J. Hernandez notes that several studies have found that:

> *the consequences of economic recessions for specific families, such as instability in husbands' work, a drop in family income, and a low ratio of family income-to-needs can in turn lead to increased hostility between husbands and wives, decreased marital quality, and increased risk of divorce.*[107]

Not surprisingly, Hernandez notes, recessions since at least the mid-1960s have been times of greater movement away from marriage. Although a society-wide trend toward children living in mother-only families has existed for many years, data produced by Hernandez indicate that this trend has proceeded about twice as rapidly during the average recession year as during the average non-recession year.[108] He writes, "these results suggest that without recession-induced increases, the proportion of children living in mother-only families with separated, divorced or widowed mothers might have increased by only 2.1 percentage points (less than one-half of the actual increase...between 1970 and 1988)." Births to never-married mothers also increase during recessions.[109]

Poor two-parent families are twice as likely as nonpoor families to break up over a two-year period, observes Hernandez, who heads the Census Bureau's Marriage and Family Statistics Branch. The pattern holds true among both Whites and Blacks. (Among Latinos, poor–nonpoor differences are smaller.) Hernandez concludes that "stresses associated with economic insecurity or need, as reflected in below-poverty income, may have contributed to marital separation,"[110] although over the longer term, sweeping changes, such as the disappearance of the farming lifestyle, greater economic freedom for women, and declining fertility resulting in fewer children to care for, probably all played major roles as well.[111]

Inequality and violence

Many social science disciplines, in addition to psychology, have firmly established that poverty and its contextual life circumstances are major determinants of violence....Violence is most prevalent among the poor, regardless of race....Few differences among the races are found in rates of violence when people at the same income level are compared.

But beyond mere income level, it is the socioeconomic inequality of the poor — their sense of relative deprivation and their lack of opportunity to ameliorate their life circumstances — that facilitates higher rates of violence.

...Not only do the poor in America lack basic necessities, but they are aware that they do not have those things most other Americans have and that they lack other opportunities needed to obtain them in the future. Media depictions of other Americans who are living "the good life" serve to compound the already untenable conditions of poverty with a heightened sense of deprivation....

American Psychological Association, *Violence and Youth: Psychology's Response*, 1993

Stress and illness. Stress also can damage family members' health by lowering their resistance to disease. Due to weakened resistance, the odds of catching a cold virus increase by more than 5 times for adults undergoing psychological stress.[112]

Parents' substance abuse. Economic problems may contribute to substance abuse. Depressed women are significantly more likely to smoke and drink alcohol during pregnancy, according to a study of more than 1,000 births to primarily low-income and minority women.[113] Alcohol sales are reported to increase during periods of economic recession.[114] According to one congressional study, deaths from liver cirrhosis — often caused by increased drinking among those with existing alcohol problems — also tend to increase following a rise in unemployment.[115]

Parents' distress and future crime and violence. Disturbingly, many of the byproducts of parent distress appear to contribute to delinquency and violence in later life. Less nurturant parenting, weak attachment between child and parents, childhood hostility and behavior problems, early learning difficulties and low IQ, marital conflict between parents, and abuse and neglect may combine to leave a child at least at slightly greater risk of becoming a violent young adult.[116] While most low-income children, like most affluent children, do *not* grow into violent adults, the indirect linkages between poverty and crime are numerous and warrant additional attention. (These linkages will be discussed more in Chapter 3.)

Money Buys a Decent Neighborhood

Poverty restricts the range of neighborhoods in which families can afford to live. Neighborhood quality affects child safety and health through the stress and danger of crime, the availability of parks and safe play areas, the level of exposure to garbage and fumes, and even the presence of lead and other toxic chemicals in the air, soil, and water. Moving to a different neighborhood can make a child more or less likely to succeed in school, not just by dictating the quality of the neighborhood school but possibly also by shaping peer influences, supervision by neighbors, access to positive adult role models, or exposure to crime, violence, drugs, or other traumas and distractions. Beyond schools, neighborhoods provide physical safety or danger, and govern a young person's proximity to well-paid jobs and to personal connections that can help build a career.

Noise. Noisy, distracting environments are one problem associated with poverty: 9.1 percent of poor children in 1989 (versus 5.9 percent of nonpoor children) lived in neighborhoods that had bothersome noise levels, according to parent reports.[117]

Crime. In 1989, 14.2 percent of poor children lived in neighborhoods that parents said had bothersome levels of crime — more than double the proportion among nonpoor children (6.0 percent).[118] Living in high-crime areas can be traumatic for children. For example, third-graders exposed to gun violence are reported to show increased symptoms associated with post-traumatic stress syndrome.[119] Disturbingly, in high-crime areas of Washington, D.C., newspapers report that elementary and high school students talk frequently about death — planning what they will wear and which friends should be invited to their own funerals — apparently in place of thinking about their future lives and careers. Further, parents who live in high-crime areas often stop taking their children places or allowing them to go outside, which limits children's range of stimulating experiences.

Opportunities for learning and work. Some neighborhoods offer children better schools, safer streets, and better opportunities to enter the work force and earn good wages. Evidence of this was provided when Black families from housing projects in Chicago received assistance moving either into middle-class suburbs or into other inner-city neighborhoods.[120] In effect the program served as an experiment in the importance of neighborhoods, as families were assigned to different neighborhoods roughly, although not perfectly, at random. Several years later, compared with the urban movers, the children and youths who moved to the suburbs were:

- *One-fourth as likely to be dropouts.*
- *Twice as likely to attend college.*
- *Almost twice as likely to be employed.*
- *Twice as likely to have job benefits.*
- *Four times as likely to earn more than $6.50 an hour.*

The study revealed major urban–suburban differences in school quality and neighborhood conditions. Compared with urban movers, the suburban families found better schools, with smaller classes and higher satisfaction with teachers and courses. Anecdotal reports from participants also suggested that the reduced fear of crime in the suburbs led to a greater sense of freedom to engage in work, learning, and safe recreational activities, improvements that may have played a role in bettering children's outcomes.

When families live in lower income neighborhoods, another study reports that the outside play environment is more likely to appear unsafe, while the apartment is more often "dark or perceptually monotonous." This difference between physical environments in poor and nonpoor neighborhoods is found even among families whose own incomes and other characteristics are similar.[121]

Toxic chemicals and pollution. Exposure to unhealthy chemicals and pollution is another problem that tends to be concentrated in low-income and minority neighborhoods. As a recent literature review found:

> *Both race and class are related to the distribution of air pollution...location of municipal landfills and incinerators...and multimedia*

exposure to pesticides....Communities with hazardous waste incinerators generally have large minority populations, low incomes, and low property values....Virtually all of the studies of exposure to outdoor air pollution have found significant differences in exposure by income and race.[122]

Potential consequences of toxic exposure and pollution for children include cancer,[123] severe lung damage,[124] and, for toxins such as lead, brain damage, school failure, and behavior problems. (See page 115 for more information on lead poisoning.) Childhood and poverty may combine to make poor children doubly vulnerable to the effects of increased pollution in their neighborhoods, according to epidemiologist Richard Rios and his colleagues. First, "Fetuses, neonates, infants, children, and pregnant women are all more susceptible to the adverse effects of some pollutant exposures," such as pesticides, PCBs, nitrates, lead, and carbon monoxide. Second, "poverty...is associated with insufficient intake of protein, calories, vitamins, and minerals...which are essential for the immune system to function normally."[125]

While poverty clearly makes it harder for individual families to move away from neighborhoods with toxic waste dumps, it is difficult to know what overall effect ending poverty would have on children's exposure to toxic wastes. In a nation with no poor children, it is very possible that toxic wastes still would be placed near some children's homes. However, if families with children had incomes comparable to childless households and had comparable freedom to move to new neighborhoods, it is also possible that they would bear a less disproportionate burden of exposure.

Similar uncertainty surrounds other issues, such as school quality. Although ending one family's poverty might allow it to move to a better neighborhood to avoid a bad school, ending all child poverty might have no impact on the number of bad schools in the nation or the number of children who must at-

'Roaches, rats...disease'

"Roaches, rats, mosquitoes, fleas, disease, chemicals," a nine-year-old Tunica, Mississippi, boy recited to an ABC Evening News reporter in an October 1985 two-part series on hunger among U.S. children.

"You've got all that around where you live? How do you feel about that?" the reporter asked.

"Terrible," the boy said. "Make[s] me feel like killing myself."

tend them. Alternatively, ending child poverty might help students focus on their classes, reduce behavior problems, and thereby improve the overall school climate and make learning, teaching, and recruiting good teachers easier.

Money Buys Health Care, Health Supplies, and Safety Devices

Poverty influences child health directly by making it harder for families to afford health services (from doctors, dentists, optometrists, psychologists, and others) as well as health supplies (ranging from dental sealants to prescription drugs to first aid supplies) and safety devices (such as special car seats for children and devices to "child-proof" a home).

Financial barriers to medical care. During the past three decades, expansions in Medicaid brought public health insurance to a growing share of poor children and successfully narrowed the gap in health care utilization between children from lower and upper income families. However, one in five poor children still had no health insurance at all during 1992.[126] Even among poor children who receive Medicaid, reports the Rand Corporation, "Poor...children less frequently had a regular source of care, more frequently used emergency rooms and other public providers for their regular care, and more frequently encountered financial barriers to health care."[127]

One barrier to health care for publicly insured patients is the difficulty of finding a regular doctor who will accept Medicaid. Many doctors refuse,[128] in part because of low Medicaid reimbursement rates from the government. In 1989 nearly one in four pediatricians said they would not accept Medicaid, up from 15 percent in 1978.[129] In a survey by the U.S. General Accounting Office, 15 percent of uninsured and Medicaid-insured women who had received inadequate prenatal care during their pregnancy said they could not find a doctor who would see them. Ten percent said they had experienced "problems with Medicaid," such as delays in being enrolled.[130]

Poor families also have trouble affording medical fees. Even poor families with health coverage through Medicaid may be required to pay fees for covered services, usually ranging from 50 cents to several dollars per visit, depending on the state and the type of service.[131] Even these small Medicaid fees may add up quickly (especially when illnesses are recurrent, when multiple follow-up visits are required, or when prescriptions must be refilled) and may cause families to seek less care than their children need.[132]

In the case of prenatal care, the General Accounting Office found that not having enough money was the largest barrier facing uninsured and Medicaid-insured women who received inadequate prenatal care during pregnancy. Two-fifths of the women with inadequate care (41 percent) reported not having enough money to pay for visits.[133]

Lack of routine medical care. When poor children *do* get medical care, its quality may be worse, even if they have health insurance through Medicaid. One of the reasons is the lack of a regular doctor. Although low-income children have some type of contact with a doctor about as often as their wealthier peers, the nature and location of the contact frequently differs by income, with lower income children going to a hospital twice as often as wealthier children.[134] Low-income children are more likely to visit clinics and similar locations and less likely to have office visits and telephone consultations. This pattern of care is of grave concern because it suggests that poor children frequently have no regular doctor, and that the doctors they see sporadically in hospitals and clinics may lack the familiarity or the medical records needed to assess and treat them properly.

Lack of routine advice from a doctor. Sporadic caregivers at a hospital or clinic may not have the time, familiarity, and trust needed to advise a child's parents on a wide range of preventive measures, as a private doctor would do. This also may help explain why a disproportionate share of low-income mothers in prenatal care never are given advice about such crucial matters as not smoking during pregnancy and the value of breast-feeding.[135]

Poorer mothers also may not receive advice about child-proofing the house, barring stairways with childproof gates, stocking ipecac syrup to administer in case of poisoning, and other routine health and safety topics. As poor children get older, they too may miss out on advice about diet, exercise, smoking, drinking, reproductive health, and other areas of prevention.

The absence of a regular doctor may help explain why many low-income parents in one study lacked knowledge about medical procedures and safety measures (such as what ipecac syrup is) that should normally be explained to parents by a doctor.[136] Further, some parents indicated that they would use emergency room services in situations (such as a minor injury to their child's head) in which the researchers considered a routine phone consultation more suitable. Emergency room visits that could have been avoided through a telephone consultation with a regular doctor represent a costly and needless burden for hospitals.

Lower quality care. Another problem for low-income children on Medicaid may be lower quality service at the hospital. "Resources for newborns covered by Medicaid were generally...less than for the privately insured" in one study of California's hospitals, even though the Medicaid newborns had worse health problems and presumably needed more care. However, even newborns on Medicaid received more care than those whose mothers were totally uninsured.[137]

Financial barriers to dental health. The use of fluoride and dental sealants makes a bigger difference in preventing tooth decay than the better-known factors of oral hygiene, diet, and regular visits to the dentist, federal health officials say.[138] Yet low-income children ages two to 16 are roughly half as likely as high-income children to use fluoride tablets or drops or other fluoride supplements (5.8 versus 9.5 percent in 1986) and are less than one-fifth as likely to have had protective dental sealants placed on their teeth (2.2 versus 12.2 percent).[139]

Financial barriers to first aid, poison control, and other safety measures. Besides making it less likely that a family will learn about routine preventive health measures from a doctor, poverty also makes it harder to purchase needed supplies, such as sterile bandages and antiseptics to stop cuts from becoming infected or other first aid materials to prevent health problems from becoming serious. The combination of less safety information and less discretionary income helps explain why, in 1990, children younger than 10 with annual family incomes below $10,000 were one-third as likely as those with family incomes above $50,000 to live in homes that had ipecac syrup to protect against poisoning (14 percent versus 45 percent).[140] Similarly, poor families may be unable to install safety latches to keep children away from medicines, cleansers, and other dangerous household supplies.

Smoke detectors and fire safety. Although smoke detectors dramatically reduce children's risk of death from housefires,[141] low-income adults (and presumably their children) are nearly 3 times more likely than the affluent to lack working smoke detectors at home.[142] Further, many smoke detectors require batteries, but poor families are less able to afford to replace batteries. More broadly, the National Fire Prevention Association warns that low-income families are "more likely to lack the discretionary income to obtain smoke detectors, or safe heating systems, or code-compliant electrical service, or firesafe security measures, or anything else that involves buying a larger measure of fire-safety."[143] Fewer working smoke detectors and other fire safety features may be one reason why a statewide study in Kansas found that low-income children are 4 times more likely than other children to die from fires.[144]

From mosquito bite to hospital stay

When "Bobby," a preschooler from a New England city, scratched a mosquito bite on his leg, the area became infected. His parents took him to a doctor, who prescribed an antibiotic. However, because Bobby's father earned very low wages at his job, the family could not immediately afford to buy the prescription. As a result of the family's poverty, the infection grew dangerously out of control and Bobby was hospitalized for three days receiving intravenous antibiotics. Each of those hospital days cost about $800, doctors estimate.

Child safety seats and childproofing devices. Poverty makes it harder to buy devices such as safety seats to protect young children in car accidents. According to a recent federal survey, only 79 percent of newborns from families with annual incomes of less than $10,000 were brought home from the hospital in car safety seats, "rising steadily to 97 percent among children whose families earned $50,000 or more."[145]

Poverty also makes it harder to afford such "childproofing" devices and procedures as gates to keep infants and toddlers from falling down stairs, or plastic plugs to cover electrical outlets and extension cords. Several thousand children each year are estimated to visit hospital emergency rooms because of electrical burns to the hands and face, most of which could be prevented with electrical safety plugs.[146]

Nationwide, more than one in six poor preschoolers in 1986 lived in homes that were ranked by trained observers as having unsafe play areas, compared with one in 14 nonpoor children.[147]

Money Buys Healthy Recreation

Poverty affects opportunities for children and adults to play, exercise, and socialize in healthy ways, with consequences for building self-esteem, physical health and fitness, and alternatives to unhealthy habits such as smoking, heavy drinking, or other high-risk behavior.

Fewer recreational facilities. Low-income families are less able to afford the cost of sports equipment or fees and uniforms for extracurricular activities. They are less able to pay even nominal fees for the local swimming pool, let alone expensive health clubs. Parks[148] and organized recreational activities such as sports teams and youth clubs tend to be less available.[148, 149] One consequence is a surplus of unstructured time. According to the Carnegie Council on Adolescent Development:

> *Unsupervised after-school hours represent a period of significant risk.... In one study,*

eighth-graders who were unsupervised for 11 or more hours a week experienced twice the rate of substance abuse as those who were under some form of adult supervision. Unsupervised teenagers are also more likely to be subject to negative peer pressure....

Unfortunately, young people from poor families are most likely to live in unsafe neighborhoods and to be unsupervised during the after-school hours. They are least likely to have access to constructive alternatives. They are at extremely high risk; they are the youth whose lives hang in the balance.[150]

Even more importantly, when fewer activities are available, children lose positive opportunities to learn skills, feel mastery, release stress, and come in positive contact with peers and adults. These opportunities are especially important for low-income children, say child development specialists at the University of Chicago:

For young people living in poverty, organized activities and facilities may off-set disadvantage by encouraging the development of their skills and abilities and providing access to opportunities that might otherwise not be available. Community facilities may provide safe havens in which children can find shelter from negative influences such as violence, drugs, gangs, or early sexual activity.... For young people living in troubled families (with parents who are ill or unavailable) community resources can put children in touch with other adults who can offer guidance, nurturance, and support.... For young people for whom academic learn-

*ing is an ongoing source of frustration,
developing skills and a sense of competence
in other areas of endeavor may off-set the
damage to self-esteem that difficulties at
school can engender....*[151]

Smoking and heavy drinking. There is evidence that psychological stress caused by economic stress may lead to increased smoking and other unhealthy habits among youths and among the adults around whom poor children are raised. One congressional study found that "other factors held constant, the unemployment rate was significantly related to increases in cigarette consumption" between 1950 and 1980; cigarette consumption was higher during years in which business failures were common, as well. Economic distress also was linked strongly with consumption of hard liquor (but not wine or beer) and, after a nine-year lag, with fatal liver disease.[152]

Besides creating economic distress, some scholars point out that poverty contributes to high-risk health habits by limiting lower income adults' choices for recreation and relaxation. Epidemiologist David Williams points out that poor adults often cannot afford the alternative coping strategies used by wealthier members of society; as a result, they may resort to unhealthy strategies such as smoking. "Cigarettes are used widely to alleviate stress and tension," Williams points out, while disadvantaged individuals "have more stress and fewer resources to cope with it." Williams notes that this may help explain why low-income Americans have not reduced smoking as much as their wealthy peers despite public education campaigns against smoking. Even though disadvantaged individuals may know that smoking and other behaviors endanger their health in the distant future, Williams says, they may rely on them as "the basic survival strategies of day-to-day existence."[153]

Unhealthy behavior in adults damages children's health and learning in several ways. Cigarette smoking by adults, for example, reaches into children's lives starting with the risk of fetal exposure during pregnancy (which has been found to

Poverty and virtues

Poverty...makes some virtues impracticable, and others extremely difficult.
Samuel Johnson

affect later IQ[154] as well as child health), continuing with exposure during childhood to secondary smoke, and lasting into adolescence with greater exposure to potential adult role models who smoke. Finally, as children grow into adulthood they themselves may resort to smoking as a way of relieving their own poverty-related stresses.

Money Buys Transportation, Communication, and Economic Opportunity

Poverty makes it harder to go places and get things done. Decreased mobility may make poor families less able to reach good child care, recreational activities, medical care, and other services for their children — exacerbating a number of problems already discussed in this chapter — while making them less able to find good employment and economical shopping to sustain the family and work their way out of poverty. Poverty also limits access to telephone service, which makes it harder to stay in touch with family and friends, use health and other professional services, shop economically, and get a job. Poverty also makes it harder to afford certification or training, or the new clothing or tools that sometimes are needed to enter a new line of work.

Lack of a car. In 1984, 42 percent of poor children (including nearly 60 percent of children in households below half the poverty line) lived in households with no car — compared with just 3 percent of children in middle-income families.[155] Many others lived in households whose vehicle or vehicles were broken and unusable. In most parts of the United States, a working vehicle is not a luxury item — especially for the majority of poor children in the United States who live outside metropolitan central cities and are less likely to have access to public transportation. As urban and suburban communities have spread outward geographically, it has become ever more difficult for families without working automobiles to reach jobs, shopping centers, and the range of services needed by children and families.

The mobility of poor families that manage to afford a working car is restricted by costs of gasoline (especially in rural areas where travel distances are long) and parking (especially in crowded urban and suburban areas).

Limited public transportation. For poor families that depend on public transportation, the round-trip cost of a bus or subway ride may restrict mobility substantially. Public transportation may be too time-consuming or too expensive, especially when children's travel must be paid for as well. It may not even take families where they need to go.

Limited access to child care, recreation, health care, and other services. Many of the problems already described in this chapter — poor access to schools, activities, health care, and other services — are made worse because poor families lack transportation.

Access to health care is a critical problem for low-income families. Medicaid is supposed to help recipients pay for transportation, but nearly 3 million poor children lacked Medicaid or other coverage in 1992. Even families on Medicaid often get no help with transportation costs. In a U.S. General Accounting Office survey of Medicaid-enrolled and uninsured women in eight states, almost one in four women who had received inadequate prenatal care — 23 percent — said they had no transportation.[156] In rural areas, transportation problems were even worse.[157]

Transportation problems similarly make it harder to take advantage of existing social services, such as parenting classes or drug counseling, and to apply for and keep public assistance in times of crisis. Lack of transportation may even cause families to lose all or part of their welfare benefits due to missed appointments with welfare officials or a parent's failure to attend the variety of activities required by welfare rules.

Limited access to good jobs. Further, poverty often makes it difficult for a family to afford bus fare or car repairs needed to seek and keep jobs, or to attend job training.

While poverty itself can create a vicious cycle because of transportation-related work barriers, current federal rules for aiding the poor ironically make the problem worse. To qualify for Aid to Families with Dependent Children (AFDC), poor families must not own a vehicle with an equity value of more than $2,500. This means an unemployed family in rural America may have to give up a reliable car — and with it the only hope of finding future work or training — just to receive assistance during a financial crisis.

Limited access to low-cost stores. Transportation problems may combine with limited choice of neighborhoods to confine poor families to shopping in places where there are few stores, banks, or other services, and where prices for food, clothing, check-cashing, and other necessities are high and selection limited. (Factors common to poor urban or rural communities, such as crime or a small volume of sales, can drive up prices. For example, a 1990 study found poor communities in rural America often relied on small, more expensive mom-and-pop stores for their food because few competitively priced supermarkets were located nearby. In these smaller stores, prices were higher, supplies were low, and there were few fresh fruits and meats.)[158]

Single-mother families (which make up slightly more than half of poor families with children) spend almost as much per person as married-couple families for food but get less nutrition — single mothers eat fewer fruits, vegetables, and milk products, and their children eat less fruit — perhaps because they cannot reach cheaper stores, according to a recent U.S. Department of Agriculture study. The study speculated that, "because transportation may be a problem for single mothers, they may have to shop at the nearest supermarket—not necessarily where food prices are lowest." At the same time, they may also need to manage their time by shopping infrequently, which also limits their supply of these healthy but highly perishable foods.[159]

No phone service. One out of every three poor children (34 percent) who receive AFDC lived in a home with no telephone in 1987, as did one in four non-AFDC poor children (25 percent). By contrast, only 4 percent of nonpoor children lacked telephone service.[160] Telephone service can improve children's lives by giving families greater access to an array of routine and emergency services and resources including teachers and schools; doctors and hospitals; poison control centers; child care, educational, and recreational options; and other human services in the community. Inability to telephone a doctor or poison control center in an emergency may help explain why poisoning is a major poverty-related health problem for children in some cities (see Chapter 3). In an increasingly spread-out society, telephones also help parents form informal networks with relatives, co-workers, and friends for helping each other in emotional or tangible ways. Telephones also permit families to spend money effectively by comparison shopping for low prices on needed items. Finally, the information available by telephone helps families to help themselves — for example, by allowing parents to find jobs that support the family or teens to find jobs that provide valuable work experience.

Poverty's Effects Add Up and Interact

Even when poverty's effects in many specific areas seem modest, the multiple risks it creates and the cumulative impact of diverse setbacks can be overwhelming. This is why poverty is so dangerous to children and why intervening at the root of the problem so important.

Consider why poor children are more likely to die in fires than nonpoor children. As already noted, 1.4 percent of poor children live in homes heated mainly by fire-prone portable electric heaters; although this is nearly triple the proportion among nonpoor children, this alone is a small risk. But add the greater likelihood that poor children will live in a poorly constructed mobile home (which makes it harder to escape in a fire) or in a house with bars on the windows that block escape in a fire (a common practice in crime-ridden inner cities). And add the higher risk that the family will have its utilities shut off and be forced to use candles as a dangerous source of lighting. Now add the increased chance that the child's home will have fire-prone faulty wiring or lack a properly functioning smoke detector (heightening the risk of fire and reducing the time available to escape). Viewed separately, none of these risks appear large. Together, they put substantial numbers of low-income children at risk of death or injury due to fires in the home.

It is even more chilling to realize that fires are only one of the factors underlying higher mortality rates among poor children. Poverty causes some parents to delay seeking medical care until a child is gravely ill. It forces many families to live in dangerous neighborhoods, exposing children to gun violence and hazardous traffic as they turn to sidewalks and busy streets in search of a place to play. It frequently leaves parents unable to find adequate child care for young children, increasing the likelihood of accidents while parents are away at work.

Poverty's effects accumulate so forcefully that some researchers believe that the *number* of problems shapes a child's future at least as much as what those problems are. In one study, more than half of adolescent delinquents, and half of adolescents with severe mental health problems, grew up with five or more separate risk factors (such as low standard of living at birth, health problems at birth, and low IQ). Among children who were neither delinquent nor seriously mentally disturbed, the majority had no more than two risk factors.[161]

Sometimes the effects of poverty do more than add up: they interact in ways that amplify their force. This pattern helps explain why poor children often suffer worse consequences than nonpoor children from the very same illnesses and setbacks.

Does it matter if poverty keeps a young child from having plenty of books and toys and an uncrowded home in which to learn? Maybe not very much by itself — that is, if the child has the kind of high quality child care that stimulates learning. In turn, not having good quality child care may not be as crucial if one's parents can pay the bills and avoid prolonged bouts of depression (so they can provide steady discipline, attention, and emotional warmth). Having distressed parents may not matter as much to a healthy, well-nourished, and good-tempered child (because most parents relate better to such children and find them easier to nurture). And not being healthy and good-tempered may be less important if a child has regular care from a good family doctor (because ongoing care helps keep health problems under control and trusted doctors can be a source of helpful, steadying advice for the parents).

But when poverty erodes many or most of these supports at once, a child is left vulnerable and the harmful effects may snowball. This may explain why, as a team of pediatrician-researchers has noted:

> *Children living in poverty experience double jeopardy. First, they are exposed more frequently to such risks as medical illness, family stress, inadequate social support, and parental depression. Secondly, they experience more serious consequences from these risks than do children from higher socioeconomic status.*[162]

These dangers can be found interacting with each other at every level of a poor child's life, at the size of a blood cell or the scale of a neighborhood.

Lead poisoning and iron deficiency. Poverty exposes children to greater risks of both lead poisoning (due to old and poorly maintained housing) and iron deficiency (due to poor nutrition). When these two consequences of poverty interact in the bloodstream, however, the combination of lead poisoning and iron deficiency is distinctly more harmful than the presence of either alone.[163] That is because the human body needs iron, and blood cells seek it out; when children lack sufficient iron, their blood cells instead grab hold of lead molecules that the child has ingested from paint dust, contaminated water, or other sources. These children therefore absorb more of the poisonous metal and it bonds more tightly to their blood cells. The result is more severe lead poisoning (see box on page 115).

Crowded housing conditions, limited recreation, limited supervision, and high residential turnover. A different type of interaction may occur between overcrowding and the lack of supervised activities for poor children — activities such as child care, youth groups, extracurricular sports and activities, and summer camps. Taken separately, none of these activities may be very influential. But poor families often cannot pay for any. When combined with cramped homes and a shortage of safe yards and playgrounds in some low-income neighborhoods, these poverty-related shortcomings may drive children to play unsupervised near busy streets or in other places where injuries are more likely to occur.[164] When large numbers of poor children also live in single-parent families, the risk of inadequate supervision grows even greater. The combination of crowded housing conditions and limited supervision is implicated in childhood injuries.

In a separate set of interactions, high concentrations of poverty within a neighborhood plus high residential turnover — but not either of these factors alone — have been linked to patterns of childhood street behavior thought to lead to delinquency and crime.[165] Even more broadly, there is evidence that "concentrated urban poverty and social disorganization combine to generate child abuse/neglect, low birthweight, cognitive impairment, and other adjustment problems," according to Robert J. Sampson of the University of Chicago, "which in turn constitute risk factors for later crime and violence."[166]

Disadvantaged backgrounds and low birthweight. When poverty combines with low birthweight, the developmental risks to children surge. One study reports that "children who are both poor and low birthweight are more likely to be in special education than the additive effects of the two variables" by themselves.[167] A well-known study on the Hawaiian island of Kauai showed that social class interacted with low birthweight, difficult labor, and other complications of pregnancy and birth. Birth complications:

> *were consistently related to later impaired physical and psychological development only when combined with persistently poor environmental circumstances (e.g., chronic poverty, family instability, or maternal mental health problems). Children who were raised in more affluent homes, with an intact family and a well-educated mother, showed few, if any, negative effects from reproductive stress unless the complications were unusually serious, such as major brain damage.*[168]

Other studies similarly have found that a disadvantaged background often makes children more vulnerable to the effects of low birthweight.[169] And, as in other interactions, the reverse is necessarily true as well: low birthweight makes children more vulnerable to the effects of poverty.

The existence of multiple, interacting risks for children has profound implications for our understanding of child poverty. If poverty triggers a deluge of problems for children — rather than just a few easily remedied problems — then attacking poverty directly by raising parents' earnings and family incomes may be a necessary part of any cure.

This does not mean that income is the only important piece of the solution. Nor does it mean that service-oriented solutions (such as better schooling, more good quality child care, better nutrition programs, or parenting education and other support for parents) are less effective for low-income children than for their wealthier peers. In fact, this section shows that poor children often suffer worse impacts than nonpoor children do when they lack a supportive environment. It follows that receiving these supports may make a *bigger* difference for poor children than for nonpoor children.

Chapter 3

Human Costs Linked to Child Poverty

That children growing up in poverty are forced to do without many basic necessities of life in a nation of unprecedented wealth should be, by itself, a national embarrassment. But the implications of children's poverty do not stop there. They continue on, through countless "pathways" such as those described in Chapter 2, ultimately leading to shortened lifespans, more severe diseases, and thwarted potential for learning and education. These and other grave outcomes are among the human costs of child poverty.

For any individual poor child, the deprivations caused by child poverty may or may not inflict serious or lasting damage. Children from all backgrounds and income groups are by nature remarkably resilient. The great majority of children who experience poverty overcome the obstacles it strews in their paths and successfully negotiate the transition to adulthood.

What poverty *does* do is expose children to greater risks. It tips the odds against poor children, making it much harder for them to survive, grow, develop, and reach their full potential. Across an astonishing range of outcomes — including premature death, stunted growth, physical impairment, injury, learning disability, low educational achievement, school failure, abuse and neglect, extreme behavioral problems, and delinquency — poor children fare worse than children who grow up in families that are able to meet their basic needs.

Chapter 2, focusing on family budgets and what money buys, revealed how poverty sows the seeds of future suffering and failure. This chapter provides a glimpse of the bitter harvest that poor children and their families reap because of our willingness to tolerate high and persistent rates of child poverty in America.

The dividing lines between Chapter 2's discussion of the ways that poverty hurts children and Chapter 3's summary of final results or human costs for children growing up poor are not always neat or clear. For example, nutritional problems such as iron deficiency and related anemia are important "pathways" to future learning problems such as learning dis-

Children's health conditions by family income

Low-income children's higher risk

Death during infancy:	1.3 times more likely
Death during childhood:	3 times more likely
Low birthweight:	1.2 to 2.2 times more likely
Stunted growth:	2 to 3 times more likely[b]
Partly or completely deaf:	1.5 to 2 times more likely
Partly or completely blind:	1.2 to 1.8 times more likely
Physical or mental disabilities:	about 2 times more likely
Mild mental retardation:	more likely
Overall injuries:	no more likely
Days in bed because of injuries:	1.8 times more likely
Hospitalization for injuries:	at least 3 times more likely[a]
Fatal accidental injuries:	2 to 3 times more likely
Hospitalization for poisoning:	5 times more likely[a]
Fair or poor health:	3 times more likely
Iron deficiency in preschool years:	3 to 4 times more likely
Frequent diarrhea or colitis:	1.5 times more likely
Pneumonia:	1.6 times more likely
Repeated tonsillitis:	1.1 times more likely
Overall asthma:	more likely
Severe asthma:	about 2 times more likely
Decayed, missing, or filled teeth:	more likely
School days missed due to acute and chronic health conditions:	1.4 times more likely

[a] Based on income data for child's neighborhood, not family.
[b] For children in long-term poor families.

Children's education outcomes by family income

Low-income children's higher risk

Average IQ scores at age 5:	9 test points lower [ab]
Average achievement scores for ages 3 and older:	11 to 25 percentiles lower[b]
Learning disabilities:	1.3 times more likely
In special education:	2 or 3 percentage points more likely [a]
Below the usual grade for child's age:	2 percentage points more likely for each year of childhood spent in poverty[a]
Being a dropout at age 16 to 24:	2 times more likely than middle-income youths and 11 times more likely than wealthy youths
Enrolling in any postsecondary education:	less likely than the U.S. average or than wealthy students
Enrolling in a four-year college:	two-thirds as likely as the U.S. average and half as likely as wealthy students
Finishing a four-year college:	one-half as likely as the U.S. average and one-fourth as likely as wealthy students

[a] Holding other factors constant.
[b] For children in long-term poor families.

abilities, low educational achievement, and subsequent school failure. They are also important human costs in themselves — critical outcomes indicating serious medical trouble. Other poverty-related problems also have a dual impact on the lives of poor children, inflicting direct harm now while at the same time exposing children to new dangers and longer term developmental consequences for months and years to come.

Rarely if ever is a shortage of income the *sole* cause of the gaps between poor and nonpoor children's risks of disease, school problems, or other bad outcomes. Poverty often is intertwined with other difficulties, such as low parental education or the effects of race and racism, which contribute to poor children's unequal risks, as well. Overall, poverty plays a large role in some problems, a smaller role in others. Yet the weight of evidence suggesting that poverty itself is the source of *a major portion* of many of the gaps between poor and nonpoor children is all but overwhelming. Time and time again, when state-of-the-art research has exhausted every available means of isolating poverty's effects and "holding constant" other factors that might influence outcomes for children, sizable impacts remain that researchers can only attribute to poverty.

Finally, it is worth remembering that the greater risks confronting poor children must never become an excuse for parents, teachers, or others to diminish their expectations of or commitment to any child. Growing up in poverty does not make failure inevitable. Neither school failure, out-of-wedlock childbearing, nor any of a host of other potential pitfalls in life are unavoidable simply because a child's family is poor. In fact, the most remarkable success stories in the face of seemingly insurmountable odds often start with a dedicated parent, teacher, or other adult who never gave up on a child he or she was determined to save. And those stories remind us that, by improving the odds for poor children in America, we can help ensure that no child is left behind.

Poverty, education, illness

People already burdened by poverty and lack of education should not also carry a disproportionate share of illness.

Excerpted from information appearing in the *New England Journal of Medicine,* July 8, 1993

Health

The added health problems of low-income children are startling, both in their variety and in their severity, and range from greater risk of death to disability to lost school days. "Low-income children are twice to three times more likely to be of low birthweight, to have delayed immunizations, to get bacterial meningitis, to be lead poisoned, and, at least until recent years, to contract rheumatic fever," observes Barbara Starfield, M.D., director of health policy studies at Johns Hopkins University.[1]

Just as important, poor children's health problems tend to hit harder. "Problems, when they occur, are...more likely to be severe," notes Starfield.[2] "Low-income children are often at triple to quadruple risk of serious problems compared with other children," she explains. "This is the case for illness progressing to death, for injuries progressing to death, for complications of various illnesses, for severely impaired vision, and for severe iron-deficiency anemia."[3] Poor children's outcomes may be more serious because they are exposed to more potent illnesses or injuries, more frequent multiple illnesses, because their resistance to disease is weakened by inadequate nutrition or other factors, or because they receive less adequate medical treatment and attention.

Deaths

Poverty's starkest and most unmistakable health effects are those leading to death. Poor children are more likely to die at every age and from every cause. Their risk of death ranges from 1.1 times greater for cancer to 5 or more times greater for infectious diseases and parasites.

Deaths during infancy. Low-income children in Kentucky are about 1.3 times more likely than others to die before their first birthday, according to that state's Department for Health Services.[4] The Kentucky 1982-1983 infant mortality rate for

---

Infant deaths

The baby death rate rises as the fathers' earnings fall.

U.S. Children's Bureau, 1918

CHILDREN'S DEFENSE FUND

low-income infants was 13.7 deaths per 1,000 live births, compared with 10.8 per 1,000 for non-low-income babies, a difference accounted for by very high death rates from sudden infant death syndrome and fatal infections among low-income infants.

This infant mortality "gap" is not simply the product of differences in race, gender, mother's age (including teen birth), mother's education, or even birthweight. When these characteristics are accounted for, Kentucky's low-income children still are consistently and significantly (1.1 to 1.4 times) more likely to die before their first birthday.

When the last nationwide comparisons of infant deaths by income were made (for 1964-1965 deaths), babies born to poor White married women were 1.5 times more likely to die than babies born to similar women who were not poor, according to Harvard researcher Steven Gortmaker.[5] This comparison held other factors constant (such as health insurance, both parents' education, mother's age, birthweight, number of siblings, and whether the birth occurred in a hospital). Gortmaker said poor families may experience:

> ...inferior housing, poor sanitary facilities at home, lack of adequate food and clothing, inadequate hospital or postnatal medical care, lack of transportation facilities — meaning difficulty in obtaining needed services. Finally, those in poverty are often vulnerable to the experience of stressful situations. All of these factors can have damaging effects upon the health of newborns.

"Income supports and employment programs" could lower infant mortality, according to Gortmaker. The Kentucky researchers also concluded that "efforts aimed at reducing the number of families living in poverty" clearly are warranted.

Deaths during childhood. Low-income children are more likely than others to die during childhood, in every age group and

Infant mortality linked to economic changes

Broad economic trends have been linked to infant deaths. Infant mortality rates tended to rise in years of increasing unemployment and fall in years of decreasing unemployment, according to a congressional study covering 1950 to 1980. Such patterns of changing mortality suggest a link between hard times and infant deaths that cannot be attributed simply to an unhealthy "culture of poverty," to possible inherited health problems, or to other unchanging attributes of disadvantaged parents themselves.[6]

Death rate per 100,000 children in Kansas, 1985-1987

	Low-income children	Non-low-income children	Comparison: low-income to non-low-income
All causes	241.0	75.4	3.2 times greater
Accidents	42.5	18.9	2.2 times greater
Motor vehicle	9.1	11.5	1.7 times greater
Fire	7.5	1.7	4.3 times greater
Drowning	9.8	3.1	3.1 times greater
Other	6.1	2.5	2.4 times greater
Suicide	2.3	1.9	1.2 times greater
Homicide	10.3	1.2	8.4 times greater
Other external causes	2.8	0.5	5.4 times greater
Congenital anomalies	27.6	14.0	2.0 times greater
Perinatal conditions	57.9	17.2	3.4 times greater
Symptoms, signs, and ill-defined conditions	33.6	6.8	5.0 times greater
Infectious and parasitic diseases	5.6	1.0	5.4 times greater
Malignant neoplasms (cancer)	4.2	4.0	1.1 times greater
Other diseases	54.2	9.8	5.7 times greater

Based on state records for all 214,113 low-income and 1,725,168 non-low-income children ages 0 to 17 in Kansas from 1985 to 1987.

Source: Elizabeth W. Saadi, *Children's Deaths in Kansas: 1985 to 1987* (Topeka, KS: Kansas Department of Health and Environment and Kansas Department of Rehabilitation Services, 1989).

across every cause of death, according to statewide studies in Maine and Kansas. In 1976-1980, Maine's low-income children were 3.1 times more likely to die from all causes combined, including motor vehicle accidents (2.21 times), fire accidents (5.01 times), drowning (4.09 times), suicide (1.58 times), homicide (5.25 times), birth defects (3.75 times), perinatal conditions (2.29 times), and other diseases (3.61 times).[7]

Likewise, in 1985-1987 low-income Kansas children were 3.2 times more likely than other children to die.[8] Low-income children were at greater risk for every cause of death.

Low-income White children younger than 10 (with annual family incomes less than $10,000) were found to be about 1.4 times more likely to die than their non-low-income peers, in a study of 1975 nationwide data (the most recent available) on child mortality by family income level.[9] "Higher income children have an advantage for all race–sex groups except Black girls," according to Robert D. Mare, who studied Census Bureau data for June 1975.[10] "Economic effects are as strong as those of mother's schooling," Mare says. Among children whose mothers finished high school, poor boys are nearly 1.3 times more likely, and poor girls are 1.7 times more likely, to die than their nonpoor peers.[11, 12]

Low Birthweight and Stunted Growth

Low birthweight. Children born at low birthweight (less than 2,500 grams, or about 5.5 pounds) are far more likely than others to die in infancy[13] — one factor in the higher death rate for poor babies, who are 1.2 to 2.2 times more likely to be born too small. Low-birthweight babies also have a doubled risk of learning problems (learning disability, hyperactivity, emotional problems, and mental illness) and significantly greater risk of neurodevelopmental problems (seizures, epilepsy, water on the brain, cerebral palsy, and mental retardation) and loss of eyesight or hearing.[14]

The effects of poverty on birthweight are often dramatic. Between 1979 and 1988, 10.3 percent of babies born to White women who were poor when they conceived had low birthweights — a figure 2.2 times higher than among nonpoor Whites (4.6 percent). Among poor Black women, 12.1 percent of births were at low birthweight; this was 1.2 times higher than for nonpoor Black women overall, and 1.4 times higher than for Black women who were neither poor nor near-poor, although these differences among Black mothers were not statistically significant.[15] (A statistically significant difference is one that is probably not due to chance variations among children. Seemingly large differences between poor and nonpoor children sometimes do not meet standards of statistical significance — that is, are not reliable — because too few children were compared, or for other reasons.)

Accounting for other factors — such as mother's education, marital status, teen birth, and smoking — does relatively little to shrink poor women's higher risk of having low-birthweight babies. With these factors held constant for the 1979-1988 births, poor White women still were about 1.8 times more likely than their nonpoor peers to have low-birthweight babies. These data also indicate that a mother's poverty *before* pregnancy, as well as during pregnancy, may affect her child's birthweight significantly.

In Kentucky, among babies born in 1982-1983 to families poor enough to receive food stamps or AFDC, 8.8 percent were born at low birthweight, a rate 1.4 times higher than among the nonpoor there (6.3 percent).[16]

A nationwide survey in 1982 also showed a gap: the low-birthweight rate of women whose incomes were below 1.5 times the poverty line was about 1.2 times higher than the rate among women with larger incomes.[17] Among women on Medicaid (who were presumably even poorer), the low-birthweight rate was 10.2 percent — 1.6 times higher than among the more affluent group.

In a sample of births between 1978 and 1982 from the Oakland, California, area, financial problems noted in the mother's medical record — such as inability to meet a rent payment or buy food, loss of medical insurance, or insufficient

---

Prenatal drug exposure and poverty

Exposure to crack cocaine in the womb is a much-publicized problem. Yet at least one study by a highly respected team of researchers suggests that the presence of poverty plays a key role in the success or failure of these drug-exposed children. Ira J. Chasnoff and others, in a report in the February 1992 issue of *Pediatrics* magazine, wrote:

"The long-term effects...of drug-exposed children will not be explained by drug exposure alone. Before we can predict the development outcomes for these high-risk children

we need further research into the additive and interactive effects of the multiple risk factors to which they are exposed, including in many cases the global effects of poverty...."

A commentary by Barry Zuckerman and Deborah A. Frank in the same issue observed:

"Prenatal drug exposure is only one of multiple treatable or preventable biologic and social stressors experienced by children living in poverty. By focusing on cocaine and not on

lack of adequate nutrition, health care, and education, we conveniently can blame mothers and not the conditions of poverty. Although the present study shows that with intervention children prenatally exposed to cocaine can do as well in their global [intellectual and motor] development scores at age 2 years as their social class-matched peers, both groups function below national norms, reflecting the double jeopardy afflicting children living in poverty."

money for bus fare to prenatal appointments — increased the odds of low birthweight nearly six-fold, holding other factors constant. Financial problems had a stronger effect on low birthweight than did lack of prenatal care, self-reported smoking or other substance use, not living with a partner, being Black or a refugee, previous miscarriage, and other pregnancy-related factors with the exception of previous history of low-birthweight birth.[18]

Because information on mothers' incomes seldom is collected in medical records, other researchers have investigated instead the effect of living in low-income neighborhoods. White and Black mothers from the poorest neighborhoods of Los Angeles were found to be about twice as likely to bear low-birthweight babies as mothers from the wealthiest neighborhoods. When the mothers were grouped into risk categories (by race, age, and adequacy of prenatal care), those from low-income areas remained generally more likely to have underweight babies.[19] Low-birthweight rates also have been found to be higher for mothers in Chicago's low-income neighborhoods than among women in similar risk categories but from affluent neighborhoods there.[20]

Stunted growth. In 1988, the odds of having stunted growth — that is, being in the shortest 10 percent of children for their age — were 2.5 times greater for long-term poor children than for children with long-term incomes above triple the poverty line, according to data from the National Longitudinal Survey of Youth. The odds remained about 2 times greater even after the researchers held constant a long list of other factors (such as race, marital status, mother's age at first birth, mother's skills and education, mother's physical size, and the child's height and weight at birth).[21]

Similarly, the 1976-1980 National Health and Nutrition Examination Survey found that two- to five-year-old poor boys were more than twice as likely as nonpoor peers (11.1 versus 5.3 percent) to have stunted growth. Girls from poor families were almost 3 times more likely to be stunted (14.7 versus 5.3 percent).[22]

Disabilities and Sensory Impairments

Partial or complete deafness. Poor children have been found to be 1.5 to 2 times more likely than others to be partly or completely deaf, according to nationwide surveys conducted between 1971 and 1983. Among non-Latino White six- to 17-year-olds, those living in poverty were 1.6 times more likely than their nonpoor peers to have inadequate hearing in their worst ear (6.1 percent versus 3.7 percent). Poor Mexican-American children in the same age range were 1.5 times more likely to have inadequate hearing (4.9 percent versus 3.3 percent). And among non-Latino Black children, those in poverty were 2.1 times more likely than their nonpoor peers (5.7 percent versus 2.7 percent) to have inadequate hearing in their worst ear.[23]

Partial or complete blindness. Similarly, poor children have been found to be 1.2 to 1.8 times more likely to be partly or completely blind. Poor non-Latino White children ages six to 17 were 1.5 times more likely than their nonpoor peers to have inadequate vision in their worst eye (13.5 percent versus 9.1 percent), according to nationwide surveys taken between 1976 and 1983. Poor Mexican-American children were 1.2 times more likely to have inadequate vision (15.5 percent versus 12.7 percent). And among non-Latino Black children, those in poverty were 1.8 times more likely than their nonpoor peers to have inadequate vision in their worst eye (18.7 percent versus 10.5 percent).[24]

Physical or mental disabilities serious enough to limit daily activities. Nationwide, 9.4 percent of children with family incomes below $10,000 have chronic health conditions serious enough to limit them to some extent in their daily activities — a disability rate that is 1.8 times higher than for children with annual family incomes of $10,000 or more (5.3 percent), according to National Health Interview Survey data for 1990 through 1992. Fully 651,000 low-income children had some activity limitation.[25]

More seriously, nearly half a million (494,000) low-income children in 1990-1992 were limited in performing the major activity for their age — that is, attending school or, in the case of very young children, playing — because of their disabilities. Low-income children, therefore, are 1.9 times more likely than others (7.2 percent versus 3.8 percent) to have major activity limitations.

Most seriously of all, 72,000 low-income children in 1990-1992 were completely unable to carry on the major activity for their age. Low-income children are more than twice as likely as others (1.1 percent versus 0.5 percent) to have such complete disabilities. If low-income and wealthier children faced equal odds, more than half of the 72,000 low-income children suffering worst-case disabilities would be spared.

And the relative risk that low-income children will have disabilities is growing. In 1976-1977 low-income children were about 1.6 times more likely than children in nonpoor families to have a chronic disability (defined as a major activity limitation), according to government researchers. By 1988-1989, "poor children were...about twice as likely as higher-income children to have a disabling chronic condition."[26]

Low income also accounts completely for the higher disability rate of Black children: "The effect of race was eliminated from the disability measure" when low-income status was held constant, the researchers found.

Mild mental retardation. The rate of mental retardation among children from low-status backgrounds (based on measures such as parents' occupation and education) has been found to be 4 to 20 times greater than among more privileged children, according to a National Academy of Sciences research review. (Few if any studies examine direct links between income and retardation; social status is the best available proxy for income in this area.) Having a low social status increases the risk of retardation for both White and Black children, and in small-town America as well as inner cities. Low-status children seem to be at particular risk of mild retardation.[27]

Several poverty-related factors may cause mental retardation, starting as early as pregnancy with "cytomegalovirus [a virus that can cause mental and physical abnormalities if trans-mitted to the fetus], alcohol, complications during the newborn period related to prematurity and/or low birthweight, and early childhood insults such as malnutrition and lead intoxica-tion," according to the National Academy of Sciences study. "These threatening influences and many others exist with greater frequency among poor and minority populations. The unequal distribution of these risk factors is certainly influenced by social and economic forces," the study concludes.[28]

Serious Injuries and Poisoning

Overall injuries. Although the numbers of children's injuries reported by parents do not vary greatly by income, low-income children appear to suffer more serious consequences. From 1990 to 1992 low-income children averaged slightly fewer reported injuries than their wealthier peers nationwide, a ratio of about 0.8 to 1.[29] (These differences could result from higher income children having larger numbers of minor injuries, their parents being more likely to report minor injuries, or other fac-tors.) Lower income children's injuries, however, are more likely to result in death, days in bed, and hospitalizations.

Days spent in bed because of injuries. Low-income children spent a combined total of 2 million days per year confined to bed because of injuries in 1990-1992. This came to about 31 days per 100 low-income children, compared with 17 days per 100 children with family incomes over $10,000.[30]

Hospitalization for injuries. Poorer neighborhoods often have higher injury rates. In New York City, for example, children in the most poverty-stricken neighborhoods have hospital dis-charge rates 3 times higher for arm and leg fractures and twice as high for traumatic stupor and brief coma (although slightly lower for concussions) than children in low-poverty neighborhoods.[31]

Motor vehicle accidents also have been linked to neighborhood poverty. In Montreal during 1981, pedestrian and bicycle injuries (but not passenger injuries) in the poorest neighborhoods were 4 to 9 times greater than those in more affluent areas.[32] Hartford, Connecticut, neighborhoods where many accidents occurred in 1986 and 1987 had twice the poverty rate and nearly 3 times the rate of overcrowded households as neighborhoods with few or no accidents.[33]

In Memphis, 210 children were hit by motor vehicles during 1982, usually while crossing streets from between parked cars or not crossing at an intersection. In neighborhoods where accidents occurred the family poverty rate was nearly 1.5 times higher, the rate of overcrowded housing was 2 times higher, and the density per acre of overcrowded housing was 3 times higher than in neighborhoods that had no accidents.[34]

Fatal accidental injuries. Low-income children in Kansas were found to be 2.2 times more likely than others to die from accidental injuries, and low-income children in Maine were 2.6 times more likely.[35] This may reflect the worst consequences of having no safe place to play and limited resources to provide safe child care and supervision.

Hospitalization for poisoning. In New York City, children from the poorest neighborhoods are more than 5 times more likely to be hospitalized for poisoning than children from the wealthiest areas (35.6 versus 6.8 hospital discharges per 10,000 children), making poisoning the childhood medical problem with the greatest income-related disparity in New York City.[36]

Perceived Health Status and Specific Diseases

There is considerable evidence that poor children experience more illness and, especially, greater severity of illness. Parents of poor children more frequently report that their children are in ill health, and rates of several specific illnesses have been found to be higher among poor children.

Poverty and fire deaths

Poor rural households, particularly those in warm climates, are also more likely to lack the resources for central heating, leading them to push portable or space heaters beyond safe limits. When electrical bills can't be paid, unsafe electrical practices and makeshift heating, cooking, and lighting arrangements are more likely.

The electricity in the rural Texas mobile home of Mary Elizabeth S., 3, her sisters Nancy Michelle, 2, and Melissa Torene, 7 months, was supplied by a heavy-duty power cord that ran from the home next door. The three little girls died in 1985 when an electrical problem, possibly a short circuit, in a window fan, started a fire that destroyed the mobile home.

Reprinted with permission from *NFPA Journal*® (January/February). Copyright © 1989, National Fire Protection Association, Quincy, MA 02269 (*NFPA Journal*® is a registered trademark of the National Fire Protection Association)

Between 1990 and 1992, 6.6 percent of low-income children were rated by their parents as in fair or poor health — 3 times more than among children with annual family incomes above $10,000 (2.1 percent).[37] (While subjective, such health assessments provided by families closely match doctors' determinations, according to medical researchers.)

The link between income and health status appears to be growing stronger. According to government health specialists:

> *In 1976-1977, children in poor families were twice as likely as children in [nonpoor] families to be in fair-poor health.... In 1988-1989, poor children were nearly three times more likely to be in fair or poor health.... In addition, poverty was a stronger predictor than race of fair/poor health and of disability in children.*[38]

Iron deficiency and anemia. Poor preschoolers are 3 to 4 times more likely than better off children to have abnormally low iron levels in their blood. In a series of nationwide health examinations from 1976 to 1980, 20.6 percent of poor one- and two-year-olds had iron deficiency — triple the rate among non-poor toddlers (6.7 percent).[39] At ages three and four, 9.7 percent of poor children had low iron levels — nearly quadruple the rate among nonpoor children (2.5 percent). Iron deficiency is the most common cause of anemia (the inability of red blood cells to carry enough oxygen to the body). Although childhood anemia has declined since 1975,[40] it continued to afflict more than 1 million low-income young children in 1992, including about one in five low-income children younger than age two.[41]

Frequent diarrhea and colitis. Frequent diarrhea and colitis are significantly related to income, according to the 1988 National Health Interview Survey on Child Health. These illnesses occur at an annual rate of 2.0 cases per 100 children in families with annual incomes below $10,000, compared with fewer than 1.4 cases per 100 in families with incomes of $10,000 or more.[42]

Pneumonia. Pneumonia also is significantly related to income, according to the 1988 National Health Interview Survey on Child Health. Pneumonia occurs at an annual rate of 2.6 cases per 100 children in families with annual incomes below $10,000, compared with 1.6 cases per 100 in families with incomes of $10,000 or more.[43]

Repeated tonsillitis. Repeated tonsillitis, as well, is related to income, occurring at an annual rate of 5.2 cases per 100 children in the lower income families, compared with 4.7 per 100 in the higher income families.[44]

Asthma. Poor children are more likely to have asthma — the most common chronic medical condition among children — and more likely to suffer severe effects from the condition. A reliable (statistically significant) link between poverty and asthma among children was found in an analysis of data from the 1988 National Health Interview Survey by researchers Neal Halfon and Paul Newacheck, although the size of the difference was modest (4.8 cases per 100 poor children, compared with 4.2 per 100 nonpoor children).[45] A similar study reported that children from low-income families (with annual incomes of less than $10,000) were 1.3 times more likely to suffer asthma: 5.4 percent of low-income and 4.1 percent of non-low-income children had asthma. Asthma rates for all children have risen by more than one-third since 1981.[46]

Halfon and Newacheck also found that poor asthmatic children were about 1.8 times more likely than nonpoor asthmatic children to be hospitalized during the year (10.6 percent versus 6.0 percent) or to spend at least one week bedridden because of asthma (16.4 percent versus 9.1 percent). Other measures of severity are worse for poor children with asthma, as well, although the differences are not statistically significant. Poor children with asthma averaged twice as many days sick in bed; missed twice as many school days; spent 3 times as many days in the hospital; and were one-third more likely to say they are bothered often or all the time by their disease. However, poor

---

Asthma prevention barriers

"Asthma is really a chronic disease that requires special knowledge and behavior...," said Floyd Malveaux, an associate professor at the Howard University College of Medicine. Yet many asthma patients cannot afford to make even simple changes, such as purchasing mattress covers, vacuum cleaners and dehumidifiers, which can improve their condition, he said. "In order to practice prevention, you...can't be concerned about where your next meal is coming from, or how to pay the rent."

Copyright © 1994. *The Washington Post.* Reprinted with permission

children with asthma had significantly fewer doctor visits, likely because of their lack of a source of routine care.

Hospitalization for asthma in Maryland is reported to be 3.2 times higher for children who receive Medicaid than for other children (with hospital discharge rates of 4.83 per 1,000 children versus 1.52 per 1,000). Within racial groups, White children receiving Medicaid were 2.8 times more likely, and Black children 1.9 times more likely, to be hospitalized for asthma than their peers who did not receive Medicaid.[47]

Similarly, hospitalizations for childhood asthma are much more common in poor neighborhoods. In New York City, hospital discharge rates for asthma and bronchitis were 4 times higher among children from the poorest neighborhoods than among children in affluent neighborhoods.[48] In Maryland, the hospital discharge rate for asthma was 3 times higher in the poorest districts than in the districts with the least poverty. Among Black children, the rate was 4 times higher in the poorest districts.[49]

Dental problems no child should have

Six-year-old "Melinda" has dental problems that no child in American should have today. But Melinda grew up without the basics of preventive oral health that most children take for granted. With an annual income of less than $5,000, her parents — Navaho migrant farmworkers — barely can scrape together enough food for her, her sister, and themselves. Nutritionally sound food, essential for strong teeth, often is an unaffordable luxury. Regular medical and dental care are out of the question.

Although Medicaid would have covered dental care for Melinda, her parents, deterred by a combination of language barriers and general distrust of the White culture's systems, didn't try to enroll her.

In late 1993, Melinda developed a bad decay in one of her baby molars. By the time her mother took her to a local public health clinic, the girl was in severe pain, her face was swollen from the decay-caused infection, and she had a temperature of 100 degrees. Melinda was given an antibiotic, and her mother was told to buy some penicillin for the girl and bring her back the next day for follow-up care. Unable to afford the $12 penicillin at a drug store, embarrassed to tell clinic staff that fact, and afraid that more contact with the health care system would mean more bills she could not pay, the mother decided not to take her daughter back to the clinic.

Three days later, Melinda was in the public health clinic again, this time brought in by her school nurse. Without the penicillin, Melinda's infection had worsened. Dentist Charles Belting had no choice but to extract the tooth. While that cured the infection, premature loss of baby teeth can lead to later problems, including crooked permanent teeth and jaw pain in adolescence or adulthood, says Belting. Not only that, Melinda has other decaying teeth that can bring on infections which, if left untreated long enough, could spread to her sinuses. "Those other teeth are time bombs waiting to go off," says Belting.

Decayed, missing, or filled teeth by age 12. In a study of 10 U.S. cities, children of low socioeconomic status had more dental problems. In areas without fluoridated water, the lowest-status one-fourth of children had an average of almost three additional cavities, missing permanent teeth, and fillings by age 12, compared with the highest status one-fourth of children (9.47 versus 6.70). In areas with fluoridated water, the differences were smaller (5.71 versus 4.91). In both types of sites, differences between low- and high-status children widened with age. The study did not show income differences separately but noted that all three attributes used to gauge socioeconomic status (family income, parent education, and parent occupation) were related to these dental problems "to about the same degree."[50]

School Days Missed Due to Illness

Even minor health problems can affect every aspect of a child's life, starting with a baby's ability to learn and interact energetically with his or her parents. Frequent illnesses cause school children to miss more classes and may do lasting damage to their education.

School days missed. Low-income school children miss 1.7 more school days a year than their wealthier peers due to illness and injury. School-age children from families with annual incomes below $10,000 stayed home from school an average of 6.4 days per year between 1990 and 1992 because of ill health — together missing a total of 29 million school days per year — compared with an average of 4.7 days for children with family incomes of $10,000 or more.[51] This disparity costs low-income children a total of nearly 8 million school days each year.

Low-income children's high rate of lost school days cannot be explained by differences in mothers' employment, race, parents' marital status, or mothers' education. In a study of 1981 data, even after these and other factors were held constant,

---

'Learning-threatening' ailments

The children Geneva Ballou sees in her school nurse's office here can neither breathe nor hear well, and cannot calm themselves when they are upset. They are part of a silent plague in America's schools: children whose ailments are not life-threatening, but learning-threatening.

Copyright © 1991 by The New York Times Company. Reprinted by permission

the odds of missing school because of poor health were 2 times greater for low-income White children than for their non-low-income White peers.[52]

Education and Learning

Besides missing more school days due to ill health, poor children are most likely to suffer numerous other problems that can hamper their learning and school completion, ranging from lead poisoning and hunger to stressful relationships with parents and lack of money to attend college. The cumulative results of impaired health and nutrition, fewer learning opportunities at home, family distress leading to emotional and behavioral problems, lack of appropriate schooling, and other disadvantages can be seen in every area of poor children's learning and education. In the poorest schools served by the Chapter 1 compensatory education program, more than half of principals believed poor nutrition and lack of rest are "moderate" or "serious" problems for their students.[53] Behavior problems — linked to poverty-related family stress — can interfere with learning both for the disruptive children and for their classmates. Ironically, although the vast majority of poor children can succeed in the right learning environment[54] and are possibly more sensitive to quality of education than their more advantaged peers,[55] they tend to be stranded in the worst schools with the least stimulating teaching methods.

Lower Test Scores
Average IQ scores at age five. Children who spend their first five years of life in poverty score 9 points lower on an IQ test than children whose families never were poor (after accounting for differences in race, family status, parental education, and other factors), according to a study that followed nearly 900 low-birthweight, premature infants born in eight U.S. hospitals.[56]

'They solve problems all day'

"Some of them get up with the problem every morning of: How do you wake up without an alarm clock or a parent there to wake you? How do you get up and go to school when you probably didn't have a bed to sleep in the night before and people were up drunk and fighting all night?...These kids could beat anybody. They solve problems all day."

Louisville science teacher, describing how students in her heavily impoverished school district won a statewide academic competition. Copywight © 1993. The [Louisville, Kentucky] *Courier-Journal.* Reprinted with permission

Achievement scores. Nationwide, on four tests of vocabulary, reading, and math achievement for children age three and older, long-term poor children ranked 11 to 25 percentile points below children whose long-term incomes were above triple the poverty line. (If children were ranked by score and separated into 100 groups of equal size, each percentile difference would equal the difference between the scores of one such group and the next.)[57]

Achievement score differences cannot be explained away by parents' own characteristics (see sidebar, this page). Even after holding these factors constant, long-term poor children still had significantly lower scores than middle- or high-income children. Adjusting for these factors shrank the size of poverty's effect on test scores only modestly — to between 6 and 11 percentiles, or about one-half of the original gap. (The study also tentatively explored what aspects of poverty did explain its harmful effects. Consistent with the importance of family stress and other aspects of home life described in Chapter 2, poor mothers' parenting behavior and physical home environment explained a substantial share of the remaining gaps, although never more than half.)[58] One area where poor children did not fare significantly worse, holding other factors equal, was on a test of verbal memory.

Learning Disabilities and Special Education
Learning disabilities. Nationwide in 1988, 8.4 percent of three- to 17-year-olds with family incomes below $10,000 were reported by their parents to have learning disabilities. This was 1.3 times more than the proportion among children in higher income families (about 6.4 percent).[60]

Special education. Family poverty increases the chances that a child will be in special education by more than 2 percentage points, holding other factors equal, according to an analysis of 8,000 six- to eight-year-olds in the 1988 National Health Interview Survey. Overall, about 7 percent of children are in

Factors that do *not* explain poor children's lower test scores

Poor children's worse academic scores cannot be attributed to their mothers' lower academic skills, less formal education, teen childbearing, race, single-parent status, or the mother's smoking or drinking behavior.

Even when researchers "held constant" these factors — in effect by comparing poor and nonpoor children who were as similar as possible on all these characteristics — poor children still fared much worse. Holding these factors constant reduced the effect of poverty by roughly one-half. The results suggest that maternal and family characteristics can explain only a portion of the gaps between poor and nonpoor children.[59]

special education because they are developmentally delayed, learning disabled, or emotionally disturbed. But (after adjusting for race, family structure, parents' education, low birthweight, rural residence, region, and age) being from a poor family increases this risk by 2.4 percentage points. Using a slightly broader definition of special education, the research found that poverty increases the risk by 2.7 percentage points.[61]

Although poverty was not the focus of the study, it found that poverty has as large an effect as low birthweight in predicting specified categories of special education and almost as large in predicting special education overall. And as noted in Chapter 2, poverty and low birthweight appear to interact harmfully: when a child experiences both, the combined effect on special education is even larger than one would expect from adding the two separate effects together.

Similarly, a small local-level study found that the odds of ending up in special education in New York City are greater for children born to families on Medicaid (and therefore generally in poverty) than for other children. Poverty's effect was particularly strong among non-Black children: those born on Medicaid had 11 times greater odds of being in special education. For Black children, being born on Medicaid increased the odds of special education 1.4 times.[62]

Falling Behind Grade Level

The chance that a student will fall behind in school increases by 2 full percentage points for every year he or she spends growing up in poverty, according to a U.S. Department of Education study. Poor children's pattern of being below the most common grade level for students of their age is a strong indication that they are having trouble academically, have been kept back a grade, or are at risk of dropping out.

The study holds constant several other key factors, including the mother's education, her involvement in the child's schooling, and the student's gender. Several commonly cited

---

The legacy of lead poisoning

"Lana" had been worried for a long time about the lead-based paint in her Holyoke, Massachusetts, apartment hurting her three children's health. She wanted to move but, with welfare her only source of income, didn't have the money. When her one-year-old twins tested positive for lead poisoning in 1982, she ditched her fears about money, packed up her children and belongings, and left. For the next three months, Lana and the children were homeless.

With help from The Care Center, a local education and support program for young mothers and children, Lana eventually became employed and gained a measure of economic security. She successfully sued her former landlord on behalf of one of the twins, who suffered lasting health and learning problems from the lead poisoning and has needed special education since he started school. But none of that can reverse her son's brain damage. Now 13, the boy has speech difficulties and problems with memory loss that doctors say will plague him for life.

factors — including race, having a teen parent, or living in a one-parent home — were found to have no significant independent effect on falling behind grade level when duration in poverty and other factors were held constant.[63]

The odds of school failure (defined as either having failed a grade or being rated by one's mother as performing "below the middle" or "near the bottom" at school) are nearly 1.9 times greater for low-income White children than their wealthier White peers, other risk factors being equal, according to another study.[64]

Dropping Out of High School

Poorer youths are twice as likely as their middle-income peers, and almost 11 times more likely than wealthy youths, to drop out of high school. In 1992, 24.6 percent of the 16- to 24-year-olds from the poorest one-fifth of families were considered high school dropouts (that is, they were out of school and had no diploma), compared with 2.3 percent among the wealthiest one-fifth of youths and 10.1 percent among middle-income peers. The dropout rate of low-income youths consistently has been twice as high as the rate for middle-income youths since 1972.[65] Among both Whites and Blacks, the dropout rate of low-income youths is more than twice as high as their middle-

Dropout rates
(proportion not in school and not high school graduates),
ages 16 to 24, October 1992

	Poorest 20 percent of youths	Middle 60 percent of youths	Wealthiest 20 percent of youths	Total
All races	24.6%	10.1%	2.3%	11.0%
Non-Latino White	19.0	7.9	1.9	7.7
Non-Latino Black	24.0	9.6	0.8	3.7
Latino	44.7	25.2	9.6	29.4

Source: National Center for Education Statistics, *Dropout Rates in the United States: 1992* (Washington, D.C.: U.S. Department of Education, 1993), p. 17, table 9.

income peers, and it is nearly twice as high among Latinos.

In one nationally representative sample of families, which researchers followed for 20 years, each year spent in poverty (between ages three and 16) reduced by 3 percentage points the likelihood that a child would finish high school by age 19. Even after holding constant a very large number of factors (such as race, parents' marital status and family instability, parents' education, religion, welfare use, region, rural residence, number of siblings, and parents' employment), poverty continued to have a large and significant effect, with each year of poverty reducing the likelihood of on-time high school com-

---

The effects of long-term poverty and single-parent families on children

It is often argued that the prevalence of single-parent families, not poverty, lies at the heart of children's problems. Without question, family structure plays a major role in children's lives and in their risks of poverty. Yet numerous studies indicate that the effects of long-term poverty on children are distinct from — and in many cases may be much *stronger* than — the effects of growing up in single-parent families. This appears to be especially true for young children and for outcomes related to children's learning.

• Long-term poverty had powerful effects on the IQs of five-year-olds who were born with low birthweights, even among children with otherwise similar family backgrounds, one study found. "Family income is a far more powerful correlate of a child's IQ at age five than maternal education, ethnicity, and growing up in a single-parent family," it concluded.[66]

• Long-term poverty was significantly associated with lower scores on six separate tests of mental ability and skills, other things being equal, according to a study that examined the test scores in the National Longitudinal Study of Youth. The study found no evidence that out-of-wedlock birth or divorce contributes to low test scores when poverty status is held constant. Children with single parents fared no differently on five skill tests when other factors were held constant, and actually fared better on the sixth. Never-married and divorced families were judged less positive childrearing environments, however, and there was evidence that children from these families had more behavioral problems, even among families with similar incomes.[67]

• Each year spent in poverty while growing up significantly worsens the risk that a child will fall behind grade level in school by age 18, when other factors are held constant, according to the U.S. Department of Education.[68] Living with a single parent was not a significant factor when long-term poverty and other key factors were held equal, the department found, using data from the Panel Study of Income Dynamics (PSID). The findings suggest that children are kept back in school (or drop out) because of problems associated with poverty — not because they have single parents.

• Child abuse by mothers is a function of poverty, not family structure, according to a nationwide study of violence in 1986.[69] Low-income mothers (whether single or married) were consistently 60 percent more likely than higher income mothers to inflict severe violence on their children. Within each income group, family structure made no difference to mothers' rates of severe violence.

• Child development expert Urie Bronfenbrenner stated that the "developmental risks associated with a one-parent family structure are relatively small" compared with poverty.[70]

• Single-parent families *are* more strongly linked to other types of problems for children. For example, single parenthood and number of years spent in poverty were each found to be strongly and independently related to children's behavior problems in a number of recent studies.[71]

pletion by at least 2 percentage points, depending on precisely which other factors were held constant.[72] Nationwide, 35 percent of 19-year-olds had not finished high school in this study.

Attending College

The erosion of educational and career opportunities for poor children does not stop with high school. Even when poor children manage to finish high school, they are more likely to stop there rather than continue on to any higher education. And they are dramatically less likely to enter a four-year college and complete a bachelor's degree.

• Although growing up in divorced families is associated with a higher level of behavior problems — such as aggression, disobedience, and substance abuse — some of these problems actually predate the marital breakup, according to research by Andrew Cherlin and others.[73] This suggests that problems which appear to be linked with divorce may in reality be, in part, the symptoms of longstanding family difficulties such as stress or conflict between parents. Such longstanding problems would not necessarily be improved if single parents got married or stayed married.

Moreover, single-parent families are not the cause of most childhood poverty. More than one in three poor children (5.3 million in 1992) lives in a two-parent family. And many other poor children come from single-parent families that are so far down the economic ladder that they would be poor even if the parents got married or stayed married. As Donald J. Hernandez, the chief of the Marriage and Family Statistics branch of the Census Bureau explains:

[T]he fathers associated with mother-only families tend to have lower incomes than do other fathers. Taking this into account, the post-1959 rise of mother-only families probably accounts for 2-4 percentage points in current childhood poverty rates.[74]

Further, he said, even if all "fathers who do not live with their wives and children were (re)united with them...," for both [B]lacks and [W]hites [child] poverty rates would have been about two-thirds as large" as they are now (for example, the difference between the actual child poverty rate of 21.9 percent in 1992 and a projected poverty rate of close to 15 percent).[75]

All of the studies discussed above are made more complicated by the overlap between poverty and family structure: single parenthood is known to cause some (but probably not most) poverty and poverty is known to cause some (but probably not most) single parenthood. Further, about half of children's lifelong problems associated with

parental divorce appear to result from income lost due to the divorce.[76]

The close connection between the problems of child poverty and single-parent families has important implications for public policy toward absent parents. Presently, few absent parents are both legally obligated to pay child support and paying the full amount (only one in four in 1990). A combination of stronger child support enforcement — together with a new system to assure that single parents receive the security of at least a minimal payment from the government if the absent parent cannot or does not pay — can help lower the poverty level for children in single-parent families. At the same time, other antipoverty policies are needed for poor children who live with two parents, or whose absent parent is unable to lift them out of poverty.

Enrolling in any postsecondary education. About half (52 percent) of all 1980 high school graduates who came from families with incomes below $7,000 had enrolled in some form of postsecondary education by 1986. In contrast, four out of five graduates from families with annual incomes above $38,000 (83 percent), and two out of three graduates overall (66 percent), had enrolled in postsecondary institutions.[77] (These institutions included four-year colleges, two-year community colleges, private for-profit trade schools such as secretarial schools, and other programs. Not all students who enrolled received degrees.)

Enrolling in four-year colleges. Thirty-one percent of high school graduates from families making less than $7,000 per year in 1980 went on to enroll in four-year colleges or universities during the next six years. This enrollment rate was only two-thirds that of all high school students graduating in 1980 (48 percent) and was less than half the four-year college enrollment rate of 1980 graduates with family incomes of at least $38,000 (76 percent).[78]

Four-year college completion. Low-income high school graduates are about half as likely as graduates overall — and one-quarter as likely as more affluent students — to complete a bachelor's degree. Of the 1980 high school graduates from families with incomes below $7,000, only about 9 percent completed four-year degrees by 1986. The college completion rate for all 1980 high school graduates was 18 percent; for graduates whose family incomes were at least $38,000, the rate was 36 percent.[79]

Other Problems Linked to Child Poverty

Child Abuse and Neglect
Most poor parents provide loving, nurturing care to their children. But the stress and depression caused by becoming poor (and sometimes the resulting substance abuse, as noted in

Income and success

[T]he most consistent, and typically the most powerful, predictor of adolescent success and well-being is family income. Adolescents growing up in families experiencing economic hardship are at high risk for health and behavioral problems, for school failure, and for becoming involved in criminal activities.

Reprinted with permission from *Losing Generations: Adolescents in High-Risk Settings.* Copyright 1993, National Academy of Sciences. Courtesy of the National Academy Press, Washington, D.C.

CHILDREN'S DEFENSE FUND

Proportion of 1980 high school graduates who enrolled in or finished college by February 1986, by income of student's family in 1980

	Less than $7,000	$38,000 or more	All incomes
Total who enrolled in any postsecondary institution	52%	83%	66%
Four-year college	31	76	48
Completed bachelor's degree	9	36	18
Two-year college	19	27	26
Completed associate's degree	4	7	7
For-profit (proprietary) school	6	5	6

Percentages may not sum to total because of rounding, because of overlap between categories, and because some categories of postsecondary institutions are not shown.

Source: U.S. Department of Education, Center for Education Statistics, tabulations of the High School and Beyond Survey.

Chapter 2) can, in the extreme, drive some parents to abuse or neglect their children.

There is growing agreement that child abuse and neglect occur at a higher rate among poor families — although experts also agree these problems exist in families at all income levels, with wealthier families keeping the incidents better concealed.[80] While maltreatment is not "entirely, or even primarily, a poverty phenomenon," a recent literature review concludes, "poverty is perhaps the single most predictable risk factor" for child abuse and neglect.[81]

Poverty-related circumstances also put children at increased risk of abuse or neglect by persons other than their parents. For example, poor working parents who cannot afford child care may be forced to leave their children with inexperienced caretakers or in other makeshift and unsafe child care arrangements. Similarly, children living in inadequate housing are at great risk of harm, a situation that is sometimes construed as neglect.

Abuse. The rate of abuse for children in families with annual incomes below $15,000 was 19.9 per 1,000 in 1986 — 4.5 times more than in higher income families (4.4 per 1,000), according to the second National Incidence Study on abuse and neglect.[82]

Poverty and child abuse

Deeply rooted attributes of parents — such as alleged character flaws or cultural differences among the poor — cannot by themselves explain the link between child abuse and economic hard times.

Child development expert James Garbarino notes anecdotally that after an Oregon community suffered widespread layoffs in the logging industry, child maltreatment there soared by 46 percent.[83]

Less dramatic but similar trends were documented in a highly rigorous study of two neighboring California counties over a period of 30 months.[84]

Reports of child abuse in each county tended to go up or down, respectively, two months after local employment levels worsened or improved, the study found. The researchers ruled out the possibility that these results were caused by broad region-wide trends, or by unchanging personal or cultural traits of the parents.[85] They concluded that their findings are "consistent with the hypothesis that undesirable economic change causes family stress, resulting subsequently in child abuse."

This pattern of abuse is echoed in milder parenting behavior nationwide. Mothers who recently escaped poverty administer far fewer spankings than mothers who recently entered poverty (and fewer even than other nonpoor mothers), as described in Chapter 2.[86] This suggests that the very same parent may treat her child harshly after becoming poor, but stop when the strain of poverty is lifted.

By definition, none of these patterns of *changing* behavior can be explained entirely by parents' deep-set, *unchanging* traits.

Low-income children suffered more abuse of all types, including physical abuse, sexual abuse, and emotional abuse. Lower income children also were more likely to be seriously injured or impaired by abuse (6.0 per 1,000 low-income children, compared with 0.9 per 1,000 higher income children).

Such findings may partly reflect under-reporting of abuse and neglect among wealthier families and greater scrutiny of poorer families, both of which are known to skew reports of abuse and neglect by individuals and by some schools, hospitals, and other institutions.

Neglect. The rate of neglect for children in families with annual incomes below $15,000 was 36.8 per 1,000 in 1986 — 9 times more than in higher income families (4.1 per 1,000), according to the second National Incidence Study.[87] Low-income children suffered more neglect of all types, including physical neglect, educational neglect, and emotional neglect.

The definition of neglect used in the National Incidence Study encompasses many direct results of poverty. These include such actions as delays in getting immunizations or

CHILDREN'S DEFENSE FUND

Rates of abuse and neglect per 1,000 children, by family income, 1986

	Less than $15,000	$15,000 or more	Ratio of low- to high-income families
All abuse and neglect	54.0	7.9	7 times greater
All abuse	19.9	4.4	5 times greater
Physical abuse	10.2	2.5	4 times greater
Sexual abuse	4.8	1.1	4 times greater
Emotional abuse	6.1	1.2	5 times greater
All neglect	36.8	4.1	9 times greater
Physical neglect	22.6	1.9	12 times greater
Educational neglect	10.1	1.3	8 times greater
Emotional neglect	6.9	1.5	5 times greater

Source: U.S. Department of Health and Human Services, National Center on Child Abuse and Neglect, *Study of National Incidence and Prevalence of Child Abuse and Neglect: 1988* (Washington, D.C.: U.S. Department of Health and Human Services, 1988), p. 5-29, table 5-6.

health care for a child — delays which, in practice, sometimes reflect the lack of insurance, transportation, time to reach clinics (which often are open only during parents' working hours), and other byproducts of poverty. Also counted as neglect are some cases of failure to thrive — a condition that often reflects poverty's symptoms, such as lack of healthy food, parental stress, and noisy or distracting living conditions (as described in Chapter 2). In the same study, a child with "inadequate nutrition, clothing, or hygiene" may be considered a victim of physical neglect. Although technically parents who are unable to provide for their children through no fault of their own should not be included in such figures, these distinctions are seldom made in practice. For example, families sometimes are charged with neglect for being homeless, or are brought to the attention of child protective services for living in grossly substandard housing.

Violence, Delinquency, and Crime

Most poor children are not violent and do not become criminals. However, childhood poverty appears to increase the chances that children will become delinquent or violent and, if they do not receive help, may move on to the adult criminal justice system.

Crime and violence rates in poorer neighborhoods. Many experts believe poverty is an important cause of crime and violence. "Indeed," the National Academy of Sciences concludes, "data from the Centers for Disease Control indicate that personal and neighborhood income are the strongest predictors of violent crime."[88]

Crime and poverty often go hand in hand. Detroit — the poorest big city in the nation in 1989 — had the highest rate of homicide. Within cities, the highest poverty neighborhoods tend to have the most crime. For example:

- *In the poorest of Los Angeles's six planning areas (South Central), the murder rate is 3 times higher and the robbery rate is 4 times higher than in the area with the least poverty (West Los Angeles). If the entire city had crime rates as low as those in West Los Angeles, the total number of murders citywide would drop by half.[89]*
- *In New York City, the two poorest communities (Mott Haven and Hunts Point, both in the Bronx) have felony arrest rates more than 14 times higher than the communities with the lowest poverty rates (Bayside in Queens and Tottenville on Staten Island). If all of New York City had crime rates as low as those in Bayside and Tottenville, felony arrests in the city would drop by 80 percent.[90]*
- *In Washington, D.C., the poorest part of the city (Ward 8) has a violent crime rate 13 times higher than in the ward with the least poverty (Ward 3). If overall District of*

Poverty and victimization

Most homicide victims are poor.... Numerous studies point to the fact that it is poverty rather than race that makes victims vulnerable to homicide.... Increasingly, being poor in America means living in a devastated, crime-ridden neighborhood.

Deborah Prothrow-Stith, with Michael Weissman, *Deadly Consequences*

Columbia crime rates were as low as those in Ward 3, violent crime in the nation's capital would drop by 90 percent.[91]

The underlying reasons behind these apparent links between poverty and crime are poorly understood. (See Chapter 2, pages 38 and 55, for discussion of some of these reasons.) There are at least two general ways in which hard economic times may contribute to crime: by increasing the motivation for theft and other property crimes immediately among youths and adults who are short of money, and by increasing the long-term likelihood that children will lack hope and will grow up to have violent and criminal behavior.

Youth and adult theft rates. The effects of economic problems on adult and youth crime can be almost immediate, according to several studies. In 1984 the Joint Economic Committee of Congress quantified the historical link between unemployment and economic inequality on one hand, and rising rates of arrest, imprisonment, and violence on the other. Holding other factors constant, a one-tenth increase in unemployment, such as from 10 percent to 11 percent, was associated with a significant rise of more than 400,000 arrests per year; a one-tenth increase in the ratio of young men's unemployment to older men's unemployment was associated with an increase of more than 400 murders.[92] A 1991 study found that "an increase in the unemployment rate triggers a subsequent increase in the crime rate" and that "there are economic forces and motivations" behind this link.[93] Tulane University sociologist Joel Devine and his colleagues found that, other factors being equal, burglary rates tend to go up in years when unemployment goes up, and decrease when unemployment goes down. Increased public cash assistance for poor Americans also was associated with falling burglary rates — contradicting the notion that welfare causes crime.[94]

Devine and his colleagues also found that changes in the economy and public assistance were good predictors of short-term changes in burglary rates (which rose when assistance payments fell), but were weaker predictors of violent crimes such as robbery and murder. This difference may reflect the fact that hard times may drive some persons to commit burglary out of what they feel is economic necessity.

A separate set of explanations for the poverty–crime link emphasizes poverty's effects on children. These effects take years to develop and manifest themselves; hard times reach into childhood and adolescence to shape a younger generation's patterns of violence.

Aggressive and violent acts during adolescence. A study of more than 350 White families with seventh-grade children in rural Iowa found that family economic problems in 1989 (specifically, low or declining income, unstable work, or debt) were linked to significantly greater aggression in the children by 1991 — meaning that the youths were more likely to "beat up someone; purposely damage or destroy others' property; throw objects at people; attack someone with a weapon; use a weapon or force to get money or things from someone; [or] set fire to a building."[95]

Economic problems appeared to heighten the children's anger and aggressiveness by first causing a string of bad family interactions, including parental depression, marital conflict, arguments between parents and adolescents about money, and hostility between parents and adolescents.

Extreme behavior problems during childhood. Poor children were twice as likely as wealthier children to have extreme behavior problems, as reported by mothers in one nationwide study. Among children with annual family incomes of $5,000 or less in 1980 (an income level of about three-quarters of the poverty line for a three-person family in 1980), 16.8 percent were reported to have extreme behavior problems — double the rate among children with family incomes over $25,000 (8.6 percent). The odds of extreme behavioral problems were still 1.3 times greater among the poorest children when parents' marital status, mother's education, mother's age at childbirth,

Urban crime

The high levels of crime among [B]lack American youth are causally associated with the concentration of poverty in urban neighborhoods. Patterns of ethnic, especially racial, segregation have created the conditions in which economic downturns and concentrated poverty have torn the social fabric of [B]lack American communities.

Reprinted with permission from *Losing Generations: Adolescents in High-Risk Settings.* Copyright 1993, National Academy of Sciences. Courtesy of the National Academy Press, Washington, D.C.

CHILDREN'S DEFENSE FUND

race, child's age and sex, and presence of chronic health conditions were held constant.[96] In a separate study, the odds of having three or more behavior problems reported by the mother were nearly 1.5 times greater for low-income White four- to 11-year-olds than for their wealthier peers, other factors being equal.[97]

Similarly, children in long-term poverty have been found to rank an average of 7 percentiles worse than those whose long-term incomes are above triple the poverty line, according to a nationwide study that asked mothers to report on behavior problems. The analysis holds constant a sweeping list of other factors, such as home environment and mothers' parenting practices, mothers' academic skills, mothers' smoking or drinking history, and child nutritional status as well as more conventional factors such as race, age, and parents' marital history.[98] Strong effects of long-term poverty on acting out and withdrawn behaviors also have been found for high-risk (low-birthweight) five-year-olds, even after accounting for single parenthood, race, gender, and parent education.[99]

Juvenile delinquency and warning signs of adult crime. Among children raised during the Depression in Boston, delinquency was found in one recent analysis to be higher in poorer families, apparently because poverty made it harder for families to control their children.[100]

Poverty was tied to two types of delinquency: officially delinquent youths who were committed to correctional schools because of persistent delinquency ("many of whom can be labeled 'career criminals'," according to the researchers); and delinquency based on reports by youths, parents, and teachers of acts such as crime and truancy. "Poverty appears to inhibit the capacity of families to achieve informal social control, which in turn increases the likelihood of adolescent delinquency," the researchers concluded. Poverty seems to damage family relationships regardless of the children's initial temperament, the parents' own tendencies toward crime or deviance or mental instability, marital status, and other factors. One optimistic finding in an otherwise grim report is that, when poor families managed to keep steady control of their children, poverty did not increase delinquency.

The study is striking because it uses a "[W]hite sample that is largely 'underclass' by today's economic definition" to show that poverty can break down the capacity of families in any ethnic or racial group to control their children, thereby increasing the risk of later crime.

Similarly, among all children born in 1955 on the Hawaiian island of Kauai, low socioeconomic status was a good predictor of delinquency by age 18, even when learning problems, parents' education, family stability, health status at birth, and other factors were held constant.[101]

Criminal records in adulthood. Of the relatively few (21) serious juvenile offenders in Kauai who went on to commit further crimes as adults, three out of four "had grown up in chronic poverty as children." (The majority also had other problems, such as low IQ scores and learning problems at age 10, and had spent time in single-parent families.)[102] Although this group is too small to generalize from, the findings regarding poverty appear to be consistent with other studies.

Other warning signs of later crime and violence. The childhood and adolescent behavior problems described above are disturbing in part because early violence fosters later violence. "The strongest developmental predictor of a child's involvement in violence," according to the American Psychological Association, "is a history of previous violence."[103] In a 22-year study, aggression at age eight was a good predictor of the number and seriousness of convictions by age 30.[104]

Besides childhood behavior problems, other warning signs of delinquency and violence include early learning difficulties and the need for remedial education by age 10;[105] disability at an early age or pronounced mental health problems at age 10;[106] difficult relationships with parents;[107] childhood abuse and neglect;[108] family disruption and discord;[109] living in a high-crime neighborhood;[110] a crowded home;[111] and lead poisoning.[112] Each of these factors is more common among children living in poverty.

Evidence from Randomized Experiments

Would raising poor families' incomes really help their children avoid the unfair risks described in this chapter?

The answer appears to be yes, according to a series of federally funded experiments. Although these experiments were limited in important ways, they nonetheless offer persuasive evidence that reducing child poverty really can improve children's health and learning.

From a scientific perspective, the firmest possible proof that raising incomes helps children would come from a well-conducted "randomized" experiment. A group of poor families would be split at random into two identical groups: one group (the treatment families) would receive the extra assistance needed to lift them out of poverty, the other (the control group) would not receive this additional assistance. The experiment would measure important effects on children carefully, and would be large enough and would last long enough to ensure a clear result. What makes this type of research design so persuasive is that there is little doubt about cause and effect: Differences between the two groups almost certainly would be caused by the extra help that the treatment group was provided.

A series of experiments that met some of these conditions was conducted between 1968 and 1982 in several urban and rural sites around the country. A group of low-income families was chosen and split at random. The treatment group was offered cash assistance that kept their incomes above a particular level, and treatment and control groups then were studied. Unfortunately, because the experiments were designed principally to focus on adult behavior, impacts on children received spotty attention and the results for children frequently were inconclusive. In most sites, information was gathered on relatively few children, on very few types of child outcomes, and over too short a period to measure the full impacts on many long-term outcomes. (For example, the sole study of high school completion to emerge from the experiments was based on only 138 teenagers in New Jersey who participated for just three years.) Even the precise level of income assistance being guaranteed was often unclear, since families in the experimental group were not all placed in the same antipoverty program but rather were assigned to several very different programs that provided different levels of assistance and varying incentives to stay employed.

Despite these many limitations, the findings for children in some instances were dramatic and encouraging. According to an overview of experiments' results for children:

> The quality of *nutritional intake* was higher in the experimental than in the control group.... Three of the experiments found higher *school attendance* levels among experimental children.... Receiving the [guaranteed income] was associated with higher *grades and achievement test scores*, which act as powerful reinforcers for increased self-esteem, affecting as well the value that is placed on education by the individual.... In New Jersey educational level was higher among experimental than control children.[113] (Italics in original.)

Especially strong results for school enrollment. One of the more striking results showed that offering more cash assistance to low-income youths caused more of them to be enrolled in school. The finding was from the Seattle/Denver income maintenance experiment (known as SIME/DIME). Young people ages 16 to 21 whose families were offered greater income security through SIME/DIME were one-fifth more likely than unassisted youths to be enrolled in school (51 percent of youths participating in the treatment group for more than 18 months, versus 42 percent of the controls, a large and significant difference).[114] Because SIME/DIME was the largest and longest running of all the income maintenance experiments, the study was able to examine more than 2,000 young people, enough to permit considerable confidence in the results.

The SIME/DIME findings echoed the results of the earlier New Jersey experiment in revealing that many low-income youths who hold jobs will switch from work to school when their families are ensured a more adequate family income.[115] Together, the studies provide strong evidence that many low-income youths are torn between a long-term goal of education and a short-term goal of bolstering their own or their families' income, and that a better income allows them to finish more schooling. (Chapter 4 describes the positive results of the New Jersey experiment on raising young people's years of schooling. Unfortunately, researchers in the larger SIME/DIME program never studied the possible effects of income assistance on school completion or on other educational outcomes such as test scores or grades.)

Higher benefits did not trigger more births. The experiments also provided an opportunity to answer other politically significant questions about cash assistance to the poor. Many Americans are reluctant to increase cash benefit levels to low-income families, fearing that this may induce women to have more children to get the benefit. However, the research showed that women who received the more generous guaranteed income actually had lower fertility rates than the control group.[116]

Higher benefits were used responsibly. Many Americans also fear that low-income families will misuse cash assistance, buying alcohol or other items that will not help their children. However, when some of the income maintenance experiments explored this possibility, the results did "not suggest that payments were used in ways that taxpayers would view as purely frivolous or immoral." In the rural North Carolina site, where nutrition levels were especially low before the experiment, recipients bought more food and improved their nutrition.[117] In other sites, recipients generally used the money to buy more of what they usually bought "in the same general proportions as before, and in the same proportions as people with higher incomes."[118]

In contrast to these generally encouraging results for children, the experiments may have had some unintended negative consequences for adults, particularly in the area of work disincentives.[119] For this reason, an effective antipoverty strategy for children may need to include provisions designed to maintain strong work incentives among adults and promote continued labor force attachment.

———

In each of the subject areas in this chapter, there clearly are gaps in our current research and more that we must learn about the costs of child poverty. While the data presented here have been drawn from the most recent, careful, and nationally representative studies available, a number of poor children's problems (such as higher death rates) simply have received too little attention in the federal government's data collection efforts. The only information available on some topics is from studies that are now relatively old, narrowly focused on local communities, or of limited usefulness because they measure children's circumstances and outcomes imprecisely. These limitations should be taken seriously and responses to them should form the core of a future research agenda on poverty's impact on children. At the same time, only dramatic and surprising new results from further research would alter the central findings of the broad range of studies already completed: poverty plays a powerful role in shaping the lives of children, resulting in tragic human costs for poor children and (as Chapter 4 will describe in detail) large social and economic costs for the rest of the nation.

Chapter 4

The Economic Costs of Child Poverty

The children who suffer poverty's effects are not its only victims. When children do not succeed as adults, all of society pays the price: businesses are able to find fewer good workers, consumers pay more for their goods, hospitals and health insurers spend more treating preventable illnesses, teachers spend more time on remediation and special education, private citizens feel less safe on the streets, governors hire more prison guards, mayors must pay to shelter homeless families, judges must hear more criminal, domestic, and other cases, taxpayers pay for problems that could have been prevented, fire and medical workers must respond to emergencies that never should have happened, and funeral directors must bury children who never should have died.

Continuing to permit so many of our children to grow up in poverty is enormously expensive. In an effort to quantify at least a portion of this expense, the Children's Defense Fund (CDF) examined the work of leading academic researchers specializing in fields such as poverty, economic growth, and the value of education and, where necessary, commissioned new research. CDF performed the final step of work — piecing together the necessary figures to form cost estimates — under the supervision of a group of eminent economists.[1] According to the estimates, even the fraction of child poverty's consequences that we are able to measure is costing society tens or even hundreds of billions of dollars for every year that we tolerate current child poverty levels. The good news is that ending this poverty should save the same amount of money.

Our cost estimates are tentative and conservative — tentative because no one, to our knowledge, ever before has attempted to evaluate the burden of child poverty; conservative because we look at only a fraction of the ways child poverty may create costs. Other types of costs are promising subjects for future research. Still others — such as the feelings of a hungry or ill-clothed child — are so deeply personal that they never can be described adequately by dollars or numbers.

This chapter has three sections. The first provides a range of estimates of child poverty's effects on future earnings and

Poverty, mounting problems, and what it costs

Sam and Sarah, an Indiana couple, could not afford prenatal care. Their son Josh was born two months prematurely and was subject to chronic ear infections. When Amy was conceived, Sarah and Sam's relationship deteriorated, and Sam left the state.

Sarah applied for food stamps and Aid to Families with Dependent Children (AFDC), which provided assistance far below the poverty line. She had to make difficult choices among food, housing, clothing, and incidental expenses for her children.

At the grocery in the winter of 1980, three-year-old Josh pulled a jar out of a display and a pyramid of grape jam toppled over on him, breaking half the items on display. The storekeeper insisted that Sarah pay for the damage, which amounted to $27. This figure represented a sizable portion of her monthly income. Sarah paid for the damage at the expense of Amy's diaper budget. After Sarah rationed Amy's disposable diapers, Amy developed a diaper rash, which became infected. Amy was unable to sleep and developed a fever. Concerned, Sarah took both children to the public health clinic.

The nurse who examined Amy was legally compelled to report the child's condition to the family's welfare caseworker. Josh was rambunctious in the doctor's office. Tired, overwhelmed, and angry with Josh, Sarah lost control. She slapped Josh in the face and blamed him for her current situation.

An inexperienced, newly hired caseworker was assigned to investigate the referral from the nurse. The rural county welfare department did not have sufficient staff to keep up with the high volume of referrals. Unable to monitor Sarah's situation, the caseworker recommended temporary foster care. The court removed both children to a foster home 30 miles away. The new caseworker could provide transportation for monthly visits only.

- Separated from their mother, the children stayed in foster care for years. Total foster care expenses for both children grew to an estimated $104,000.
- Josh never adjusted well to his foster placements. He became delinquent and required an additional estimated $58,400 in Boys' School and residential care.
- Josh's latest caseworker reported that he met the profile of many children who pass through the child welfare system. "Prognosis for the future is poor. If his behavior doesn't improve, Josh will likely spend as much time incarcerated in the adult correctional system as he will on the streets" — at an estimated cost of $25,000 per year of incarceration.

Adapted from Indiana Youth Institute Occasional Paper No. 1, 1991

economic output. The estimated future costs range as high as $192 billion in lifetime earnings for each year of the current high child poverty level. Looked at another way, ending child poverty is estimated to add as much as $192 billion per year in long-term worker earnings and production in the economy. Even the lowest estimates (which are intended to capture only one piece of child poverty's total effects on productivity) are about $35.4 billion in lost lifetime earnings for each year we allow the current 14.6 million children to be poor.

The second section describes some of child poverty's other costs to society, such as the cost of repeated grades, special education, and medical care. Data generally are not available to calculate reliable estimates of these other costs. Instead, in certain cases we have tried to indicate the potential scale in rough terms. (For example, repeated years of schooling due to each year of child poverty are expected to cost hundreds of millions of dollars.) Although our confidence in these estimates is lower than for those in the first section, we present these ranges as the best figures possible with available data; further research should be able to refine them considerably. In many other areas, however, we have not made estimates at all — including crucial areas such as crime and delinquency. These omissions suggest that the total cost of childhood poverty may greatly exceed its impact on lifetime worker output or the school system alone. If that is true, the economic benefits of ending child poverty would be much larger, as well.

The third section compares the range of estimates in the previous two sections with the costs of ending child poverty. Although we conclude there is not yet enough information to create a single accurate benefit–cost comparison, it is clear that child poverty's costs are large by any standard. The heartening implication is that ending child poverty will generate substantial long-term savings to help offset the costs of doing so — it is much cheaper than commonly realized. On balance, *ending child poverty is likely to save considerably more than it costs.*

Child Poverty Reduces Lifetime Worker Output

CDF used four separate methods to estimate the impact of children's poverty on the value of their paid work later in life — and thus on the economy. Each method uses a different kind of data and has its own strengths and weaknesses, which are discussed below. Each approaches the question from a different angle, using different research tools to help isolate the effects of low income and hold other factors constant.

No matter which approach is used, the costs of poverty are enormous. It is no surprise that the results differ from each other somewhat, because each looks at children who have different age ranges and other characteristics; therefore, each measures slightly different things. None of these four esti-

---

Investment choices

"Joanna" is one year old. She is the second daughter of hard-working migrant farm workers. Joanna was born with a congenital heart defect, and has spent the majority of her infancy in a highly specialized pediatric hospital in Seattle, Washington. Her devoted parents make repeated trips from their rural farming community, endangering their lives on snowy, icy roads to spend days at her side.

Ironically, Joanna could have been discharged safely long ago — except for her family's poverty. According to her nurse, "[Joanna's] home is the best her parents can afford, but it is inadequate to support her...because [Joanna's] delicate cardiopulmonary system is vulnerable to repeated pneumonias and the ever-present threat of deterioration.

"There is no doubt in my mind, as her pediatric nurse practitioner, that her parents could provide more developmental, emotional and physiologic support for this child than we are capable of. However, they must be given the stability of a home with guaranteed heat, light, and safety — a few steps beyond survival living."

Warm, adequate, middle-class housing, observes Joanna's nurse, would help her more — and would cost society less — than the tens of thousands of dollars needed each year to keep a child like Joanna in a hospital room.

Measuring the cost of child poverty

	Indicator of child poverty	Measure of outcome during adulthood	Type of analysis
Method 1 (PSID data analyzed by Robert Haveman, Barbara Wolfe, and Donna Ginther)	Years poor, ages 6-15	Years of school completed, ages 21-27	Multiple regression (tobit) analysis of individual-level data
Method 2 (New Jersey Income Maintenance Experiment data analyzed by Charles Mallar)	Whether family was assigned to a guaranteed income plan, starting age 16 or 17, ending age 19 or 20	Years of school completed, ages 19-20	Random-assignment experimental design
Method 3 (PSID data analyzed by Amy C. Butler)	Generosity of state's AFDC policies in the 5 years following end of parents' marriage, for children ages 2-16	Years of school completed, ages 19-32	Multiple regression analysis (OLS), using state public assistance policies as the instrumental variable
Method 4 (PSID data analyzed by Mary Corcoran & Terry Adams)	Proportion of childhood spent in poverty; starting age varied from 3-14, ending age was 16	Average annual earnings, age 25+ (ending ages varied from 25-34), on a logarithmic scale	Multiple regression analysis (OLS) of individual-level data

mates is definitive. Instead, each reinforces the others and supports the finding that child poverty is acting as a costly brake on the U.S. economy.

The first three methods take an indirect approach based on children's years of education. Education is one of the major pathways by which child poverty may affect the economy. Education affects a child's skills and his or her capacity to follow complicated directions, learn new skills on the job, and become a productive worker. One of the many ways in which poverty affects education is to reduce the number of years of schooling a child completes before giving up, dropping out, or feeling compelled to go to work. In turn, years of schooling is a powerful predictor of an individual's hourly wages — that is, how much an employee's time is worth to employers, and, by implication, how much value he or she contributes to the economy.[2] By combining these different estimates of child poverty's effects on schooling with existing estimates of the impact of schooling on wages,[3] CDF calculated partial estimates of child poverty's effects on future worker output.

Methods 1 through 3 provide an incomplete picture because they trace only one pathway of effects from child poverty to economic output — the pathway from child poverty to fewer years of schooling and, from there, to lower hourly wages (which economists consider a reasonable measure of a worker's productivity or hourly output).

The three methods, therefore, do not capture all the ways child poverty can hamper the economy. Childhood poverty also may lead to lower wages and productivity during adulthood by subtly lowering an individual's basic skills and ability to learn on the job, for example, by lowering the quality of education children receive, or by causing brain damage from sources such as lead poisoning. In addition, poverty can impair the development of interpersonal skills needed for teamwork, create lasting scars on outlook and motivation, or cause chronic poor health or mental health.

Beyond its effect on hourly wages and productivity, moreover, child poverty is likely to affect the economy further by causing unemployment,[4] involuntary part-time employment, or work hours lost due to teenage parenthood, ill health, or death at an early age. Poverty experienced in later adolescence — as children get older and begin to enter the world of work — may restrict a young person's opportunities to look for the right job (by restricting transportation and telephone service, for example) and make it harder to afford the special certifications,

Estimated costs to the economy resulting from one year of child poverty

Reduced worker output, as measured by lower lifetime earnings
(mid-range estimates, discounted to present value, 1992 dollars)

	For 1 poor child	For 14.6 million poor children
Method 1*	$2,466	$36.0 billion
Method 2*	$6,759	$98.8 billion
Method 3*	Between $0.92 and $1.51 lost for every dollar decrease in payments	
Method 4	$12,105	$176.9 billion

* Methods 1 through 3 show only one part of the total impact of child poverty on lifetime earnings — namely, reductions in hourly wages associated with poor children's reduced years of schooling. Method 4 represents a direct estimate of the total impact of childhood poverty on future annual earnings (including effects on work hours and unemployment and effects related to quality of schooling, poor health, or other factors).

Note: Conversely, these estimates also show the expected gain to the economy from eliminating one year of child poverty. For example, Method 3 implies that every dollar of assistance returns between $0.92 and $1.51 in future lifetime earnings and economic output.

clothes, union dues, or equipment that often are needed to enter a trade. All of these potential impacts of poverty on wages, productivity, employment, and longevity may be only partly reflected, or not reflected at all, by Methods 1 through 3.

To encompass some of these additional impacts on the economy, therefore, Method 4 takes a direct approach. It relies on a specially commissioned study that follows a sample of children through adulthood, and directly measures the effects of childhood poverty on adult earnings.

In none of these four methods can the results be attributed to single-parent families, race, or parental education: these and other measurable factors have been held constant. Two of the methods go further. They appear to rule out other, harder-to-measure attributes of poor families — such as low motivation or lack of informal connections that might help a young person get started in a career — as the reasons for lowered adult earnings.

Specifically, Method 2 employs data from a set of experiments that actually gave money to low-income families: when families were assigned at random to more generous income assistance programs, their children completed more schooling (compared with essentially identical low-income children whose families did not receive extra assistance). Similarly, Method 3 employs data on family income differences caused by differing state cash assistance policies, which are relatively unlikely to reflect family characteristics such as motivation or job connections. These data, too, indicate large effects of family income on children's education.

Together, all four estimates provide strong evidence that child poverty is having very large and negative effects on the U.S. economy.

Method 1: Effects through education only. Each year of child poverty at current levels reduces future economic output by $36.0 billion solely due to the effect of reduced years of schooling on productivity. Conversely, eliminating child poverty for one year would save $36.0 billion because of increases in schooling that would improve future worker productivity.

For Method 1, CDF commissioned University of Wisconsin economists Robert Haveman and Barbara Wolfe to estimate poverty's effect on education, holding other factors constant. Haveman and Wolfe, assisted by Donna Ginther, used data from an ongoing federally supported survey of families — the Panel Study of Income Dynamics (PSID) — to follow a group of 1,705 children who were six or younger in 1968. They found that, on average, each year a child spent in poverty between ages six and 15 reduced the amount of education he or she completed by between .042 and .05 years, depending on what other factors the researchers held constant. The middle estimate from their three most extensive models is .045 years.[5] (Technical information regarding this analysis is available from CDF.)

CDF then estimated the value of a year of education. We assumed that, on average, each year of education increases a worker's hourly wages by between 6 and 14 percent, based on recent research and advice from our academic advisory board. Our mid-range estimates assume 10 percent.[6] To see what this means in dollars, we applied this increase to the future lifetime earnings of an average American. Future lifetime earnings of an average American child were estimated to be about

$814,000, based on 1992 earning patterns.[7] We then adjusted this number in two ways. First, we "discounted" downward to account for the fact that most people would rather have a dollar now than in the future, because a dollar today can be invested or used in other ways. And we adjusted upward to reflect government projections of economy-wide growth in productivity and wages.[8] Together, these steps yielded a present value of about $548,000. Ten percent of these earnings is $54,800 — the estimated lifetime value of one additional year of schooling.[9]

Combining these effects of poverty and education yields a mid-range estimate equal to $2,466[10] in future lifetime earnings lost for each year a child spends growing up in poverty. Multiplying the mid-range estimate by 14,617,000 children (the number of children who experienced poverty during 1992, the most recent year for which Census Bureau figures are available) yields about $36.0 billion in future lost earnings for every year in which we allow this many American children to experience poverty.

The mid-range result of $36.0 billion is our best estimate using Method 1. Higher or lower estimates are also possible, using alternative assumptions about the effects of poverty and education. At the extremes, our lowest and highest estimates using Method 1 are $14 billion and $68 billion, respectively.[11]

A particular strength of Method 1 is that the results are as up-to-date as possible. Moreover, they represent a straightforward analysis of nationally representative data using techniques widely accepted by academic economists. The results cannot be explained away by factors such as single parenthood, race, parental education, religious affiliation, or even, in one of Haveman and Wolfe's models, the type of neighborhood a child grows up in, because all of these factors are held constant.[12] (Methods 2, 3, and 4 likewise hold various factors constant.) One unavoidable weakness in Method 1 is that it cannot account fully for unobserved factors (such as innate ability) that some believe separate poor and nonpoor families; to this extent the estimates could be criticized for possibly being too high. On the other hand, the estimates may be too low in other ways. Because of limitations in the PSID, the estimates cannot measure several aspects of poor children's educational disadvantages, such as the type of schools a child attended or how much the child learned and retained. Notably, they do not take account of lost productivity among one large group of poor youths: those who finish high school late, after age 18 or 19.[13] Youths in this group may have received GEDs rather than regular diplomas, and probably have lower skills and a less attractive educational record from the perspective of an employer. Method 1 ignores these likely disadvantages. Because of these and other potential weaknesses, two other methods are used below to bolster the findings and provide alternate estimates of the effects of poverty operating through education.

Method 2: Effects through education only. Each year of child poverty at current levels reduces future economic output by $98.8 billion solely due to the effect of lost years of schooling on productivity. Conversely, eliminating child poverty for one year would save $98.8 billion because of increases in schooling that would improve future worker productivity.

Method 2 uses data from the New Jersey Income Maintenance Experiment conducted from 1968 to 1972. In the experiment, low-income families were divided into two groups essentially at random and one group was guaranteed a minimum income (the exact amount varied). The other group received either no support or the state's normal (generally less generous) public assistance. Educational outcomes were studied for youths from two-parent, low-income working families who entered the experiment at age 16 or 17. After three years in the program, the youths who received the higher benefits "completed, on average, from one-half to a whole year more of formal education."[14]

Members of the experimental group were assigned to a variety of different income maintenance plans. One plan in particular guaranteed an income at or above the poverty line and provided moderate work incentives for family members to remain in the paid labor force (families could keep half of their earnings without losing assistance benefits). Low-income children from these families were estimated to complete an average of 0.37 years of schooling more than similar children in the control group (a very conservative estimate given that under some scenarios the study found schooling outcomes as much as 3 times higher).[15] Dividing 0.37 by three, CDF calculated that each single year of poverty reduction would increase youths' years of schooling by about 0.12 years. Multiplying this schooling impact by the mid-range value of schooling used in Method 1 yields an average increase in expected lifetime earnings of $6,759.[16]

Multiplied across all 14,617,000 poor children in the United States in 1992, the mid-range estimate implies lost future earnings and output of $98.8 billion. (The sensitivity of this result to assumptions about the value of education and discount rates is described in the endnotes.[17])

The overriding strength of Method 2 is the randomized, scientific design of the New Jersey experiment from which the education data are taken: the results reflect what actually happens when low-income families receive more income, and so are free of research issues (regarding unknown differences between poor and nonpoor families) that arise in other types of studies. A possible weakness of Method 2 is the age of the underlying experimental data, which were collected more than 20 years ago. A more serious problem is the small size of the sample: schooling was studied for only 138 youths, who were spread across eight distinct experimental benefit plans with different income levels and work incentives, plus the control group. The small number of youths makes comparisons in the study less reliable.[18] The positive findings from New Jersey are bolstered somewhat by findings from other income maintenance experiments, where school enrollment rates and other educational outcomes often showed significant improvement; however, none of the other experiments collected data on children's years of education. (See Chapter 3, page 93 for more information on what the income maintenance experiments found about poverty and children.)

Method 3: Effects through education only. Each dollar cut from monthly AFDC assistance levels reduces future economic output by between $0.92 and $1.51 solely due to the effect of lost years of schooling on productivity. Conversely, increasing AFDC levels by $1.00 is estimated to generate between $0.92 and $1.51 because of increases in schooling that improve future worker productivity.

The best antipoverty policy for children probably would focus on a variety of job- and tax-related supports for working families, on child support enforcement and assurance, and on reducing rather than increasing the need for AFDC — the nation's primary cash welfare program for low-income families with children. Nonetheless, the safety net provided by AFDC does have positive effects for children and for society, and indiscriminate cuts in AFDC may have substantial costs. Method 3 shows some of these costs.

Method 3 uses estimates in a 1990 study by Amy C. Butler, currently at the University of Iowa School of Social Work.[19] Butler used the PSID to examine 574 children who lived with divorced, separated, or widowed mothers — that is, previously married (versus never-married) mothers. Butler found that "an increase of $100 per month in the AFDC guarantee (in 1988 dollars) is associated with a predicted increase of 0.095 years of completed education after age, family characteristics, and community characteristics have been controlled" — a statistically significant difference.[20] Holding constant the family's resource networks (the reported number of "friends and relatives who can help" in various emergencies), the effect rose to 0.157 years and became even more strongly significant.[21] Both of these effects are larger than they appear because they are averaged over all children in previously married families, including families that never actually received AFDC.

To estimate the potential costs and benefits of this added income, CDF first considered the case of an average family with a previously married mother in 1992. Multiplying Butler's weaker finding — that an average child in a previously married family completed 0.095 years of education for every $100 per month increase in AFDC levels — by the previously derived mid-range estimate of the value of education, indicated that each child's lifetime earnings will increase by $5,206.[22]

Alternately, taking Butler's larger and statistically stronger finding — an increase of 0.157 years of education — the estimated value of the increased education for each child comes to $8,604.[23]

Next, CDF estimated the costs of increasing the maximum AFDC benefits available to this average previously married family by $100 per month. CDF assumed that the children Butler studied received AFDC for 49.1 percent of the time their fathers were absent from the home.[24] Because of a lack of good data, CDF also assumed that every child's father was absent for the full 18 years of childhood; this extreme assumption is likely to overstate greatly the true cost of raising AFDC for children in previously married families (and therefore understate the relative benefits of raising AFDC).[25] For an average previously married family, therefore, increasing monthly AFDC levels by $100 would cost an estimated $10,601.[26] Because the AFDC levels considered by Butler are expressed in 1988 dollars, CDF adjusted for price changes between 1988 and 1992, yielding a total cost of $12,572 per family in 1992 dollars.[27] (These are benefit payment costs only; they include neither additional costs — such as administrative expenses or labor market effects — nor offsetting savings, such as reduced food stamp or housing assistance payments.) Since the average previously married family that receives AFDC has about 2.21 children,[28] CDF divided this increased payment by 2.21, which yields an estimated cost of $5,689 for 18 years of higher benefits per assisted child.

Comparing benefits to costs, the additional spending of $5,689 for an AFDC increase for an average child in a previously married family was estimated to generate higher future economic gains of $5,206 based on Butler's lower estimate — equivalent to $0.92 in economic output for each dollar of assistance paid. Butler's higher estimate implies a $1.51 payback per dollar of assistance.[29] As mentioned previously, these figures are likely to overstate greatly the costs, and therefore understate the relative payoff to society, of the income increase.

A major strength of Method 3 is that it makes use of the wide differences in state income assistance policies to measure the effects of income on children. These state-to-state policy differences are a good way to test the influence of income, because they create a source of differences between family incomes that is by and large beyond the control of poor families themselves. Method 3 therefore somewhat resembles Method 2 in being largely immune to the criticism that unmeasured characteristics of poor families (such as lack of motivation) are to blame for both the low income of the family and the foreshortened education of the children.

A potential weakness unique to Method 3 is that comparisons based on AFDC levels in the child's home state could inadvertently reflect other state characteristics such as funding for schools. If that were true, AFDC levels would just be a proxy for these other state characteristics, and the apparent positive impact of AFDC as a source of income would be misleading. However, Butler took several steps to rule out this possibility, turning this potential weakness into a methodological strength. She accounted statistically for possible differences in each state's educational profile (using high school and college graduation rates) as well as other state and county economic characteristics (median income and unemployment). More convincingly, she studied a comparison group of children who were unlikely to receive AFDC because of program eligibility rules (children with two parents); as expected, she found that AFDC benefits were unrelated to years of schooling completed for this non-AFDC group. This rules out the possibility that state AFDC generosity is simply a proxy for some other statewide factor that would increase education for children of both married and previously married families in a state.

A final attribute of Method 3 — the limited sample — is both a strength and a weakness. The weakness is the inability to generalize. Because Butler's data did not allow her to make estimates for never-married families, she cautions that her results may not apply to children in those families; nor can AFDC differences reveal much about the effects of income on children in two-parent families, since few of these families receive AFDC (especially in the time period Butler studied). A strength of this narrow sample is that the results are not "contaminated" by purported differences between family types such as never-married families and always-married families.

Method 4: Total effect on future worker output. Each year in poverty at present levels reduces future economic output by $176.9 billion. Conversely, eliminating child poverty for one year would save $176.9 billion because of increases in future economic output.

To estimate the impact of child poverty directly, CDF commissioned estimates by University of Michigan researchers Mary Corcoran and Terry Adams. Corcoran and Adams used the PSID to follow a group of young people from childhood (various ages younger than 17) to early adulthood (various ages 25 and older)[30]

Corcoran and Adams found that children who spent a smaller proportion of childhood in poverty tended to earn significantly more as young adults. For each one-year reduction in the time a boy spent growing up in poverty, Corcoran and Adams' study predicts that future adult annual earnings increase by about 2.5 percent.[31] For girls, each year of poverty reduction was predicted to raise adult annual earnings by almost 1.65 percent.[32]

Applying these proportional increases to men's and women's lifetime earnings yields an earnings gain of $12,105 per child,[33] or $176.9 billion for all 14,617,000 children in poverty in 1992. (Estimates range from $125 billion assuming a 5 percent inflation-adjusted discount rate up to $214.5 billion assuming a 2 percent discount rate.)

The strength of Method 4 is that it represents a direct measurement, unlike Methods 1 through 3, which rely on predictions and projections using the value of lost schooling. More importantly, it reflects all of child poverty's effects on employment and productivity, not just reduced hourly pay due to lost years of schooling. Like previous methods, these estimated effects are not due to single-parent families, race, or mother's education: Corcoran and Adams held these factors constant. The weakness of Method 4 is that it also may encompass additional disadvantages of poor children (beyond those in Methods 1 and 3) that would not necessarily be cured by raising their families' incomes — disadvantages such as their parents' relative lack of personal connections with employers who could hire their children in well-paid jobs. From this perspective, the estimates based on Method 4 could be too high. On the other hand, these estimates still could be too low for a number of reasons. For instance, they probably do not measure the full labor-market impact of any educational deficits or health problems that may have resulted from child poverty. That is because educational and health effects often only hit with full force after individuals are past the ages observed by Corcoran and Adams.[34] Nor do they measure the impact of poverty on work hours lost when poor children die young.

Summary of impacts on the economy. Methods 1 through 4 suggest that every year of child poverty at current levels is costing tens — if not hundreds — of billions of dollars in future productivity. The mid-range estimates vary from $36 billion to nearly $177 billion.

Most of these estimated impacts on future worker output would be substantially higher if education's effects on unemployment, underemployment, and labor force nonparticipation were taken into account, along with additional effects of poverty on productivity, employment, ill health, and mortality that are not captured by years of schooling.

What We Have Left Out

The true financial cost of child poverty extends far beyond the impact on children's future output on the job. A full accounting of costs also would include expenditures for preventable problems such as:

- *Public education for students who fall behind in school and who must repeat grades for reasons related to poverty. Child poverty's annual costs in this area potentially are hundreds of millions of dollars.*[35]
- *Added special education costs for students from poor families. Child poverty's costs in this area appear to be a minimum of $800 million. (Unlike other estimates in this chapter, this cost is not per year of poverty; instead, it represents the effects of currently poor children's present and past experience in poverty.)*[36]
- *Medical care during childhood and adulthood for illness and chronic disabilities acquired due to child poverty. Child poverty's lifetime costs could potentially come to tens of billions of dollars in medical expenses. (Unlike other estimates in this chapter, this estimate does not hold other factors constant, and represents poor children's present and past experience with poverty rather than a cost per year of poverty.)*[37]

Among the most important costs whose size we could *not* estimate is the cost of crime. Even a small effect of child poverty on crime rates would have a very large price tag for society since federal, state, and local governments spent $74.2 billion in 1990 alone for police, prisons, and other criminal justice expenses.[38] In addition, recent estimates of the annual costs of stolen property and private-sector security measures exceed $80 billion, while the direct medical and mental health costs of violent crime have been projected to be $11 billion.[39] Although Chapters 2 and 3 present evidence that child poverty may be driving up crime rates, we cannot yet tell how large this effect is. If, hypothetically, it accounted for just 5 percent of crime costs, that would add at least $8 billion to the annual costs of child poverty.

In addition, we have left out child poverty's effects on:

- *The value of lost life.*
- *Costs of teen pregnancy and childbearing.*
- *Costs of litigation caused by poverty (rental evictions, consumer collections, divorce,*

Lead poisoning as a cost of child poverty

Lead poisoning is one of the most potent health risks children face, affecting an estimated 2.5 million children below age 12—including more than one in four Black children younger than age six in 1988 to 1991. Children are exposed to lead primarily through lead-based house paint, and the dust that forms as paint deteriorates. Children may eat the sweet-tasting paint chips and eat or breathe lead paint dust.

Low-income one- to five-year-olds are four times more likely than their peers in high-income families and three times more likely than those in moderate-income families to have lead levels in their bloodstream of at least 10 micrograms of lead per deciliter of blood (ug/dL), a level at which harmful effects have been documented (and federal guidelines recommend intervention).

Lifting families out of poverty would enable their parents to afford measures to reduce the effects of lead exposure on their children, such as:

- Improving children's nutrition. Adequate levels of iron, calcium, and other nutrients greatly reduce the absorption of lead into the bloodstream.

- Moving into newer or better-maintained homes.
- Screening children for lead poisoning, and testing paint and water supplies for contamination.
- Regularly repainting and cleaning homes to reduce the lead dust from old layers of paint.
- Saving toward the high cost of lead paint abatement.

The health risks begin prior to birth. Studies have linked prenatal lead exposure with low birthweight and premature birth, which in turn are associated with increased infant mortality. Lead exposure, especially at very young ages, also causes stunted growth, hearing loss, and damage to children's vitamin D metabolism, blood production, and kidney development.

Lead exposure also damages the brain and central nervous system, often with devastating lifelong effects. In one study, second grade children with high lead levels were 7 times more likely to drop out of high school, were 6 times more likely to have a reading disability, and had significantly lower IQ scores, attendance rates, class rank, and vocabulary test scores. Lead exposure also

has been associated with Attention Deficit and Hyperactivity Disorder (ADHD), a significant risk factor for delinquency and anti-social behavior.

Some of the costs of lead exposure can be reliably estimated. According to the Department of Health and Human Services, each additional ug/dL in a child's bloodstream costs an average of $1,147 in lifetime earnings. Using this estimate (and adjusting to 1992 dollars), CDF calculated that each year poor children's lead levels are reduced to those of children slightly above the poverty line would save $440 million in future lifetime earnings alone. Government analysts also calculate large potential savings in earnings and in other areas — including health, special education, infant mortality, and neonatal care. If other costs — such as crime linked with ADHD — were included as well, this figure would be even higher.

*abuse and neglect proceedings, and other
conflicts related to poverty among families
with children).*

• *Costs of inefficient medical usage (families using the emergency room because they
have no doctor for routine care or advice, or
families using ambulances because they cannot afford taxicabs).*

• *Costs of poverty in future generations,
including future generations' ability to raise
their children effectively.*

The Cost of *Ending* Child Poverty

How much would it cost to end all child poverty in the United
States? Census Bureau figures show that poor families with
children needed a total of $39.4 billion to fill the gap between
their actual income levels in 1992 and the poverty line — just
over $2,800 per child living in a poor family. In theory, then,
child poverty could be ended for about $39 billion per year.

In practice, the answer is far more complicated and
depends on the kind of policies one considers. Certain
antipoverty strategies — such as raising the minimum wage or
toughening enforcement of absent parents' child support
duties — cost taxpayers relatively little. And putting a jobless
parent to work in a badly needed occupation, such as Head
Start instructor, may be cost-effective in the long term even
apart from the beneficial effect that comes from reducing the
children's poverty with a parent's paycheck.[40]

Other strategies to end child poverty could cost much more
per poor child than the $2,800 implied by the Census Bureau.
In direct cash assistance programs for low-income families
with children, for example, it is generally considered necessary
to reward families for private-sector work; under some scenarios, maintaining strong work incentives by rewarding people for their work could potentially double the cost of an
antipoverty cash assistance program. And, regardless of the

CHILDREN'S DEFENSE FUND

Estimated cost to taxpayers of ending one year of child poverty, 1992 dollars

	For 1 poor child	For 14.6 million poor children
Poverty deficit method*	$2,800	$39.4 billion
Targeted policies method**		
Gross cost	about $4,300	about $62 billion
-Value of work performed by parents	about $1,100	about $16 billion
= Cost minus value of parents' work	about $3,200	about $46 billion

* Average amount per child by which poor families' incomes fall below the poverty line. (Figures are for the 13.9 million poor related children living in families; official data not available for all 14.6 million poor children.)

** Estimates based on one possible combination of public sector job creation and child care for targeted families and additional cash transfers and work incentive payments. (The value of reduced food stamp payments are counted as offsetting savings.) Estimated costs would be lower if child support enforcement and assurance policies and a minimum wage increase were adopted as well.

type of antipoverty strategy used, it would have administrative expenses and imperfectly targeted payments.

To illustrate the possible magnitude of costs associated with eliminating child poverty, CDF chose a hypothetical mixture of policies and estimated its costs. This mixture includes giving jobless parents part-time jobs and providing child care, wage supplements, and direct cash assistance. This blend of strategies not only would end (or drastically diminish) child poverty, but it also would improve incentives and opportunities for low-income parents to work and form stable families. Although we estimated costs for this scenario, it is only intended as one example. It is *not* CDF's recommended strategy. Rather it is one strategy for which it is possible to estimate costs, that is politically plausible, and that sends much stronger messages of support regarding work and marriage than the present system is sending.

To estimate the approximate costs of this hypothetical policy change, CDF looked at the Census Bureau's most recent data (for 1992) on children in poverty. Our analysis included several steps. First, looking child-by-child, we calculated how much each family's income fell short of the poverty line — the family's actual "poverty gap." Next, we estimated the effect of allowing approximately 3 million work-ready unemployed parents (and severely underemployed parents who worked less than 500 hours per year) to take half-time, public-sector jobs at $5.00 per hour.[41] Together, these steps eliminated more than one-third of the combined "poverty gap" for all families with children. To eliminate the remaining poverty for families with children, we hypothesized a series of tax credits and increased benefits, including work-incentive payments to poor and near-poor parents already in the private labor market.

CDF calculated the annual taxpayer cost of these measures to be about $62 billion, of which more than $16 billion[42] would be returned to society immediately in the form of public sector work performed. The detailed expenditures include $16 billion in wages for newly created jobs, $28 billion in other payments to families below the poverty line, and about $29 billion in costs of child care, incentive payments to working families just above poverty to reward them for working, and costs of administering assistance payments and generating public sector jobs. CDF counted the estimated decrease in the need for food stamps (close to $8 billion) as a savings.

As we did when estimating the costs of continuing poverty, we also left out some costs of ending poverty. These include remaining work disincentives for assisted families and potential work disincentives for wealthier taxpayers (if antipoverty programs are financed through new taxes). Economists dis-

Comparison of gains and costs to the economy of ending one year of child poverty
(mid-range estimates in present value, 1992 dollars)

	Taxpayer costs*	Gains to the economy	
		Long-term	Long-term plus immediate**
Method 1	$62 billion	$36 billion	$52 billion
Method 2	$62 billion	$99 billion	$115 billion
Method 3	Not calculated	$0.92 to $1.51 gained for every $1 spent	
Method 4	$62 billion	$177 billion	$193 billion

* Under one hypothetical mixture of public sector job creation and increased cash assistance.
** In Methods 1, 2, and 4, immediate gains are assumed to be $16 billion, which reflects the value of public sector work performed by poor children's parents. In Method 3 — which represents the estimated impact of changes in cash assistance levels — parents are not assumed to get public sector jobs; therefore, no immediate gains are assumed.

CHILDREN'S DEFENSE FUND

agree over how substantial these costs would be.[43]

Comparison of Benefits and Costs of Ending Child Poverty

When long-term benefits and costs are compared, ending child poverty appears highly affordable. In fact, it may result in a large net financial gain for society over time — even when only a limited portion of the benefits of ending child poverty are considered.

The taxpayer costs of ending poverty under this hypothetical policy mix are estimated at roughly $62 billion per year, but they carry immediate economic benefits of $16 billion because of increases in work done by parents.

Adding these immediate benefits (from parents' paid employment) to the long-term benefits from poor children's increased lifetime economic output (which we previously estimated to range from $36 billion to $177 billion) yields $52 billion to $193 billion in combined gains to the economy. Across Methods 1 through 4, the estimated economic gains to society either largely offset the taxpayer costs or, more often, greatly exceed the costs of eliminating children's poverty. Since these comparisons represent only a portion of the expected economic benefits of ending child poverty — they include none of the impacts on crime, health care spending, or repeated years of education, for example (nor any of the human costs such as lost lives or needless suffering) — a fuller accounting probably would show even greater benefits.

Endnotes

Chapter 1
Chapter 2
Chapter 3
Chapter 4

Chapter 1 Endnotes
Who Are Poor Children and How Poor Are They?

1. $541 equals the federal government's 1992 nationwide Fair Market Rent for a modest two-bedroom apartment. Unpublished calculations, Economic and Market Analysis Division, Office of Policy Development and Research, U.S. Department of Housing and Urban Development, February 1994. The nationwide Fair Market Rent represents the cost of a private, unsubsidized apartment or housing unit ranked somewhat below the middle of the price range (calculated for a weighted average of housing markets in the United States).

2. Human Nutrition Information Service, "Cost of Food at Home for Food Plans at Four Cost Levels, July 1992, U.S. Average" (Hyattsville, MD: U.S. Department of Agriculture, 1992). Data are for a mother age 35 and two children, ages seven and 10. Calculations by the Children's Defense Fund.

CDF chose the Agriculture Department's Low-Cost Food Plan rather than the even-lower-cost Thrifty Food Plan for this comparison because the Agriculture Department has long warned that: "If the standard [for food costs in public assistance programs] is to be a reasonable measure of basic needs for a good diet, it should be as high as the cost of the low-cost plan. Of families spending at even this level, many will have poor diets. The agency that sets its food cost standard as low as the cost of the economy plan should recognize that almost one-half of the families that spend this amount for food are likely to have diets that fall far short of nutrient needs." Betty B. Peterkin, "USDA Food Plans and Costs— Tools for Deriving

Food Cost Standards for Use in Public Assistance," *Family Economics Review* (March 1965): 19-23, p. 21. See also note 13 below.

3. The average parent with children ages five to 14 in paid child care spent $40.40 per week on child care in Fall 1991, or about $175 per month. Parents below the official poverty line tend to pay less for child care on average, but only very slightly (5 percent) less, according to figures for all ages of children.

U.S. Census Bureau [Lynne M. Casper and others], *Who's Minding the Kids? Child Care Arrangements: Fall 1991,* Current Population Reports P70-36 (Washington, D.C.: U.S. Government Printing Office, 1994), p. 37, table 10.

Bus fare expenses of $40 per month represent a round-trip fare of $1.00 each way for five days per week for four weeks.

4. In addition to the poverty thresholds used by the Census Bureau, there is another set of federal poverty lines called poverty guidelines. These guidelines are a simplification of the poverty thresholds, and are published every February in the *Federal Register* by the U. S. Department of Health and Human Services to help determine eligibility for a variety of federal programs. By contrast the Census Bureau's poverty thresholds are used primarily for statistical purposes and are published in the Census Bureau's annual poverty report.

5. Charles L. Skoro and David A. Johnson, "Establishing an Updated Standard of Need for AFDC Recipients," *Social Work Research and Abstracts* 27, no. 3 (September 1991):22-7, p. 26.

6. Lawrence Neil Bailis and Lynn Burbridge, *Report on Costs of Living and AFDC Need and Payment Standard Options: Executive Summary,* (Concord, NH: State of New Hampshire, Committee

for SB 153, 1991). The commission's list of expenses did not even count child care or other work expenses.

7. U.S. Census Bureau, *Poverty in the United States: 1992,* Current Population Reports Series P60-185 (Washington, D.C.: U.S. Government Printing Office, 1993), p. 4, table 3. Unless otherwise mentioned, all poverty data in this chapter are from the U.S. Census Bureau.

8. U.S. Census Bureau, unpublished tables from the Current Population Survey. Calculations by the Children's Defense Fund.

9. Karl Ashworth and others, "Economic Disadvantage During Childhood," Leicestershire, England: Centre for Research in Social Policy, Loughborhough University of Technology, 1992). Using a definition of poverty that is about 25 percent higher than the official definition, the study finds that 38 percent of children are ever poor before turning 16. Information about this study is available from its coauthor, Martha S. Hill, Institute for Social Research, University of Michigan, Ann Arbor.

10. U.S. House of Representatives, Committee on Ways and Means, *Overview of Entitlement Programs: 1993 Green Book* (Washington, D.C.: U.S. Government Printing Office, 1993), p. 665. This decline represents a weighted average of states' AFDC and food stamp benefits for a family of three persons with no other income.

11. For a comparison of how much economic conditions and marital and other family changes contributed to poverty trends for White and Black children, see Peter Gottschalk and Sheldon Danziger, "Family Structure, Family Size, and Family Income: Accounting for Changes in the Economic Well-Being of Children, 1968-1986," in Sheldon

Danziger and Peter Gottschalk, eds., *Uneven Tides: Rising Inequality in America* (New York, NY: Russell Sage, 1993). For a discussion of how many conventional analyses (including that of Danziger and Gottschalk, above) may overstate the impact of single parent families on child poverty, see Donald J. Hernandez, *America's Children: Resources from Family, Government, and the Economy* (New York, NY: Russell Sage, 1993), especially pp. 308-13. For data on earnings, family structure, and government benefits, and a detailed discussion of child poverty and family income in America's families headed by someone younger than 30, see Clifford M. Johnson and others, *Vanishing Dreams: The Economic Plight of America's Young Families* (Washington, D.C.: Children's Defense Fund, 1992). For a discussion of the falling value of wages as a contributor to poverty for all age groups, see Rebecca M. Blank, "Why Were Poverty Rates So High in the 1980s?" in Dimitri B. Papadimitriou and Edward N. Wolff, eds., *Poverty and Prosperity in the USA in the Late Twentieth Century* (New York, NY: St. Martin's Press, 1993). For cross-national comparisons of levels and trends in income assistance, see Timothy M. Smeeding, "Cross-National Perspectives on Income Security Programs," testimony for the Congress of the United States, Joint Economic Committee, September 25, 1991.

12. Betty Peterkin, "Family Food Plans, Revised 1964," *Family Economics Review* (October 1964), p. 12.

13. 45 *Federal Register* 22001 (1980). Federal studies confirmed that most families whose food expenditures were equal to the dollar amount of this food plan were falling substantially short of the recommended allowance of one or more major nutrients. Betty B. Peterkin and Richard L. Kerr, "Food Stamp Allot-ment and Diets of U.S. Households," *Family Economics Review* (Winter, 1982), pp. 23-6.

To better reflect families' true nutritional needs, the government economist who designed the present official poverty line also proposed an alternative poverty line that was 25 percent higher. For many years the Census Bureau published much of its poverty data using both definitions.

14. Patricia Ruggles, *Drawing the Line: Alternative Poverty Measures and Their Implications for Public Policy* (Washington, D.C.: Urban Institute Press, 1990), p.53, table 3.4. Ruggles calculated the updated poverty line the same way the original poverty line was calculated but substituting the assumption that families spend about one out of every 5.6 dollars on food (or 17.7 percent of their budgets) rather than one out of every three dollars (33.5 percent) as was the original assumption. She therefore multiplied the cost of the Thrifty Food Plan by about 5.6 instead of by three.

15. Ida C. Merriam, who supervised the work of the Social Security Administration economist who invented the poverty line (Mollie Orshansky), wrote in 1967 that "obviously today's measure, even if corrected year by year for changes in the price level — the purchasing power of money — should not be acceptable twenty, ten or perhaps even five years hence.... What changes over time is the kinds of goods and services actually available and the perception of the relevant groups in society as to what constitute necessities...ready-made dresses becoming standard, for example." I.C. Merriam, "The Meaning of Poverty-Effectiveness," interdepartmental memorandum, draft, January 4, 1967.

16. Under the definition of income used for the official poverty estimates, 21.9 percent of persons younger than 18 were poor in 1992, up from 19.6 percent in 1989 and 16.4 percent in 1979. Counting the estimated cash value of food stamps and housing benefits, the comparable child poverty rate was 19.2 percent in 1992, up from 17.0 percent in 1989 and 13.3 percent in 1979. Under the official definition, the number of persons younger than 18 in poverty rose from 10,377,000 in 1979 to 12,590,000 in 1989 and then to 14,617,000 in 1992 — an increase of 41 percent from 1979 to 1992. Counting the cash value of food stamps and housing assistance and the impact of federal taxes (without making any corresponding adjustments in the poverty threshold dollar amounts), 8,620,000 children would have been poor in 1979, 11,300,000 would have been poor in 1989, and 12,694,000 would have been poor in 1991 — an increase of 47 percent from 1979 to 1992. Wendell Primus, unpublished tabulations of the Current Population Survey, U.S. Department of Health and Human Services, Office of the Assistant Secretary for Planning and Evaluation, 1993.

17. While counting food stamps and housing benefits as income would have lowered the child poverty rate by about 3 percentage points in 1992, updating the poverty definition to account for changes in consumer expenditure patterns since 1965 would have boosted the 1987 child poverty rate from about 21 percent to about 35 percent — an increase of 14 percentage points. See Ruggles, *Drawing the Line....*

18. See Robert Rector, "Thumbs on the scale when poverty is weighed," *Washington Times* (September 26, 1993); Heritage Foundation, "How 'Poor' Are America's Poor" (Washington, D.C.: September 21, 1990).

19. See Robert Greenstein, "Attempts to Dismiss the Census Poverty Data" (Washington, D.C.: Center on Budget and Policy Priorities, 1993).

20. Over longer time periods, many analysts feel the poverty definition may become outdated and may tend to understate the true amount of poverty. In this respect, long-term trends in child poverty may be worse than they appear. See, for example, Ruggles, *Drawing the Line....*

Chapter 2 Endnotes
What Money Buys for Children and Families

1. See, for example, Emmy E. Werner and Ruth S. Smith, *Vulnerable But Invincible: A Longitudinal Study of Resilient Children and Youth* (New York, NY: McGraw-Hill, 1982).

2. Betty B. Peterkin and Mary Y. Hama, "Food Shopping Skills of the Rich and the Poor," *Family Economics Review 3* (1983):9.

3. The poorest one-fifth of American households spent $68 per household member on alcoholic beverages in 1992, while the middle one-fifth spent $130 per person and the wealthiest one-fifth spent $193.

Out of every dollar of expenditures on food or alcoholic drink in 1992, alcoholic beverages consumed an average of 5 cents among the poorest one-fifth of American households, 7 cents among the middle one-fifth of households, and 8 cents among the wealthiest one-fifth of households — over 50 percent more than among the poorest one-fifth. For all U.S. households combined, alcohol consumed about 7 cents of every dollar spent on food or drink. U.S. Bureau of Labor Statistics, *Consumer Expenditures in 1992* (Washington, DC: U.S. Bureau of Labor Statistics, December 1993), table 1. Calculations by the Children's Defense Fund.

4. U.S. Census Bureau, *Poverty in the United States: 1992,* Current Population Reports, Series P60-185 (Washington, D.C.: Government Printing Office, 1993), table 22, p. 144.

5. Human Nutrition Information Service, *Nationwide Food Consumption Survey — Continuing Survey of Food Intakes by Individuals: Women 19-50 Years and Their Children 1-5 Years, 4 Days,* CSFII Report No. 85-4, (Hyattsville, MD: U.S. Department of Agriculture, 1987), pp. 68-75.

6. U.S. Department of Health and Human Services and U.S. Department of Agriculture, *Nutrition Monitoring in the United States: An Update Report on Nutrition Monitoring* (Washington, D.C.: U.S. Government Printing Office), p. 150, Iron Table 1.

7. Alan Meyers and others, Letter to the Editor, "Public Housing Subsidies May Improve Poor Children's Nutrition," *American Journal of Public Health* 83, no. 1 (January 1993):115.

8. Ernesto Pollitt, "Developmental Impact of Nutrition on Pregnancy, Infancy, and Childhood: Public Health Issues in the United States" in Norman W. Bray (Ed.), *International Review of Research in Mental Retardation,* vol. 15 (Academic Press, 1988): 52-58; Frank A. Oski and Alice S. Honig, "The effects of therapy on the developmental scores of iron-deficient infants," *Journal of Pediatrics* 92, no. 1 (January 1978); Frank Hoski and others, "Effect of Iron Therapy on Behavior Performance in Nonanemic, Iron-Deficient Infants," Pediatrics 71, no. 6 (June 1983); Betsy Lozoff and others, "Long-Term Developmental Outcome of Infants with Iron Deficiency," *New England Journal of Medicine* 325, no. 10 (September 5, 1991):687-94.

9. Personal communication, Cheryl Wehler, director, National Community Childhood Hunger Identification Project (June 3, 1993). The Pontiac study looked at 606 children; 33 percent of those with family incomes at or below the poverty line were identified as experiencing hunger, compared with 12 percent of children above poverty. The non-poor hungry children were concentrated just above the poverty line, and none had family income above three times the poverty line. These figures suggest that the official poverty line may be set too low to capture all families who have hunger problems.

10. Food Research and Action Center, *Community Childhood Hunger Identification Project: A Survey of Childhood Hunger in the United States* (Washington: Food Research and Action Center, 1991).

11. Food Research and Action Center, *Community Childhood Hunger Identification Project...,* p. 16.

12. Jane E. Miller and Sanders Korenman, "Poverty and Children's Nutritional Status in the United States," *Journal of Epidemiology* 140, no. 3 (August 1, 1994).

13. Personal communication with Deborah Frank, M.D., director, Failure to Thrive Unit, Boston City Hospital, June 13, 1994.

14. Deborah A. Frank and Steven H. Zeisel, "Failure to Thrive," *Pediatric Clinics of North America* 35, no. 6 (December 1988).

15. Frank and Zeisel, "Failure to Thrive."

16. Ernesto Pollitt, "Developmental Impact of Nutrition on Pregnancy, Infancy, and Childhood: Public Health Issues in the United States" in Norman W. Bray (Ed.), *International Review of Research in Mental Retardation,* vol. 15 (Academic Press, 1988), p. 45.

17. Deborah A. Frank and others, "Failure to thrive: Mystery, myth, and method," *Contemporary Pediatrics* (February 1993):114-43, p. 130.

18. Frank and Zeisel, "Failure to Thrive," p. 1195.

19. Dennis Drotar, "The Family Context of Nonorganic Failure to Thrive," *American Journal of Orthopsychiatry* 61, no. 23 (1991).

20. Frank and Zeisel, "Failure to Thrive," p. 1196.

21. Drotar, "The Family Context of Nonorganic Failure to Thrive."

22. Pollitt, "Developmental Impact of Nutrition...", p. 39.

23. C. Keith Conners and Arthur G. Blouin, "Nutritional Effects on Behavior of Children," *Journal of Psychiatric Research* 17, no. 2 (1982/83):193-201.

24. Ernesto Pollitt and others, "Brief fasting, stress, and cognition in children," *American Journal of Clinical Nutrition* 34 (August 1981):1526-33.

25. Pollitt, "Developmental Impact of Nutrition...," pages 39-41; Barbara H. Kehrer and Charles M. Wolin, "Impact of Income Maintenance on Low Birth Weight: Evidence from the Gary Experiment," *Journal of Human Resources* 14, no. 4 (1979):453-6.

26. Steven L. Gortmaker, "Poverty and Infant Mortality in the United States," *American Sociological Review* 44 (April 1979):280-97.

27. Centers for Disease Control, "Recommendations for the Use of Folic Acid to Reduce the Number of Cases of Spina Bifida and Other Neural Tube Defects," *Morbidity and Mortality Weekly Report* 41 no. RR-14 (September 11, 1992); Editorial, "Folic acid-preventable spina bifida and anencephaly," *Journal of the American Medical Association* 269, no. 10 (March 10, 1993):1292-3.

28. Human Nutrition Information Service, *Nationwide Food Consumption Survey — Continuing Survey of Food Intakes by Individuals: Women 19-50 Years and Their Children 1-5 Years, 4 Days,* CSFII Report No. 85-4, (Hyattsville, MD: U.S. Department of Agriculture, 1987), p. 72. Calculations by the Children's Defense Fund.

29. Editorial, "Folic Acid-Preventable Spina Bifida and Anencephaly," *Journal of the American Medical Association* 269, no. 10 (March 10, 1993):1293.

30. Human Nutrition Information Service, *Women 19-50 Years...,* p. 23. The report indicates that low-income women are also less likely to eat other common sources of folic acid, such as tomatoes, other vegetables, and prepared cereals.

31. National Academy of Sciences, Institute of Medicine, *Homelessness, Health and Human Needs* (Washington: National Academy Press, 1988).

32. United States Conference of Mayors, *A Status Report on Hunger and Homelessness in America's Cities: 1993, A 26-City Survey* (Washington, D.C.: United States Conference of Mayors).

33. See Lisa Klee Mihaly, *Homeless Families: Failed Policies and Young Victims* (Washington: Children's Defense Fund, 1991); David L. Wood and others, "Health of Homeless Children and Housed Poor Children," *Pediatrics* 86, no. 6 (1990):858-66.

34. U.S. Census Bureau and U.S. Department of Housing and Urban Development, American Housing Survey, 1989. (Hereinafter, "1989 American Housing Survey.") Tabulations of public use data on compact disk, by the Children's Defense Fund. Figures refer to children who have resided in their current home since previous winter; recent movers are excluded.

35. These figures represent the number of children living in households that pay more than 30 percent of income for housing (essentially rent or mortgage payments plus utilities). Federal rental assistance programs assume that households should not be required to pay more than 30 percent of their monthly income for housing, in order to leave enough income for other necessary expenditures.

36. 1989 American Housing Survey. Tabulations by the Children's Defense Fund. Data are for children in households with serious or moderate housing problems.

37. In 1989, 21.1 percent of poor children and 11.1 percent of nonpoor children had moved since the previous winter. 1989 American Housing Survey. Tabulations by the Children's Defense Fund.

38. Robert Haveman and others, "Childhood Events and Circumstances Influencing High School Completion," *Demography* 28, no. 1 (February 1991): 133-57, p.147, table 3. The study looks at high school completion of 19- through 23-year-olds in 1987.

39. Figures refer to children who have resided in their current home since last winter; recent movers are excluded. Data are from 1989 American Housing Survey. Tabulations by the Children's Defense Fund.

40. 1989 American Housing Survey. Tabulations by the Children's Defense Fund.

41. John R. Hall, *U.S. Home Heating Fire Patterns and Trends Through 1990* (Quincy, MA: National Fire Protection Association, 1992), p. 30, figure 5.

42. Hall, *U.S. Home Heating Fire Patterns*, p. 40, figure 13.

43. 1989 American Housing Survey, tabulations by the Children's Defense Fund.

44. Stephen D. Platt and others, "Damp Housing, Mould Growth, and Symptomatic Health State," *British Medical Journal* 298 (June 1989):1673-8; Claudia J. Martin and others, "Housing Conditions and Ill Health," *British Medical Journal* 294 (May 1987):1125-7; P. McCarthy and others, "Respiratory Conditions: Effect of Housing and Other Factors," *Journal of Epidemiology and Community Health* 39 (1985):15-9.

45. Stella Lowry, "Temperature and humidity," *British Medical Journal* 299 (1989):1326-8.

46. Kevin B. Weiss and others, "An Economic Evaluation of Asthma in the United States," *New England Journal of Medicine* 326, no. 13 (March 26, 1992): 864.

47. Vann Kang, "Cockroach Allergies and Cockroach Asthma," *Journal of Asthma and Allergy for Pediatricians* 3 (1990):228; Vann Kang and others, "Analysis of Indoor Environmental Atropic Allergy in Urban Populations with Bronchial Asthma," *Annals of Allergy* 62 (January 1989):30; Harry Bernton, "Cockroach Allergy: The Relation of Infestation to Sensitization," *Southern Medical Journal* 60 (August 1967):852.

48. 1989 American Housing Survey, tabulations by the Children's Defense Fund.

49. Mark Swanson and others, "An Immunochemical Approach to Indoor Aero-Allergen Quantitation: Studies with Mite, Roach, Cat, Mouse Allergens," *Journal of Allergy and Clinical Immunology* 76 (1985):724.

50. 1989 American Housing Survey, tabulations by the Children's Defense Fund.

51. 1989 American Housing Survey, tabulations by the Children's Defense Fund.

52. Diana B. Dutton, "Socioeconomic Status and Children's Health," *Medical Care* 23 (1985):152.

53. For Black children differences related to crowded housing were not statistically significant. Peggy J. McGauhey and Barbara Starfield, "Child Health and the Social Environment of White and Black Children," *Social Science Medicine* 36, no. 7 (1993):867-74.

54. Frederick P. Rivara and Melvin Barber, "Demographic Analysis of Childhood Pedestrian Injuries," *Pediatrics* 76, no. 3 (1985):375-81.

55. M.A. Mendall and others, "Childhood living conditions and *Helicobacter pylori* seropositivity in adult life," *Lancet* 339 (April 11, 1992), p. 896.

On the relation of the bacterium to a number of stomach cancers and ulcers, see Editorial, "Gastric Lymphoma and *Helicobacter Pylori*," *New England Journal of Medicine* 330, no. 18 (May 5, 1994):1310-1; and National Institutes of Health Consensus Development Panel, "*Helicobacter pylori* in Peptic Ulcer Disease," *Journal of the American Medical Association* 272, no. 1 (July 6, 1994):65-9.

56. Walter L. Peterson, "*Helicobacter Pylori* and Peptic Ulcer Disease," *New England Journal of Medicine* 324, no. 15 (April 11, 1991):1043-8.

57. Richard Sporik, "Exposure to House-Dust Mite Allergen and the Development of Asthma in Childhood: A Prospective Study," *New England Journal of Medicine* 323, no. 8 (August 23, 1990):502-7, finding "exposure in early childhood to house-dust mite allergens is an important determinant of asthma."

58. 7.4 percent of poor children and 4.8 percent of nonpoor children live in mobile homes. 1989 American Housing Survey, tabulations by the Children's Defense Fund.

59. In a North Carolina study, fires in mobile home were 3.3 times more likely than other homes to cause fatalities when children younger than five were present, versus 1.4 times more likely when young children were not present. Carol W. Runyan and others, "Risk Factors for Fatal Residential Fires," *New England Journal of Medicine* 327 (September 17, 1992):859-63.

60. Lynn M. Casper and others [U.S. Census Bureau], *Who's Minding the Kids? Child Care Arrangements: Fall, 1991* (Washington, D.C.: U.S. Government Printing Office, 1994), p. 37, table 10; Sandra Hofferth and others, *National Child Care Survey, 1990* (Washington, D.C.: Urban Institute, 1991). Both studies find that poor women who use paid child care pay 27 percent of their incomes for it.

61. U.S. General Accounting Office, *Early Childhood Education: What Are the Costs of High-Quality Programs?* (Washington, D.C.: U.S. General Accounting Office, January 1990).

62. The average income of families with related children younger than 18 in 1992 was $7,541. U.S. Census Bureau, *Poverty in the United States: 1992,* p. 123, table 20.

63. Nearly two in three eligible poor children do not receive Head Start according to data from the Head Start Bureau and the Census Bureau (unpublished calculations by the Children's Defense Fund). For evidence of shortages and waiting lists in states' child care subsidy systems for working poor families, see Nancy Ebb, *Child Care Tradeoffs: States Make Painful Choices* (Washington, D.C.: Children's Defense Fund, January 1994), appendix B, table 2.

64. Helen Blank, *Protecting Our Children: State and Federal Policies for Exempt Child Care Settings* (Washington, D.C.: Children's Defense Fund, January 1994).

65. Ellen Galinsky, *The Study of Children in Family Child Care and Relative Care: Highlights of Findings* (New York, NY: Families and Work Institute, 1994).

66. According to the National Child Care Staffing Study of child care centers for children younger than six in 1988, "when significant differences were found for the children from low- and high-SES [socioeconomic status] families, the high-SES group tended to receive better quality care" on measures such as ratios of children to staff, whether children were given developmentally appropriate activities, and whether the center complied with the 1980 Federal Interagency Day Care Requirements regarding ratio of children to adult care givers, the group size in classrooms, and the child-related training of the teaching staff. However, the relationship between family income and child care quality was not simple. "Children from middle-SES families appear to fare the worst" among the three SES groups, in fact. Marcy Whitebrook and others, *Who Cares? Child Care Teachers and the Quality of Care in America—Final Report, National Child Care Staffing Study* (Oakland, CA:

Child Care Employee Project, 1989), p. 150.

Among three- to eight-year-olds whose families had low incomes (below $10,000) and who were in any form of child care in 1991, about three out of four (78 percent) were in center-based care — the same as for families of all incomes. Jerry West and others [National Center for Education Statistics], *Profile of Preschool Children's Child Care and Early Education Program Participation* (Washington, D.C.: U.S. Department of Education, 1993), p. 9 (table 1) and p. 20 (table 5); calculations by the Children's Defense Fund. Children younger than three, however, are more often in relative or family child care.

67. Marianne Cederblad and Börje Höök, "Daycare for Three-Year-Olds: An Interdisciplinary Experimental Study," in E. James Anthony and Colette Chiland, eds., *The Child in His Family*, vol. 7 (New York: John Wiley and Sons, 1982).

68. For example, in the National Day Care Study, "Higher ratios (i.e., more children per adult caregiver) were found to be associated with more distress in infants as well as toddlers. For infants, it was also associated with more child apathy and with more situations involving potential danger to the child." Other research has shown the importance of training, group size, caregiver continuity, structure of daily routine, and adequacy of physical facilities. National Research Council, *Who Cares for America's Children? Child Care Policy for the 1990s* (Washington, D.C.: National Academy Press, 1990), p. 88.

69. Lawrence J. Schweinhart and David P. Weikart, "A Summary of *Significant Benefits: The High/Scope Perry Preschool Study Through Age 27*," (Ypsilanti, MI: High/Scope Educational Research Foundation, 1993).

70. National Research Council, Commission on Behavioral and Social Sciences and Education, *Losing Generations: Adolescents in High-Risk Settings* (Washington, D.C.: National Academy Press, 1993), p. 117.

71. In high-poverty schools (with more than 24 percent of students poor), 47.5 percent of students have low achievement scores (scores below the 25th percentile) — more than four times higher than the proportion (11.9 percent) in low-poverty schools where less than 7 percent of students were poor. Even non-poor students were much more likely to be low achievers in high-poverty schools (36.9 percent) than low-poverty schools (11.0 percent). Poor students, while worse off than nonpoor students in every setting, were likewise at greater risk of having low achievement scores if they attended high-poverty schools (56.0 percent) than in low-poverty schools (27.6 percent). Office of Educational Research and Improvement, *Poverty, Achievement and the Distribution of Compensatory Education Services* (Washington, D.C.: U.S. Department of Education, 1986), pp. 20-22.

72. "The more frequent use of Mastery Learning methods in high-poverty schools appears to indicate a greater emphasis on basic skills, than on higher-order thinking skills." U.S. Department of Education, *Prospects: The Congressionally Mandated Study of Educational Growth and Opportunity* (Washington, D.C.: U.S. Department of Education, 1993), p. 292.

More broadly, see Jeannie Oakes, *Keeping Track: How Schools Structure Inequality* (New Haven, CT: Yale University Press, 1985).

73. The lowest poverty schools are those in which fewer than 20 percent of students are poor. U.S. Department of Education, *Prospects...*, pp. 278-9, exhibits 3.36 and 3.37. The highest poverty schools are those in which at least 75 percent of students are poor.

74. Roger W. Hamm and Sandra Crosser, "School Fees: Whatever happened to the notion of a free public education?" *American School Board Journal* (June 1991):29-31; Roger W. Hamm and Sandra Crosser, "School Fees: A Review of National Policies and Practices," unpublished paper (Ada, OH: Ohio Northern University, 1990), p. 6.

75. See Pat Doe *et al.,* v. Utah State Bd. of Ed. *et al.,* Civ. Action No. 920903376 (3rd district court of Utah, 7/22/92) for a pending state court injunction addressing widespread non-compliance by local school administrators with state rules requiring schools to waive fees for low-income families. For more information contact Utah Legal Services, Salt Lake City.

76. Shirley Weathers and Bill Crim, *School Fees in Utah: The Law and the Practice* (Salt Lake City, Utah: Utah Issues Information Program, Inc., 1992), p. ii.

77. The poorest one-fifth of consumer units spent $66 dollars on reading materials in 1992. The middle one-fifth spent $147. Adjusting for the number of persons in the unit, these differences were slightly smaller: the poorest one-fifth of consumer units spent about $37 per person on reading, compared to $59 per person in the middle-income group. U.S. Bureau of Labor Statistics, "Consumer Expenditures in 1992," (Washington, D.C.: Bureau of Labor Statistics, December 1993), p. 6, table 1.

78. Fifty-one percent of children on AFDC, and 59 percent of poor children not on welfare, had 10 or more books in 1986, contrasted with 81 percent of nonpoor, non-welfare children, in a study of three- to five-year-olds born to mothers aged 14 to 25 at the time of birth. Nicholas Zill and others, "The Life Circumstances and Development of Children in Welfare Families: A Profile Based on National Survey Data" (Washington, D.C.: Child Trends, 1991), table 9.

79. Barbara Heyns, "The Influence of Parents' Work on Children's School Achievement," in Sheila B. Kamerman and Cheryl D. Hayes, eds., *Families that Work: Children in a Changing World* (Washington, D.C.: National Academy Press, 1982), p. 236, summarizing Barbara Heyns, *Summer Learning and the Effects of Schooling* (New York: Academic Press, 1978).

80. National Center for Education Statistics, *Digest of Education Statistics: 1991* (Washington, D.C.: U.S. Department of Education, 1991), table 395, p. 415.

81. National Center for Education Statistics, *The Condition of Education, 1991, Volume 1, Elementary and Secondary Education* (Washington, D.C.: U.S. Department of Education, 1991), table 1:15-1, p. 193. Calculation by the Children's Defense Fund.

82. Alan B. Krueger, *How Computers Have Changed the Wage Structure: Evidence from Microdata, 1984-89,* NBER Working Paper #3858 (Cambridge, MA: National Bureau of Economic Research, 1991).

83. Laurence Steinber and Sanford Dornbusch, "Negative Correlates of Part-Time Employment During Adolescence: Replication and Elaboration," *Developmental Psychology* 27, no 2 (1991):304-13, p. 310.

84. National Center for Education Statistics, *Dropout Rates in the United States: 1992* (Washington, D.C.: U.S. Department of Education, National Center for Education Statistics, 1992), p. 36, table 20.

85. National Center for Education Statistics, *The Condition of Education, 1993* (Washington, D.C.: U.S. Department of Education, National Center for Education Statistics, 1993), p. 32.

86. National Center for Education Statistics, *The Condition of Education, 1993,* p. 34. "Low-income" students in this study were defined as the least wealthy one-fourth of students who were still dependent on their families (students with family incomes below $22,030).

87. For reviews, see Vonnie C. McLoyd, "The Impact of Economic Hardship on Black Families and Children: Psychological Distress, Parenting, and Socioemotional Development," *Child Development* 61 (1990):311-46; Ramsay Liem and Joan Liem, "Social Class and Mental Illness Reconsidered: The Role of Economic Stress and Social Support," *Journal of Health And Social Behavior* 19 (June 1978):139-56; Steven Parker and others, "Double Jeopardy: The Impact of Poverty on Early Child Development," *Pediatric Clinics of North America* 35, no. 6 (December 1988):1227-39, especially 1231-4. See also Leonard I. Pearlin and others, "The Stress Process," *Journal of Health and Social Behavior* 22 (December 1981):337-56; and Jacques D. Lempers and others, "Economic Hardship, Parenting, and Distress in Adolescence," *Child Development* 60 (1989):25-39.

88. It is plausible that mental health problems in the family could cause adults to experience economic loss, rather than the other way around. In a majority of cases, however, economic problems seem to occur first, rather than being the consequence. Links between economic loss and adult depression have been explored in several studies that track community mental health indicators over time. Researchers find that job loss generally appears to occur first and only later do mental hospital admissions and self-reported symptoms of depression increase. See, for example, Blair Wheaton, "The Sociogenesis of Psychological Disorder: Reexamining the Causal Issues with Longitudinal Data," *American Sociological Review* 43 (June 1978):383-403; David Dooley and Ralph Catalano, "Economic Change as a Cause of Behavioral Disorder," *Psychological Bulletin* 87, no. 3 (1980):450-68; McLoyd, "Impact of Economic Hardship....," p. 319; Liem and Liem, "Social Class and Mental Illness...," pp. 140-1; U.S. Congress, Joint Economic Committee [M. Harvey Brenner], *Estimating the Effects of Economic Change on National Health and Social Well-Being* (Washington, D.C.: U.S. Government Printing Office, 1984), p. 55 and p. 68, table III. For a study finding that "the economic status of the poor does not appear to have been caused by psychological dispositions," see Mary Corcoran and others, "Myth and Reality: The Causes and Existence of Poverty," *Journal of Policy Analysis and Management* 4, no. 4 (1985):516-36.

89. Walter F. Stewart and others, "Prevalence of Migraine Headaches in the United States: Relation to Age, Income, Race, and Other Sociodemographic Factors," *Journal of the American Medical Association* 267, no. 1 (January 1, 1992): 64-9.

90. Child psychologist Vonnie McLoyd reviews the literature on psychological distress and finds, "Poverty and economic loss...increase the risk of emotional distress in adults and render them more vulnerable to the debilitating effects of negative life events. Distress associated with economic hardship is intensified if the adult is raising children alone, has dependent children, is [B]lack, socially isolated, or blames himself or herself for the economic difficulty." Vonnie C. McLoyd, "The Impact of Economic Hardship...."

91. The researchers examined the effects of unemployment on symptoms of anxiety, depression, somatization (for example, headaches), and physical health (activity-limiting conditions and overall self-assessment). Marital strain, diminished contact with co-workers, and other consequences of unemployment were found to be unimportant.

Ronald C. Kessler and others, "Intervening processes in the relationship between unemployment and health," *Psychological Medicine* 17 (August 1987):949-61.

92. "Perceived economic hardship" — feeling unable to afford enough food, clothing, or medical care for the family — was found to be a major link between low earnings and depression among married adults in one study. For wives, hardship was the only link: neither their own paycheck from work nor any other source of family income influenced depression except insofar as it affected perceived economic hardship. For husbands, having low personal earnings had some direct connection to depression, separate from its effect on hardship. (The researchers speculated that men's earnings may affect their self-image as breadwinners; for the women in this 1978 study, this did not seem to be the case.) But even for the men, low earnings influenced depression mostly by increasing perceived economic hardship. Catherine E. Ross and Joan Huber, "Hardship and Depression," *Journal of Health and Social Behavior* 26 (December 1985):312-27.

93. Vonnie C. McLoyd, "The Impact of Economic Hardship on Black Families and Children: Psychological Distress, Parenting, and Socioemotional Development," *Child Development* 61 (1990):311-46, p. 323.

94. McLoyd, "The Impact of Economic Hardship...," p. 328.

95. McLoyd, "The Impact of Economic Hardship...," p. 329-30.

96. Parker and others, "Double Jeopardy...," pp. 1233-4.

97. Rand D. Conger and others, "Economic Stress, Coercive Family Process, and Developmental Problems of Adolescents," *Child Development* 65, no. 2 (April 1994):541-61.

98. Jane D. McLeod and Michael J. Shanahan, "Poverty, Parenting, and Children's Mental Health," *American Sociological Review* 58 (June 1993): 351-66.

99. McLeod and Shanahan, "Poverty, Parenting, and Children's Mental Health," p. 361.

100. McLeod and Shanahan, "Poverty, Parenting, and Children's Mental Health," p. 359 note 7, and personal communication with Jane McLeod, May 12, 1994.

101. McLeod and Shanahan, "Poverty, Parenting, and Children's Mental Health," p. 361.

102. Vonnie C. McLoyd and others, "Unemployment and Work Interruption among African American Single Mothers: Effects on Parenting and Adolescent Socioemotional Functioning," *Child Development* 65, no. 2 (April 1994):562-89.

103. Gene H. Brody and others, "Financial Resources, Parent Psychological Functioning, Parent Co-Caregiving, and Early Adolescent Competence in Rural Two-Parent African-American Families," *Child Development* 65, no. 2 (April 1994): 590-605.

104. See, for example, Laurence Steinberg and others, "Impact of Parenting Practices on Adolescent Achievement: Authoritative Parenting, School Involvement, and Encouragement to Succeed," *Child Development* 63 (October 1992): 1266-81. Among 6,400 high school students in Wisconsin and California, students who said their parents had all three qualities had significantly greater year-to-year improvements in school performance than those whose parents had some or none of these qualities.

105. Cathy Spatz Widom, "The Cycle of Violence," *National Institute of Justice Research in Brief* (Washington, D.C.: U.S. Department of Justice, October 1992), p. 1.

106. Patricia Y. Hashima and Paul R. Amato, "Poverty, Social Support, and Parental Behavior," *Child Development* 65, no. 2 (April 1994):394-403. In the same study, the researchers confirmed the importance of the interaction between low income and low support, using a more sophisticated analysis that held constant family size, parents' age, gender, race, education, and marital status, metropolitan versus rural residence, and other factors.

107. Donald J. Hernandez, *America's Children: Resources from Family, Government and the Economy* (New York: Russell Sage Foundation), 390.

108. Hernandez, *America's Children...*, 390. Calculation by the Children's Defense Fund.

109. Hernandez, *America's Children...*, 391. He finds that recessions appear to account for about 14 percent (0.8 percentage points) of the total 6.0 percentage point increase in the proportion of children living with *never-married* mothers from 1970 to 1988. And, from 1968 to 1988, recessions appear to account

for 30 percent of the total increase in the proportion of children living in *all types* of mother-only families — that is, 3.2 percentage points of the total 10.7 percentage point increase.

110. U.S. Census Bureau [Donald J. Hernandez], *When Households Continue, Discontinue, and Form,* Current Population Reports, Series P23-179 (Washington, D.C.: Government Printing Office, 1992), p. 19, table I; p. 21.

111. Hernandez, *America's Children...*, 438-40.

Two recent studies confirm that growing economic problems among young men have played a significant role in driving down marriage rates, especially among young Black men. Although these studies provide a good test of the existence of an economically driven decline in marriage, they are not well-suited to measuring the size of this decline. Several features of the studies are likely to bias their findings downward. One of these features is a focus on young men's absolute rather than relative earnings. (Compared with their relative earnings, which have dropped substantially, absolute earnings provide a weak measure of young Black men's declining economic position in society.) A second feature is a focus on individual young men's economic status at the time of the survey. (Economic status fluctuates substantially for young men, so a better measure of their economic prospects and potential marriageability might be expected earnings based on local employment conditions for young men of their same race and education.) A third feature is a tendency to neglect the disturbing number of young men who disappear from statistical surveys, and presumably the local marriage market, due to death, homelessness, imprisonment, military service, or other

factors. It is not surprising, therefore, that the studies find that a relatively small — although still significant — portion of the decline in marriage is due to economic loss.

The studies are David T. Ellwood and David T. Rodda, "The Hazards of Work and Marriage: The Influence of Male Employment on Marriage Rates," Working Paper #H-90-5 (Cambridge, MA: Harvard University, John F. Kennedy School of Government, March 1991); and Robert D. Mare and Christopher Winship, "Socioeconomic Change and the Decline of Marriage for Blacks and Whites," in Christopher Jencks and Paul E. Peterson, eds., *The Urban Underclass* (Washington, D.C.: The Brookings Institute, 1991).

112. Researchers exposed stressed and nonstressed subjects to a cold virus and tested their likelihood of contracting symptoms, holding other risk factors constant. Sheldon Cohen and others, "Psychological Stress and Susceptibility to the Common Cold," *New England Journal of Medicine* 325, no. 9 (August 29, 1991):606-12.

113. Barry Zuckerman and others, "Depressive symptoms during pregnancy: Relationship to health behaviors," *American Journal of Obstetrics and Gynecology* 160 (May 1989):1107-11.

114. Dennis C. McCornac and Ronald W. Filante, "The Demand for Distilled Spirits: An Empirical Investigation," *Journal of Studies on Alcohol* 45, no 2 (1984):176-8; M. Harvey Brenner, "Trends in Alcohol Consumption and Associated Illnesses: Some Effects of Economic Changes," *American Journal of Public Health* 65, no. 12 (December 1975):1279-92. Brenner finds a complex relationship, where short-term downturns in the economy tend to increase alcohol consumption and signs of alcoholism, while long-term improvements in per-capita income also are related to increases in alcohol consumption, especially in lighter (social) drinking. Brenner suggests that "alleviation of the effects and aftermath of economic stress" seem to explain why some people become heavy drinkers despite the negative consequences for their health and family relationships.

115. U.S. Congress, Joint Economic Committee [M. Harvey Brenner], *Estimating the Effects of Economic Change on National Health and Social Well-Being* (Washington, D.C.: U.S. Government Printing Office, 1984).

116. For a broad literature review of childhood risk factors for violence, see Hirokazu Yoshikawa, "Prevention as Cumulative Protection: Effects of Early Family Support and Education on Chronic Delinquency and Its Risks," *Psychological Bulletin* 115, no. 1 (1994). For evidence of low IQ during early childhood on later aggression, see also L. Rowell Huesmann and others, "Intellectual Functioning and Aggression," *Journal of Personality and Social Psychology* 52, no. 1 (1987): 232-40 (finding that IQ prior to age eight was important to early and later aggression, but later changes in IQ did not affect aggression; the researchers suggest that "low intelligence makes the learning of aggressive responses more likely at an early age"). For evidence of childhood maltreatment as a risk factor for later violence, see also Widom, "The Cycle of Violence."

117. 1989 American Housing Survey. Tabulations by the Children's Defense Fund.

118. 1989 American Housing Survey. Tabulations by the Children's Defense Fund.

119. Helen L. Evans and others, "Stress Management for Children Who Have Witnessed Violence," manuscript (Chicago, IL: Illinois School of Professional Psychology, 1994).

120. James E. Rosenbaum, "Black Pioneers—Do Their Moves to the Suburbs Increase Economic Opportunity for Mothers and Children?" *Housing Policy Debate* 2, no. 4 (1991):1179-1213.

The program that assisted the families in this study, called the Gautreaux program, was created as the result of a major lawsuit, with the sole purpose of redressing racial segregation in Chicago. Future programs are being planned nationwide that will help low-income families — regardless of race — to move into more privileged neighborhoods.

121. Pamela Kato Klebanov and others, "Does Neighborhood and Family Poverty Affect Mothers' Parenting, Mental Health, and Social Support?" Draft manuscript (New York, NY: Columbia University, Center for Children and Families, January 18, 1994), pp. 8, 12.

122. Robert D. Bullard and Beverly H. Wright, "Environmental Justice for All: Community Perspectives on Health and Research Needs," *Toxicology and Industrial Health* 9, no. 5 (September-October 1993):821-41, pp. 822-4.

123. S.A. Geschwind and others, "Risk of congenital malformations associated with proximity to hazardous waste sites," *American Journal of Epidemiology* 135, no. 11 (1992):1197-1207.

124. Bullard and Wright, "Environmental Justice...," pp. 825, 828.

125. Richard Rios and others, "Susceptibility to Environmental Pollutants among Minorities," *Toxicology and Industrial Health* 9, no. 5 (September-October 1993):797-820, pp. 811-2.

126. U.S. Census Bureau, *Poverty in the United States: 1992,* Current Population Reports, Series P-60, no. 185 (Washington, D.C.: U.S. Government Printing Office, 1993), table 24.

127. The study found that, "Although having medical insurance improved access to medical care, low-income... children continued to have much less access compared with children from more affluent families, regardless of insurance status." The study looked at children nationwide in 1986 and adjusted for differences in race, health status, age, sex, and place of residence. David L. Wood and others, "Access to Medical Care for Children and Adolescents in the United States," *Pediatrics* 86, no. 5 (November 1990):666-73, p. 670.

Another study focused on less healthy children. The study found that low-income children on Medicaid who had health problems saw a doctor an average of 9.3 times in 1981 — somewhat less than middle-income children (10.0 visits) and upper-income children (10.5 visits) who had health problems. (All three groups had much greater health utilization than low-income children who did not have the benefit of Medicaid coverage: completely uninsured children with health problems only saw a doctor 7.7 times during the year, indicating that Medicaid plays a helpful but insufficient role in enhancing poor children's health care access.) Paul W. Newacheck and Neal Halfon, "Access to Ambulatory Care Services for Economically Disadvantaged Children," *Pediatrics* 78, no. 5 (November 1986), p. 815, table 3.

128. Sixty-three percent of private doctors' offices reached by phone in 10 cities said they did not accept Medicaid at all. Clinics were somewhat more likely to accept Medicaid (although between

9 and 35 percent of clinics, and 48 percent of urgent care centers, said they did not). Patients who said they needed urgent care after normal working hours, and could not afford to pay cash, had an even harder time getting an appointment: of close to 1,000 private doctors' offices, clinics, and urgent care centers that were contacted by callers posing as Medicaid recipients, only 8 percent offered after-hours care within two working days without a cash copayment. The Medicaid Access Study Group, "Access of Medicaid Recipients to Outpatient Care," *New England Journal of Medicine* 330, no. 20 (May 19, 1994): 1426-30.

129. U.S. House of Representatives, Committee on Energy and Commerce, *Medicaid Source Book: Background Data and Analysis — A 1993 Update* (Washington, D.C.: U.S. Government Printing Office, 1993), p. 779.

130. U.S. General Accounting Office, *Prenatal Care: Medicaid Recipients and Uninsured Women Obtain Insufficient Care* (Washington, D.C.: U.S. General Accounting Office, September 1987), p. 34, table 3.1.

131. U.S. Congress, Office of Technology Assessment, *Benefit Design in Health Care Reform: Background Paper— Patient Cost Sharing,* OTA-BP-H-112 (Washington, D.C.: U.S. Government Printing Office, September 1993).

132. According to a congressional study of patient cost-sharing experiences under the Rand Health Insurance Experiment, charging fees for health services deterred individuals from seeking all types of care, even potentially effective treatment and appropriate hospitalizations. Children in health plans that charged fees were significantly less likely to receive preventive care such as a well-care examination,

immunization, or a tuberculosis screening. As with adults, low-income children were affected much more than their middle- and upper-income peers. U.S. Congress, Office of Technology Assessment, *Benefit Design in Health Care Reform....*

133. U.S. General Accounting Office, *Prenatal Care...,* p. 34, table 3.1.

134. V. Benson and M.A. Marano, "Current Estimates from the National Health Interview Survey" [1990, 1991, 1992], *Vital and Health Statistics,* Series 10 (Hyattsville, MD: National Center for Health Statistics [1992, 1993, 1994]). Calculations by the Children's Defense Fund.

CDF averaged together rates for 1990, 1991, and 1992 to improve the reliability of the estimates.

135. Michael D. Kogan and others, "Racial Disparities in Reported Prenatal Care Advice from Health Care Providers," *American Journal of Public Health* 84, no. 1 (January 1994):82-8, p. 87, table 4.

136. Lisa J. Santer and Carol B. Stocking, "Safety Practices and Living Conditions of Low-Income Urban Families," *Pediatrics* 88, no. 6 (December 1991): 1112-8.

137. Paula A. Braveman and others, "Differences in Hospital Resource Allocation Among Sick Newborns According to Insurance Coverage," *Journal of the American Medical Association,* 266 (December 18, 1991):3300-8.

138. Ruth Nowjack-Raymer and Helen C. Gift, "Contributing Factors to Maternal and Child Oral Health," *Journal of Public Health Dentistry* 50, no. 6 (1990): 370-7, p. 373.

Many children may receive adequate fluoride through other sources, such as community water supplies. But only about half of the U.S. population had

fluoridated water in their communities in 1985, according to an article in the same volume. H. Barry Waldman, "Oral Health Status of Women and Children in the United States," *Journal of Public Health Dentistry* 50, no. 6 (1990):379-89, p. 382.

139. Low income means annual family income of less than $10,000. High income means $35,000 or more. National Center for Health Statistics, S. Jack and B. Bloom, "Use of dental services and dental health: United States, 1986," *Vital and Health Statistics,* Series 10, no. 165. DHHS Pub No. (PHS) 88-1593 (Washington, D.C.: U.S. Government Printing Office, 1988), p. 50, table 16.

140. Andrea L. Piani and Charlotte A. Schoenborn, "Health Promotion and Disease Prevention: United States, 1990," *Vital and Health Statistics,* Series 10, no. 185 (Hyattsville, MD: National Center for Health Statistics, 1993), p. 13, table C.

141. Using nationwide data for persons of all ages, the National Fire Protection Association reports that the presence of a smoke detector cuts the risk of death during a home fire nearly in half (or by about 40 percent). John R. Hall, *U.S. Experience with Smoke Detectors and Other Fire Detectors* (Quincy, MA: National Fire Protection Association, 1993). However, these estimates do not look separately at children, who likely are less able to escape on their own and therefore may be more vulnerable to fires.

One North Carolina study found that smoke detectors made a stronger difference when children were present. In residential fires where a child younger than five was present, not having a smoke detector increased the odds that a fire would result in death by 5.6 times. When no young child was present, absence of a smoke detector increased the odds

3.1 times. Carol W. Runyan and others, "Risk Factors for Fatal Residential Fires," *New England Journal of Medicine* 327, no. 12, (September 17, 1991):859-63, p. 861, table 2.

142. Data for children are not published. Among adults, ages 18 and older in 1990, 34.9 percent of those with annual family incomes of less than $10,000 had no working smoke detector in their home, compared with 11.8 percent of those with family incomes of $50,000 or more. The total for all adults, all income groups combined, was 21.4 percent.

Andrea L. Piani and Charlotte A. Schoenborn, "Health Promotion and Disease Prevention: United States, 1990," *Vital and Health Statistics* Series 10, no. 185 (Hyattsville, MD: National Center for Health Statistics, April 1993), p. 63, table 39.

143. Rita F. Fahy and Alison L. Norton, "How Being Poor Affects Fire Risk," *Fire Journal* 83, no. 1 (January/February 1989), p. 36.

144. Elizabeth W. Saadi, *Children's Deaths in Kansas* (Topeka, KS: Kansas Department of Health and Environment and Kansas Department of Social and Rehabilitation Services, March 1989), p. 10, table 2.

145. Piani and Schoenborn, "Health Promotion...," p. 13.

The figure of 79 percent of low-income newborns driven home in a car safety seat may seem high, relative to rate of car ownership among low-income families. It is important to remember that some children are driven home in the cars of friends, relatives, and taxi drivers, and that some hospitals pass out free safety seats to families in such situations, even when the family does not own a car.

146. McLoughlin and Crawford, "Burns...," p. 69.

147. For 17 percent of children on AFDC, and 18 percent of poor children not on welfare — compared with 7 percent of nonpoor, non-welfare children — interviewers in the National Longitudinal Survey of Labor Market Experience of Youth did not find that the child play environment appears safe. The study looked at three- to five-year-olds born to mothers aged 14 to 25 at the time of birth. Nicholas Zill and others, "The Life Circumstances and Development of Children in Welfare Families: A Profile Based on National Survey Data" (Washington, D.C.: Child Trends, 1991), table 9.

148. In New York City, for example, poor children live in neighborhoods with less than half as much park space per child as nonpoor children. The average poor child in New York City in 1989 lived in a community district that had 17 square yards of park space per child. The average nonpoor child lived in a community district with 40 square yards of park space. Citizen's Committee for Children, *Keeping Track of New York City's Children* (New York, NY: 1993), appendix table 2 (poverty status as of 1989). Calculations by the Children's Defense Fund.

149. In a striking comparison of one affluent community and one poor community in the Chicago area, children in the affluent community could choose from 3 times as many available activities per week, relative to children in the poor community. Activities in the affluent neighborhood spanned organized arts activities, classes, clubs or groups, sports, and social or civic events. Children in the poor community could choose between various personal support and tutoring programs, employment training, drop-out prevention, and pregnancy

prevention programs, and were offered a much narrower range of classes. In the affluent community, far more activities were offered through parks, schools, and churches, while non-profit social service organizations offered more activities in the poor neighborhood. Julia Littell and Joan Wynn, "The Availability and Use of Community Resources for Young Adolescents in an Inner-City and a Suburban Community," discussion paper (Chicago, IL: University of Chicago, Chapin Hall Center for Children, 1989).

150. Task Force on Youth Development and Community Programs, *A Matter of Time: Risk and Opportunity in the Nonschool Hours* (New York, NY: Carnegie Council on Adolescent Development, Carnegie Corporation of New York, 1992) p. 33.

151. Littell and Wynn, "The Availability and Use of Community Resources...," pp. 6-7.

152. U.S. Congress, Joint Economic Committee [M. Harvey Brenner], *Estimating the Effects of Economic Change on National Health and Social Well-Being* (Washington, D.C.: U.S. Government Printing Office, 1984), p. 65. See also, Dennis C. McCornac and Ronald W. Finante, "The Demand for Distilled Spirits: An Empirical Investigation," *Journal of Studies on Alcohol* 45, no. 2 (1984):1736-8.

153. David R. Williams, "Socioeconomic Differentials in Health: A Review and Redirection," *Social Psychology Quarterly* 53, no. 2 (1990):81-99.

154. See David L. Olds and others, "Intellectual Impairment in Children of Women Who Smoke Cigarettes During Pregnancy," *Pediatrics* 93, no. 2 (February 1994):228-33.

155. Middle-income here refers to children in the third quintile of the household income distribution. U.S. Census Bureau, *Extended Measures of Well-Being: Selected Data from the 1984 Survey of Income and Program Participation* Series P-70, no. 26 (Washington, D.C.: U.S. Government Printing Office, 1992), p. 285-7, table 10.

156. U.S. General Accounting Office, *Prenatal Care...,* p. 34, table 3.1.

157. The study reported that, in rural communities, 12 percent of Medicaid-enrolled or uninsured women interviewed who received either "inadequate" or "intermediate" prenatal care reported that child care for their other children was a barrier to prenatal care. In large metropolitan areas, 4 percent reported this. In mid-sized urban areas, 8 percent reported this. U.S. General Accounting Office, *Prenatal Care...,* p. 39.

158. Public Voice for Food and Health Policy, "Food Costs in Persistently Poor Rural America" (Washington, D.C.: Public Voice for Food and Health Policy, 1990).

159. Mark Lino and Joanne Guthrie [U.S. Department of Agriculture, Family Economics Research Group], "The Food Situation of Families Maintained by Single Mothers: Expenditures, Shopping Behavior, and Diet Quality," *Family Economics Review* 7, no. 1 (1994):9-21, pp. 19-20.

160. Child Trends, "Characteristics of Welfare Children and Their Families: Tables Based on the March 1988 Current Population Survey" (Washington, D.C.: Child Trends, no date), table 14. In most cases, when there was no phone in the home, family members indicated that they did not have a phone available to them elsewhere.

161. Emmy E. Werner and Ruth S. Smith, *Vulnerable But Invincible: A Study of Resilient Children* (New York, NY: McGraw-Hill, 1982), p. 48, table 9.

162. Steven Parker and others, "Double Jeopardy: The Impact of Poverty on Early Childhood Development," *The Pediatric Clinics of North America* 35, no. 6 (December 1988):1227-40.

163. U.S. Public Health Service, *Surgeon General's Report on Nutrition and Health* (U.S. Government Printing Office, 1988), p. 479.

164. Rivara and Barber, "Demographic Analysis of Childhood Pedestrian Injuries...."

165. Robert J. Sampson, "The Community Context of Violent Crime," in William Julius Wilson (ed.), *Sociology and the Public Agenda* (New York, NY: Russell Sage, 1993), p. 262.

166. Robert J. Sampson, "Concentrated Urban Poverty and Crime: A Synopsis of Prior Community-Level Research," background memorandum prepared for the Social Science Research Council Policy Conference on Persistent Urban Poverty, November 1993, Washington, D.C., p. 7.

167. Stephen Chaikind and Hope Corman, "The impact of low birthweight on special education costs," *Journal of Health Economics* 10 (1991):291-311, p. 299, endnote 22.

168. Werner and Smith, *Vulnerable But Invincible...,* p. 31.

169. One study found that having a mother with at least some postsecondary education "eliminated the difference in IQs by birth weight for all but the tiniest infants." Marie C. McCormick and others, "The Health and Developmental Status of Very Low-Birth-Weight Children at School Age," *Journal of the American Medical Association* 267, no. 16 (April 22/20, 1992):2204-8, p. 2207.

In a testament to the many interacting influences on children's lives, another study looked at the lives of children who are buffeted by a combi-

nation of low birthweight, poverty, and prematurity. Although some children withstood this triple threat to their health and development, the resilient children almost all had three or more other factors working in their favor — factors such as an uncrowded home, a safe play area, a very accepting parent, lots of learning materials, or a varied environment. The study concluded, "in the absence of having at least three protective caregiving experiences, the odds that a premature, [low birthweight] child living in poverty will show early signs of resilience are, for all practical purposes, nil." Robert H. Bradley and others, "Early Indications of Resilience and Their Relation to Experiences in the Home Environments of Low Birthweight, Premature Children Living in Poverty," *Child Development* 65, no. 2 (April 1994):346-60, p. 357.

Chapter 3 Endnotes
Human Costs Linked to Child Poverty

1. Barbara Starfield, "Childhood Morbidity: Comparisons, Clusters, and Trends," *Pediatrics* 88, no. 3 (September 1991):519-26, p. 521.

2. Barbara Starfield, "Child Health Care and Social Factors: Poverty, Class, and Race," *Bulletin of the New York Academy of Medicine* 65, no. 3 (March 1989):299-306, p. 300.

3. Barbara Starfield, "Childhood Morbidity...," p. 522.

4. Carl W. Spurlock and others, "Infant Death Rates Among the Poor and Nonpoor in Kentucky, 1982 to 1983," *Pediatrics* 80, no. 2 (August 1987):262-269. Low income in this study meant the parents received food stamps or AFDC.

5. Steven L. Gortmaker, "Poverty and Infant Mortality in the United States," *American Sociological Review* 44 (April 1979):280-97. Gortmaker notes that, by accounting for differences in low birthweight, the results tend to account as well for factors that affect fetal development such as mother's smoking behavior or height. Before holding other factors constant, Gortmaker found that babies born to families below official poverty guidelines were 1.75 times more likely to die in infancy than babies from more affluent families (compared with 1.5 times more likely after accounting for other factors). Births to non-White and single parents were not analyzed.

6. U.S. Congress, Joint Economic Committee [M. Harvey Brenner], *Estimating the Effects of Economic Change on National Health and Social Well-Being* (Washington, D.C.: U.S. Government Printing Office, 1984), p. 55 and p. 67, table II.

This finding was consistent with studies of other nations and with earlier studies of the United States which found that "All categories of fetal and infant mortality increased sharply" between birth and two years after the peak of an economic recession, according to the congressional report (p. 29).

7. William S. Nersesian and others, "Childhood Death and Poverty: A Study of All Childhood Deaths in Maine, 1976 to 1980," *Pediatrics* 75, no. 1 (January 1985):41-50. The study covered children ages 0 to 19. Income status was approximated based on participation in Medicaid, food stamps, or AFDC. The authors estimated that "in Maine approximately 90% of families earning less than 125% of the federal poverty level participate in [these programs]; therefore we feel that children enrolled in one or more of these programs are a

good representation of Maine's poor children" (p. 45). The differences were significant in each case except for suicide. Elsewhere, the authors cautioned that the numbers for both homicide and suicide were too small for a meaningful comparison of rates. Maine Department of Human Services, *Children's Deaths in Maine: 1976-1980, Final Report* (Augusta, ME: 1983), p. 26, table 1.

8. Elizabeth W. Saadi, *Children's Deaths in Kansas: 1985 to 1987* (Topeka, KS: Kansas Department of Health and Environment and Kansas Department of Rehabilitation Services, 1989), p. 10, table 2. The study determined low income based on records from a large number of programs providing public assistance, medical assistance, disability, foster care, and other services. The majority of children received public assistance and typically had family incomes equal to about 60 percent of the poverty line.

9. CDF estimated this figure based on child population and death rate data taken from Mare's study. From information in Table 3 of the study, CDF calculated that there were about 5.5 million White children up to nine years old in families with annual incomes below $10,000, of whom about 111,000 (or about 2.0 percent) died. Similarly, there were about 10.2 million children in families with incomes above $10,000, of whom about 145,000 (or roughly 1.4 percent) died. As noted, 2 percent is about 1.4 times greater than 1.4 percent. Robert D. Mare, "Socioeconomic Effects on Child Mortality in the United States," *American Journal of Public Health* 72, no. 6 (June 1982): 539-47.

10. Robert D. Mare, "Socioeconomic Effects on Child Mortality...," p. 543.

11. Robert D. Mare, "Socioeconomic Effects on Child Mortality...," table 4. Calculations by the Children's Defense Fund.

12. The effect of poverty in this study is somewhat weaker than in the more recent Kansas and Maine studies. At least some of this difference between the studies may result from what Mare himself cautions are several major weaknesses in his data. Mare used the Census Bureau's June 1975 Current Population Survey for information on both the current family income level of women and a retrospective question about possible death of children during the women's lifetimes. Mare warns that both of these questions are somewhat unreliable, as are other aspects of the data. "The CPS sample of child deaths is small, under-represents children in large families, ignores orphans, precludes calculation of age-specific death rates, relies upon the faulty memories of respondents who are asked only a single question about possible child mortality, and provides no retrospective information that might better measure children's environments than family characteristics at the survey date."

13. Unpublished data from the National Center for Health Statistics show that, nationwide, low birthweight babies were 20 times more likely than normal-weight babies to die in their first year of life. This comparison is based on the most recent available data, for 1987. It is likely that the survival picture of low birthweight babies has improved somewhat since 1987, however, as a result of new life-saving treatments (called surfactants) that allow sick babies with underdeveloped lungs to breathe.

14. Marie C. McCormick and others, "The Health and Developmental Status of Very Low-Birth-Weight Children at School Age," *Journal of the American Medical Association* 267 (April 22/29, 1992):2204-8.

15. Barbara Starfield and others, "Race, Family Income, and Low Birth Weight," *American Journal of Epidemiology* 134, no. 10 (1991):1167-74.

16. Spurlock and others, "Infant Death Rates...," p. 266, table 3. Calculations by the Children's Defense Fund.

17. National Center for Health Statistics, E.R. Pamuk and W.D. Mosher, "Health aspects of pregnancy and childbirth," *Vital and Health Statistics* Series 23, no. 16. DHHS Pub. No. (PHS) 89-1992. (Washington, D.C.: U.S. Government Printing Office), p. 53, table 26.

18. Donald B. Binsacca and others, "Factors Associated with Low Birthweight in an Inner-City Population: The Role of Financial Problems," *American Journal of Public Health* 77, no. 4 (April 1987):505-6.

The unadjusted odds of low birthweight were 7.1 times greater for mothers with financial problems. Holding other factors constant reduced the odds ratio only slightly, to 5.9.

19. The one exception was for Black teen mothers younger than 17 who had received inadequate prenatal care during pregnancy: for this group, low neighborhood income was not linked in any obvious way to greater low-birthweight births. This exception may be a statistical anomaly, or it may indicate that the effects of income were outweighed by other factors for this one very highly disadvantaged subgroup. Jeffrey B. Gould and Susan LeRoy, "Socioeconomic Status and Low Birth Weight: A Racial Comparison," *Pediatrics* 88, no. 6 (1988):896-904, p.900, table 2.

20. The study grouped infants into similar risk categories by age, race, education, and marital status of parents. In each group, those from the poorest neighborhoods fared worse. An exception was well-educated White mothers: the low-birthweight rates for this group were the same in low- and high-income neighborhoods. James W. Collins and others, "The Differential Effect of Traditional Risk Factors on Infant Birthweight among Blacks and Whites in Chicago," *American Journal of Public Health* 80, no. 6 (June 1990): 679-81, p. 681, table 3.

21. Jane E. Miller and Sanders Korenman, "Poverty and Children's Nutritional Status in the United States," *American Journal of Epidemiology* 140, no. 3 (August 1, 1994), table 2.

22. U.S. Department of Health and Human Services and U.S. Department of Agriculture, *Nutrition Monitoring in the United States—A Report from the Joint Nutrition Monitoring Evaluation Committee* (Washington, D.C.: U.S. Government Printing Office, 1986), p. 325.

23. Laura E. Montgomery and Olivia Carter-Pokras, "Health Status by Social Class and/or Minority Status: Implications for Environmental Equity Research," *Toxicology and Industrial Health* 9, no. 5 (1993):729-73, p. 756, table 21.

24. Montgomery and Carter-Pokras, "Health Status by Social Class...," p. 755, table 20.

25. V. Benson and M.A. Marano, *Current Estimates from the National Health Interview Survey* [1990, 1991, 1992], Vital Health Statistics, Series 10 (Hyattsville, MD: National Center for Health Statistics [1992, 1993, 1994]). Calculations by the Children's Defense Fund. Rates for 1990, 1991, and 1992 were averaged together to improve the reliability of the estimates.

26. Laura E. Montgomery and Olivia Carter-Pokras, "Health Status by Social Class and/or Minority Status: Implications for Environmental Equity Research," *Toxicology and Industrial Health* 9, no. 5 (September-October, 1993), p. 751. The authors define low income as family income below 1.5 times the poverty line.

27. Jack P. Shonkoff, "Biological and Social Factors Contributing to Mild Mental Retardation," in K. Heller and others, eds., *Placing Children in Special Education: A Strategy for Equity* (Washington, D.C.: National Academy Press, 1982), pp. 142-3.

28. Shonkoff, "Biological and Social Factors...," p. 171.

29. For example, data for the 1990, 1991, and 1992 National Health Interview Surveys (averaged to improve reliability) indicate that there were about 24 injuries per 100 children in families with incomes under $10,000, compared with 29 per 100 children in families with incomes over $10,000. V. Benson and M.A. Marano, *Current Estimates from the National Health Interview Survey* [1990, 1991, 1992], Vital Health Statistics, Series 10 (Hyattsville, MD: National Center for Health Statistics [1992, 1993, 1994]). Calculations by the Children's Defense Fund.

30. Benson and Marano, *Current Estimates....* Data for three years averaged together to improve reliability.

31. Natan Szapiro, "Children, Poverty, and Hospital Care in New York City," in M.I. Krasner (ed.), *Poverty and Health in New York City* (New York, NY: United Hospital Fund of New York, 1989), p. 97, exhibit 4.7.

32. I. Barry Pless, "The Epidemiology of Road Accidents in Childhood," *American Journal of Public Health* 77, no. 3 (March 1987):358-60.

33. Mary Braddock and others, "Population, Income, and Ecological Correlates of Child Pedestrian Injury," *Pediatrics* 88, no. 6 (December 1991):1242-7.

34. In census tracts in which child injuries occurred during 1982, 29.4 percent of families were poor — nearly 50 percent higher than the rate for tracts without injuries (20.1 percent). Frederick P. Rivara and Melvin Barber, "Demographic Analysis of Childhood Pedestrian Injuries," *Pediatrics* 76, no. 3 (September 1985):375-81.

35. Saadi, *Children's Deaths in Kansas;* Nersesian and others, "Childhood Death and Poverty...."

36. Natan Szapiro, "Children, Poverty, and Hospital Care in New York City," in M.I. Krasner, ed., *Poverty and Health in New York City* (New York, NY: United Hospital Fund of New York, 1989), p. 97, Exhibit 4.7.

37. Benson and Marano, *Current Estimates....* Data for three years averaged together to improve reliability.

38. Montgomery and Carter-Pokras, "Health Status by Social Class...," p. 751. The authors define low income as family income below 1.5 times the poverty line.

39. U.S. Department of Health and Human Services and U.S. Department of Agriculture, *Nutrition Monitoring in the United States: An Update Report on Nutrition Monitoring* (Washington, DC: U.S. Government Printing Office), p. 150, Iron Table 1.

40. Ray Yip and others, "Declining Prevalence of Anemia Among Low-Income Children in the United States," *Journal of the American Medical Association* 258 no. 12 (September 25, 1987):1619-23. The study uses an especially stringent definition of anemia.

41. Centers for Disease Control (CDC), Pediatric Nutrition Surveillance System (PedNSS), 1992 annual summaries, unpublished tables. PedNSS data covered more than 5.6 million children younger than five in 1992 who participated in public health programs for low-income children, principally the Special Supplemental Food Program for Women, Infants, and Children (WIC). More than 20 percent of the children tested in this age group — representing more than 1 million children in the PedNSS — had low hemoglobin (below the 5th percentile for their age, according to norms established in the Second National Health and Nutrition Examination Survey). Moreover, these numbers understate the total number of low-income children with anemia in the United States because they leave out any children who did not come in contact with WIC and other programs in the PedNSS.

For children younger than two, about 22 percent of those tested were anemic. Biases in the PedNSS sample — which arise because WIC deliberately seeks to enroll and retain anemic children — mean that the true proportion in the general population of low-income young children (including those not served by public health programs) is probably "slightly lower, not dramatically lower" than 22 percent. (Personal communication with Ibrahim Parvanta, CDC, February 1, 1994.)

For CDC's most recent (1991) published anemia data, see Ray Yip and others, "Pediatric Nutrition Surveillance System—United States, 1980-1991," *Morbidity and Mortality Weekly Report* 41 no. SS-7 (November 27, 1992).

42. Ann M. Hardy [National Center for Health Statistics], "Incidence and impact of selected infectious diseases in childhood," *Vital Health Statistics* 10, no. 180 (October 1991), table 7 and text on page 5. Calculations by the Children's Defense Fund. The National Center for Health Statistics determined that the incidence rate for this disease generally falls as income rises; unfortunately, it did not specifically test whether the comparison presented here, between families below and above annual incomes of $10,000, was statistically significant.

To obtain estimated figures on children with family incomes above $10,000, CDF combined data for several income groups. To combine these data, CDF used population figures from appendix table IV.

43. Hardy, "Incidence and impact of selected infectious diseases...." Calculations by the Children's Defense Fund. See footnote 40 for technical detail.

44. Hardy, "Incidence and impact of selected infectious diseases...." Calculations by the Children's Defense Fund. See footnote 40 for technical detail.

45. Neal Halfon and Paul W. Newacheck, "Childhood Asthma and Poverty: Differential Impacts and Utilization of Health Services," *Pediatrics* 91, no 1 (January 1993):56-61.

46. Michael Weitzman and others, "Recent Trends in the Prevalence and Severity of Childhood Asthma," *Journal of the American Medical Association* 268 (November 18, 1992):2673-7.

47. Lawrence Wissow and others, "Poverty, Race, and Hospitalization for Childhood Asthma," *American Journal of Public Health* 78, no. 7 (July 1988): 777-82.

48. Szapiro, "Children, Poverty, and Hospital Care...," p. 96, exhibit 4.7.

49. Wissow and others, "Poverty, Race, and Hospitalization for Childhood Asthma...."

50. Robert M. Bell and others, *Results of Baseline Dental Exams in the National Preventive Dentistry Demonstration Program* (Santa Monica, CA: Rand Corporation, 1982), p. 35.

51. V. Benson and M.A. Marano, *Current Estimates from the National Health Interview Survey* [1990, 1991, 1992], Vital Health Statistics, Series 10 (Hyattsville, MD: National Center for Health Statistics [1992, 1993, 1994]). Calculations by the Children's Defense Fund.

52. For Black children, the effects of low family income were not statistically significant. However, children of mothers who subjectively perceived themselves as poor did have significantly greater odds of missing school due to illness — the effect of poverty measured this way was greater among Black children (odds ratio = 2.65) than White children (odds ratio = 2.1). McGauhey and Starfield, "Child Health and the Social Environment...," p. 870, table 3.

53. Mary Ann Millsap and others, *The Chapter 1 Implementation Study: Final Report* (Washington, D.C.: U.S. Department of Education, Office of Policy and Planning, 1993), p. 1-11.

54. See for example, Hillary Stout, "Remedial Curriculum for Low Achievers is Falling From Favor," *Wall Street Journal* (July 30, 1992), and Robert E. Slavin, "Synthesis of Research on Cooperative Learning," both reprinted in Alan Backler and Sybil Eakin, eds., *Every Child Can Succeed: Readings for School Improvement* (Bloomington, IN: Agency for Instructional Technology, 1993).

55. As Chapter 2 describes, low-income children's overall development appears to be more vulnerable and sensitive to the kinds of stimulation they receive at home. The same vulnerabilities may make them more sensitive to the quality of their school, compared with nonpoor children.

56. Greg J. Duncan and others, "Economic Deprivation and Early-Childhood Development," *Child Development* 65, no. 2 (April 1994):296-318, pp. 311-2.

57. Sanders Korenman and others, "Long-term Poverty and Child Development in the United States: Results from the NLSY," *Child and Youth Services Review* 17, no's. 1-2 (forthcoming, 1995).

These comparisons hold constant a set of "basic controls." These are child's age, race, gender, number of siblings, and whether the child is the oldest sibling.

The study examined several thousand children born to women in the National Longitudinal Survey of Youth between 1979 and 1988, and used test results collected between 1986 and 1990 for children age three and older. The results discussed here are for the Peabody Picture Vocabulary Test-Revised and three sub-scales of the Peabody Individual Achievement Test: Math, Reading Recognition, and Reading Comprehension. Results on behavior problems reported by Korenman and his colleagues are reported elsewhere in this chapter.

58. Sanders Korenman and others, "Long-term Poverty and Child Development...."

59. Korenman and others, "Long-Term Poverty and Child Development...."

60. Nicholas Zill and Charlotte Schoenborn, *Developmental, Learning, and Emotional Problems,* Advance data from vital and health statistics, no. 190 (Hyattsville, MD: National Center for Health Statistics, November 16, 1990), p. 13, table 2, and p. 18, appendix table I. Calculations by the Children's Defense Fund.

61. Stephen Chaikind and Hope Corman, "The impact of low birthweight on special education costs," *Journal of Health Economics* 10 (1991):291-311.

62. Doris Goldberg and others, "Which Newborns in New York City Are at Risk for Special Education Placement?" *American Journal of Public Health* 82, no. 3 (March 1992):438-40, p. 439, table 1. The study collected data on 161 third graders in New York City, including 45 who were in special education.

63. Stephen Chaikind, "The Effects of Short-Term and Long-Term Poverty on Educational Attainment of Children," in Mary M. Kennedy and others, *Poverty, Achievement and the Distribution of Compensatory Education Services* (Washington, D.C.: U.S. Department of Education, 1986), appendix D; summarized on p. 18 and in p. 19, table 2.1.

64. McGauhey and Starfield, "Child Health and the Social Environment...."

65. National Center for Education Statistics, *Dropout Rates in the United States: 1992* (Washington, D.C.: U.S. Department of Education, 1993), p. 17, table 9; National Center for Education Statistics, *Dropout Rates in the United States: 1991* (Washington, D.C.: U.S. Department of Education, 1992), p. 254, table 20-3.

66. Greg J. Duncan and others, "Economic Deprivation and Early-Childhood Development," *Child Development* 65, no. 2 (April 1994):296-318.

67. Jane E. Miller and Sanders Korenman, "Poverty and Children's Nutritional Status in the United States," *American Journal of Epidemiology* 140, no. 3 (August 1, 1994), table 2.

68. Mary M. Kennedy and others, *Poverty, Achievement and the Distribution of Compensatory Education Services* (Washington, D.C.: U.S. Department of Education, Office of Educational Research and Improvement, January 1986), p. 19, table 2.1.

69. Richard J. Gelles, "Child Abuse and Violence in Single-Parent Families: Parent Absence and Economic Deprivation," *American Journal of Orthopsychiatry* 59, no. 4 (October 1989).

70. Urie Bronfenbrenner, "What do families do?," *Family Affairs* 4, no. 1-2 (1991):1-6.

71. Sara S. McLanahan and Gary Sandefur, *Growing Up with a Single Parent* (Cambridge, MA: Harvard University Press, 1994); Duncan and others, "Economic Deprivation..."; Korenman and others, "Long-term Poverty and Child Development...."

72. Naomi Carol Goldstein, "Why Poverty is Bad for Children," dissertation, Harvard University, John F. Kennedy School of Government (January 1991), p. 115, table 5.3.

73. National Institutes of Health, "Children of Divorce: Policy Implications from NICHD Research" (Bethesda, MD: National Institutes of Health, National Institute of Child Health and Human Development, May 1993), summarizing research by Andrew Cherlin and others.

74. Donald J. Hernandez, *America's Children: Resources from Family, Government and the Economy* (New York, NY: Russell Sage, 1993) p. 290.

75. Hernandez, *America's Children*, p. 312.

76. McLanahan and Sandefur, *Growing Up with a Single Parent*. The researchers studied the effects of single parent families on three outcomes: dropping out of high school, becoming a teen unwed mother, or becoming an unemployed out-of-school male.

77. Center for Education Statistics, "Cumulative Rates of Entry into Postsecondary Institutions by 1980 High School Graduates: September 1980

through February 1986," unpublished tabulations of the High School and Beyond survey (Washington, D.C.: U.S. Department of Education, April 1988), table 1.

78. Center for Education Statistics, "Cumulative Rates of Entry...," tables 2 and 3.

79. Eva Eagle [MPR Associates, Inc.], "High School and Beyond: Educational Experiences of the 1980 Senior Class," report prepared for Center for Education Statistics (Washington, D.C.: U.S. Department of Education, January 1988), table 9a. The Education Department data are for high school seniors rather than high school graduates. However, when CDF adjusted for the very small number of nongraduating seniors in the survey, the figures changed by less than one percentage point (that is, the rounded results were unchanged).

80. McLoyd, "The Impact of Economic Hardship..."; Richard J. Gelles, "Poverty and Violence Toward Children," *American Behavioral Scientist* 35, no. 3 (January/February 1992):258-74; Joan I. Vondra, "Childhood Poverty and Child Maltreatment," in Judith A. Chafel, ed., *Child Poverty and Public Policy* (Washington, D.C.: Urban Institute Press, 1993).

81. Vondra, "Childhood Poverty and Child Maltreatment," pp. 128-9.

82. U.S. Department of Health and Human Services, National Center on Child Abuse and Neglect, *Study of National Incidence and Prevalence of Child Abuse and Neglect: 1988* (Washington: U.S. Department of Health and Human Services, 1988), p. 5-29, table 5-6.

83. James Garbarino, "The Meaning of Poverty in the World of Children," *American Behavioral Scientist* 35, no. 3 (January/February 1992):220-37.

84. Laurence D. Steinberg and others, "Economic Antecedents of Child Abuse and Neglect," *Child Development* 52 (1981):975-85.

85. To provide an especially strict test of the hypothesis that job losses were causing abuse, the researchers carefully ruled out the notion that permanent traits of jobless families, such as parents' cultural attitudes or inherent tendencies, are enough to explain why jobless families commit more abuse (since they found that employment losses triggered statistically significant changes in reported abuse during their 30-month study period, changes which by definition cannot be triggered by permanent traits). They also ruled out weather patterns, broad cultural or seasonal influences, or any other region-wide trends (since employment losses also helped explain the changing differences in reported abuse between the two counties, differences which by definition were not caused by region-wide trends). They even ruled out the unlikely possibility that abuse causes economic loss, rather than the other way around (since there was a clear lag of two months in both counties between employment losses and increases in reported abuse).

86. McLeod and Shanahan, "Poverty, Parenting, and Children's Mental Health," p. 359 note 7, and personal communication with Jane McLeod, May 12, 1994.

87. U.S. Department of Health and Human Services, National Center on Child Abuse and Neglect, *Study of National Incidence and Prevalence...*, p. 5-29, table 5-6.

88. National Research Council Panel on High-Risk Youth, *Losing Generations: Adolescents in High-Risk Settings* (Washington, D.C.: National Academy Press, 1993), p. 156.

89. City of Los Angeles, Community Development Department, unpublished data on Community Improvement and Planning Areas (crime rates in 1991, poverty rates in 1989). Calculations by the Children's Defense Fund.

90. Citizen's Committee for Children, *Keeping Track of New York City's Children* (New York, NY: 1993), appendix table 2 (arrests in 1991, poverty rates in 1989). Calculations by the Children's Defense Fund.

91. Government of the District of Columbia, Office of Planning, *Socioeconomic Indicators by Census Tract* (Washington, D.C.: December 1992) (crime rates in 1990, poverty rates in 1989). Calculations by the Children's Defense Fund.

92. U.S. Congress, Joint Economic Committee, *Estimating the Effects of Economic Change on National Health and Social Well-Being* (Washington, D.C.: U.S. Government Printing Office, 1984).

93. Johan M. Kang and others, "Crime Rates versus Labor Market Conditions: Theory and Time-Series Evidence," NBER Working Paper no. 3801 (Cambridge, MA: National Bureau of Economic Research, 1991), summarized by authors in *NBER Reporter* (Fall 1991), p. 35.

94. Joel A. Devine and others, "Macroeconomic and Social-Control Policy Influences on Crime Rate Changes, 1948-1985," *American Sociology Review* 53, no. 3 (June 1988):407-20.

95. Rand D. Conger and others, "Economic Stress, Coercive Family Process, and Developmental Problems of Adolescents," *Child Development* 65, no. 2 (April 1994):541-61.

96. Steven L. Gortmaker, "Chronic Conditions, Socioeconomic Risks, and Behavioral Problems in Children and Adolescents," *Pediatrics* 85, no. 3 (March 1990):267-76.

97. McGauhey and Starfield, "Child Health and the Social Environment...."

98. Sanders Korenman and others, "Long-term Poverty and Child Development...."

99. Duncan and others, "Economic Deprivation and Early-Childhood Development."

100. Robert J. Sampson and John H. Laub, "Urban Poverty and the Family Context of Delinquency: A New Look at Structure and Process in a Classic Study," *Child Development* 65, no. 2 (April 1994):523-40.

101. Werner and Smith, *Vulnerable But Invincible...*, p. 47.

102. Emily E. Werner and Ruth S. Smith, *Overcoming the Odds: High Risk Children from Birth to Adulthood* (Ithaca, NY: Cornell University Press, 1992), p. 107.

103. Commission on Violence and Youth, *Violence and Youth: Psychology's Response*, vol. I: Summary Report (Washington, D.C.: American Psychological Association, 1993), p. 17.

104. Hirokazu Yoshikawa, "Prevention as Cumulative Protection: Effects of Early Family Support and Education on Chronic Delinquency and Its Risks," *Psychological Bulletin* 115, no. 1 (1994), citing L.D. Eron and L.R. Huesmann, "The stability of aggressive behavior — Even unto the third generation," in M. Lewis and S.M. Miller, eds., *Handbook of Developmental Psychopathology* (New York, NY: Plenum Press, 1990).

105. L. Rowell Huesmann and others, "Intellectual Functioning and Aggression," *Journal of Personality and Social Psychology* 52, no. 1 (1987):232-40; Werner and Smith, *Vulnerable But Invincible...*, p. 47; Werner and Smith, *Overcoming the Odds...*, p. 107.

106. Werner and Smith, *Vulnerable But Invincible...*, p. 47.

107. Sampson and Laub, "Urban Poverty and the Family Context of Delinquency...."

108. Cathy Spatz Widom, "The Cycle of Violence," *Research in Brief* (U.S. Department of Justice, National Institute of Justice, October 1992); Cathy Spatz Widom, "The Cycle of Violence," *Science* 244, no. 4901 (April 14, 1989):160-6.

109. One literature review concludes that, "although joblessness or even poverty may not have direct effects on crime, they do have significant effects on family disruption, which in turn predicts violence." Further, "the effect of family disruption...could not be attributed to unique cultural factors within the [B]lack community given the similar effect of family disruption on [W]hite crime." Robert J. Sampson, "The Community Context of Violent Crime," in William Julius Wilson (ed.), *Sociology and the Public Agenda* (New York, NY: Russell Sage, 1993), p. 274.

See also Werner and Smith, *Vulnerable But Invincible...*, p. 173, table A-2, finding that at age two, family instability is the single most powerful predictor of future delinquency for boys; however, the authors note that absence of a father has no such negative effect on girls and may even be beneficial.

Werner and Smith also found that children who were "exposed to serious conflict between family members during childhood" were more vulnerable and less resilient to factors that predicted developmental and social problems at ages 10 and 18.

110. Yoshikawa, "Prevention as Cumulative Protection...."

111. Werner and Smith, *Vulnerable But Invincible...*, p. 71.

112. Herbert L. Needleman, "Lead Exposure: The Commonest Environmental Disease of Childhood," *Zero to Three,* bulletin of the National Center for Clinical Infant Programs (Arlington, VA), vol. 11, no. 5 (June 1991).

113. Neil Salkind and Ron Haskins, "Negative Income Tax: The Impact on Children from Low-Income Families," *Journal of Family Issues* 3, no. 2 (June 1982):165-86, pp. 172, 174.

114. Significant positive impacts also were observed in both the Seattle and Denver sites, and for White youths, females, and 18- and 19-year-olds. Impacts for every other subgroup (those ages 16, 17, 20, and 21, Black youths, and males) were positive but did not achieve statistical significance.

Steven F. Venti and David A. Wise, "Income Maintenance and the School and Work Decisions of Youth," study prepared for U.S. Department of Health and Human Services (Cambridge, MA: Harvard University, 1984), p. 53, table 12.

115 Charles D. Mallar, "The educational and labor-supply responses of young adults in experimental families," in H.W. Watts and A. Rees (eds.), *The New Jersey Income Maintenance Experiment*, vol 2 (New York, NY: Academic Press, 1977), p. 165.

116. Salkind and Haskins, "Negative Income Tax: The Impact on Children...."

117. Katherine L. Bradbury, Discussion of Eric A. Hanushek, "Non-Labor-Market Responses to the Income Maintenance Experiments," in Alicia H. Munnell (ed.), *Lessons from the Income Maintenance Experiments*, Proceedings of Conference Held in September 1986 (Boston, MA: Federal Reserve Bank of Boston, 1986), pp. 122-6.

118. William J. Baumol, "An overview of the results," in Harold W. Watts and Albert Rees, eds., *The New Jersey Income Maintenance Experiment*, vol. III (New York, NY: Academic Press, 1977), p. 5.

119. Many economists agree that the experiments probably encouraged adult participants to work less than they otherwise would have; however, at a conference convened to evaluate the experiments, there was considerable debate over the size and importance of these labor market disincentives. There was even less agreement as to whether the experiments encouraged adults to leave unhappy marriages. See, generally, Alicia H. Munnell (ed.), *Lessons from the Income Maintenance Experiments*, proceedings of a conference held in September 1986 (Boston, MA: Federal Reserve Bank of Boston, no date).

Chapter 4 Endnotes
The Economic Costs of Child Poverty

1. Supervision was provided by Robert M. Solow, Institute Professor, Massachusetts Institute of Technology (chair of the Costs of Child Poverty Research Project advisory committee), Rebecca M. Blank, Professor of Economics, Northwestern University (former staff member of the Council of Economic Advisors under President George Bush), and Martha S. Hill, Professor of Economics, University of Michigan and Institute for Social Research, Ann Arbor (specialist in the Panel Study of Income Dynamics and Senior Research Advisor with the Costs of Child Poverty Research Project). Robert Haveman also reviewed the chapter and suggested important improvements.

2. Wages may not be a perfect measure of the true value of a person's work. However, economists generally consider the value of compensation to be a good indicator of the value of output at the margin.

3. CDF's mid-range assumption is that each year of schooling increases future hourly wages by 10 percent.

Recent state-of-the-art estimates report payoffs to education of about 10 percent; moreover, several studies indicate that this payoff to education is rising. One important study found that a one-year difference in education (induced by differences in state compulsory education laws and other involuntary determinants of youths' opportunities to drop out of school) raised hourly wages by 10 percent among men in 1980; this was later revised to 11 percent. Joshua Angrist and Alan Krueger, "Does Compulsory Schooling Affect Schooling and Earnings?" *Quarterly Journal of Economics* 106 (November 1991):979-1014; Joshua D. Angrist and Alan B. Krueger, "Split Sample Instrumental Variables," working paper #320 (Princeton, NJ: Princeton, University, Industrial Relations Section, 1993), p. 24.

Another major study found that each additional year of schooling added between 9 percent and 16 percent, on average, to the wage level of a twin brother or twin sister, relative to their less-educated sibling. Orley Ashenfelter and Alan Krueger, "Estimates of the Economic Return to Schooling from a New Sample of Twins," working paper #4143 (Cambridge, MA: National Bureau of Economic Research, 1992). The uppermost figure was later revised from 16 to 13 percent.

A year in a community or four-year college has been estimated to boost subsequent earnings by 8 or 9 percent, regardless of whether the student receives any type of degree. Thomas Kane and Cecilia Rouse, "Labor Market Returns to Two- and Four-Year Colleges: Is a Credit a Credit and Do Degrees Matter?" working paper #4268 (Cambridge, MA: National Bureau of Economic Research, 1993). Men who live near a college finish more education than other men, and each additional year of education gained in this way has been estimated to boost their earnings by 10 to 14 percent. David Card, "Using Geographic Variation in College Proximity to Estimate the Return to Schooling," working paper #4483 (Cambridge, MA: National Bureau of Economic Research, 1994).

To test the sensitivity of our cost estimates to assumptions about the value of education, CDF also calculated alternate estimates based on a low assumption of 6 percent and a high assumption of 14 percent per year of education.

As described below, CDF applied this 10 percent increase to the expected lifetime earnings of an average American to estimate in dollars the yield to the economy from one additional year of education.

4. For evidence of education's effects on unemployment (effects ignored in Methods 1 through 3) see Jacob A. Mincer, "Education and Unemployment," working paper #3838 (Cambridge, MA: National Bureau of Economic Research, 1991), and Jacob A. Mincer, "Education and the Unemployment of Women," working paper #3837 (Cambridge, MA: National Bureau of Economic Research, 1991).

5. Haveman, Wolfe, and Ginther analyzed their data in four ways, each time holding constant a different set of factors. The first and most basic model controlled for race (Black), sex, number of siblings (average number during childhood), education level of the most-

educated parent, number of years the head of household was disabled, the presence of only one parent at age six, and a constant term. (In this model, each year spent in poverty reduced children's average years of schooling by 0.042 years.)

The second model held these same factors constant, except that it used separate education data for mothers and fathers (mother a high school graduate or more, father a high school graduate or more), and added whether the family declared itself to have any religion, years child spent living in a metropolitan area (versus a rural area), years the mother worked, whether child was the first-born sibling, and whether the respondent perceived the grandparents as having been poor when growing up. (Impact of poverty: 0.05 years of schooling.)

The third model held constant the same factors as in Model 2, but added an interaction term for race and gender (Black Female), more detailed measures of education (mother a high school graduate, mother had some college, mother a college graduate, father a high school graduate, father had some college, father a college graduate) and more detailed measures of the family religion (Catholic, Jewish, Protestant). (Impact of poverty: 0.045 years of schooling.)

The fourth and most complete model held constant the same factors as in Model 3, but added number of parental (re)marriages during childhood, number of parental separations, and several attributes of the neighborhood in which the family lived — including average proportion of households headed by unmarried women, average proportion of young adults who are high school dropouts, average proportion in a high prestige occupation. This model is especial-

ly conservative, in that it holds constant factors that may have been caused or exacerbated by poverty during the study period (when the child was age six to 15). For example, the family may have been driven to divorce or obliged to live in a less desirable neighborhood because of poverty during this period. These factors may best be thought of as possible pathways by which poverty hurts children; holding them constant statistically therefore may understate the full influence of poverty. Nonetheless, even in this model, poverty retained most of its effect on children's education. (Impact of poverty: 0.042 years of schooling.)

For each analysis, years of education completed were measured by age 21 through 27. Haveman, Wolfe, and Ginther ran tobit regressions and used the results to simulate, for each child in the sample who experience one or more years of poverty, the effect of reducing years in poverty by one.

6. See note 3 above.

7. CDF estimated future lifetime earnings for individuals ages 22 to 64, in inflation-adjusted 1992 dollars, following a general approach used previously by the Census Bureau. (See U.S. Census Bureau, *Lifetime Earnings Estimates for Men and Women in the United States: 1979*, Current Population Reports, P-60, no. 139 (Washington, D.C.: U.S. Government Printing Office, 1983), p. 6.

For each single year of age from 22 to 64, inclusive, CDF multiplied average annual earnings per male with earnings at that age by the probability of having earnings. (Because earnings data by single years of age were not available, CDF approximated by using earnings for the appropriate five-year age group.) CDF multiplied that result by the relative number of men expected to survive to that age, out of those alive at age 22.

The sum of the resulting amounts is men's estimated lifetime earnings. We followed the same procedure for women. To get the average lifetime earnings of an American, CDF averaged together men's and women's lifetime earnings.

Data were taken from the following sources: U.S. Census Bureau, *Money Income of Households, Families, and Persons in the United States: 1992,* Current Population Reports, Series P60-184 (Washington, D.C.: U.S. Government Printing Office, 1993), table 30 (for earnings and number of earners) and table 26 (for most population numbers); U.S. Census Bureau, *Poverty in the United States, 1992* (for population age 18 to 24); National Center for Health Statistics, *Vital Statistics of the United States, 1989,* vol. II, section 6 (Washington, D.C.: Public Health Service, 1992), p. 11, table 6-2 (for number of survivors at single years of age, out of 100,000 persons born alive).

8. For our mid-range estimates, CDF discounted children's projected future earnings at an annual rate 3 percentage points above inflation. Alternate discount rates are explored below.

We also assumed that real economic output (as measured by per-capita gross domestic product) and real earnings and salaries will expand at a rate of about 1 percent annually. (The Bureau of Labor Statistics projects that GDP per worker will grow at an annual rate of 0.8 percent through 2005. See Norman C. Saunders, "The U.S. economy: framework for BLS projections," *Monthly Labor Review* 116, no. 11 (November 1993): 11-30, p. 28, table 10. Counting projected continuing increases in labor force participation would increase lifetime earnings by slightly more than 1 percent.) This implies that, in inflation-adjusted terms, general lifetime earnings will increase, which in turn will raise the dollar value of a 10 percent wage increase resulting from improved education.

Economists would describe these two steps more precisely with the following formula:

$$\sum_{n=22}^{64} \text{(Expected annual earnings at age n)} \times (1.01/1.03)^{n-22}$$

9. More precisely, our mid-range estimate is that one year of schooling will yield $54,771 in additional lifetime earnings for an average child, discounted to present value at 3 percent. The following table describes the sensitivity of this number to alternative assumptions about the discount rate and the advantage resulting from a year of schooling.

Real Discount Rate*

	2 percent	3 percent	5 percent
Total lifetime earnings	$663,124	$547,706	$387,958
Impact of an additional year of school:			
6 percent	$39,787	$32,862	$23,277
10 percent	66,312	54,771	38,796
14 percent	92,837	76,679	54,314

* All figures also assume there will be 1 percent annual general growth in earnings and output.

As the table shows, the range of values varies from $23,277 (which is about 42 percent of our mid-range estimate) assuming a 5 percent discount rate and a 6 percent return to schooling up to $92,837 (which is about 170 percent of our mid-range estimate) assuming a 2 percent discount rate and a 14 percent return to schooling.

It should be remembered that all of these estimates of the labor force impact of education are low, in that they consider only the impact on hourly wages. They leave out the impact of education on unemployment, underemployment, labor force participation, and longevity, all of which govern a person's lifetime work hours.

10. 0.045 additional years of education multiplied by an earnings increase of $54,800 per added year of education equals $2,466 in present value.

11. The extreme range of results based on Method 1 was $14.3 billion (assuming that each year of child poverty reduces schooling by 0.042 years, each year of schooling alters wages by 6 percent, and lifetime earnings of $813,000 are discounted at a rate that is 5 percentage points greater than inflation as shown in note 9 above) and $67.9 billion (assuming that each year of child poverty reduces schooling by 0.05 years, each year of schooling alters wages by 14 percent, and lifetime earnings are discounted at an inflation-adjusted rate of 2 percent). Each estimate assumes that earnings and worker output will grow at a rate of 1 percent throughout the economy.

12. See note 5 above for a complete list of factors held constant.

13. Two earlier studies indicate that each year a child spends in poverty decreases the likelihood of on-time high school completion by about 2 percentage points. Stephen Chaikind, "The Effects of Short-Term and Long-Term Poverty on Educational Attainment of Children," in Mary M. Kennedy and others, *Poverty, Achievement and the Distribution of Compensatory Education Services* (Washington: U.S. Department of Education, 1986), appendix D; summarized on p. 18 and in p. 19, table 2.1; Naomi Carol Goldstein, "Why Poverty is Bad for Children," dissertation, Harvard University, John F. Kennedy School of Government (January 1991).

Since Haveman, Wolfe, and Ginther, using similar data, estimate a considerably smaller effect on high school completion by ages 21 and older, it seems plausible that many of the youths who failed to graduate by ages 18 and 19 later got a diploma or, more likely, GED. It seems likely that these late completers would be less skilled, less productive, and less employable as a group than youths who finished high school on time; however, the effects of poverty on these youths' future earnings and output are not included in Method 1.

14. Charles D. Mallar, "The educational and labor-supply responses of young adults in experimental families," in H.W. Watts and A. Rees (eds.), *The New Jersey Income Maintenance Experiment,* Vol. II (New York, NY: Academic Press, 1977), p. 175.

15. A less conservative assumption would be that participants would receive 0.5 to 1.0 more years of education than the control group, the experiment-wide average. One relevant experimental group showed even stronger impacts: 1.12 years, or 3 times larger than the estimate we used. This group received the same guarantee of income at or above the poverty line, and a somewhat weaker work incentive (families could keep 30 percent of their earnings).

16. 0.37 years of education in a three-year program, divided by 3 (to yield the one-year impact), then multiplied by $54,800 (the estimated present value of one year of education calculated in Method 1), equals $6,759.

17. Estimates using Method 2 range from a low of $42 billion (based on a 6 percent return to education and lifetime

earnings discounted at a rate of 5 percent, as described in Method 1) to a high of $167 billion (based on a 14 percent return to education and lifetime earnings discounted at a rate of 2 percent, as described in Method 1).

18. The sample sizes were especially small within the eight specific plans that were being tested, making comparisons between plans difficult or impossible. This may explain why the researcher who studied the experiment found what he called an "anomalous" pattern in one analysis, which showed that the most generous of the eight plans actually reduced the children's school completion. Other data on the educational status of youths from the New Jersey experiment showed no negative effects of being enrolled in a more generous plan. Mallar, "The educational and labor supply responses...," p. 177.

19. Amy C. Butler, "The Effect of Welfare Guarantees on Children's Educational Attainment," *Social Science Research* 19 (1990):175-203.

20. Butler reports that the level of statistical significance is $p \leq .05$, meaning that there is at least a 95 percent estimated likelihood that the positive finding is genuine and not due to random variations in the sample.

21. Butler reports that the level of statistical significance is $p \leq .01$, meaning that there is at least a 99 percent estimated likelihood that the positive finding is genuine and not due to random variations in the sample.

22. CDF multiplied the increase in years of education (0.095) by the middle estimate of the value of a year of schooling from Method 1 ($54,800) to yield $5,206.

23. CDF multiplied the increase in years of education (0.157) by the mid-

dle estimate of the value of a year of schooling from Method 1 ($54,800) to yield $8,604.

24. This assumption reflects the fact that in FY 1977, about the middle of Butler's study period, 49.1 percent of children in previously married families were receiving AFDC in any given month. Calculated by the Children's Defense Fund, based on Social Security Administration, *1977 Recipient Characteristics Study—Part 1, Demographic and Program Statistics* (Washington, D.C.: U.S. Department of Health and Human Services, 1980), p.28, table 15; U.S. Census Bureau, *Household and Family Characteristics: March 1977,* Current Population Reports, Series P-20, no. 326 (Washington, D.C.: U.S. Government Printing Office, 1978), p. 102, table 12.

25. Since most previously married families were in fact probably married for some of their children's lives, and not receiving AFDC, this assumption is likely to overstate greatly the true AFDC costs incurred by the types of single-mother families Butler studied.

26. Multiplying the cost of the AFDC increase per month by the maximum amount of time a child with a previously married mother can be expected to receive AFDC yields ($100 x 0.491 x 12 months x 18 years) or $10,601.

27. The Bureau of Labor Statistics consumer price index for all urban consumers for 1992 was 140.3. For 1988 it was 118.3. Dividing 140.3 by 118.3 yields the factor by which prices increased between 1988 and 1992 (approximately 1.19). Multiplying $10,601 by this factor yields $12,572.

28. The average divorced, separated, or parent-deceased family on AFDC contained 2.21 children in FY 1991, the most recent available data. Calculated by the Children's Defense Fund, based on Office of Family Assistance, *Characteristics and Financial Circumstances of AFDC Recipients, FY 1991* (Washington, D.C.: U.S. Department of Health and Human Services, no date), tables 14 and 15.

29. Estimates using Method 3 range from $0.39 per dollar spent (based on Butler's lower estimate and assuming a 5 percent return to education) up to $2.56 per dollar spent (based on Butler's higher estimate and assuming a 2 percent discount rate and 14 percent return to education). All of these estimates assume a general economic growth rate of 1 percent, as shown in note 9.

30. Data collection for individuals in their sample started between age three and age 14, depending on the individual, and ceased between age 25 and age 34, depending on the individual. In the analysis, "childhood" consisted of at least three years of observations, from age 14 (or younger) to age 16. "Adulthood" consisted of at least one year of observations, at age 25 (and also included data for subsequent years if data was available).

31. One year is considered to be the same as one-eighteenth (or 5.56 percent) of a boy's total 18-year childhood. A one-year reduction of poverty therefore equals a reduction in poverty of 5.56 percent of his childhood.

Corcoran and Adams found that every percentage-point decline in the proportion of measured years during childhood spent in poverty was associated with a 0.00444 increase in the natural logarithm of annual earnings among the men in their sample. CDF calculated the effects of a one-year decline in poverty by assuming that this relationship applies to all 18 years of childhood, from ages 0 to 17. Conse-

quently, a one-year decline in the proportion of childhood years spent in poverty will be the same as a decline of 1/18, or 5.556 percent. Applying this to Corcoran and Adams' formula yields roughly 5.556 x 0.00444, or about 0.02467.

32. Specifically, Corcoran and Adams found that every percentage-point decline in the proportion of childhood years spent in poverty was associated with a 0.00294 increase in logged annual earnings among the women in their sample. CDF calculated the effects of a one-year decline in poverty by assuming that this relationship applies to all 18 years of childhood, from ages 0 to 17. Consequently, a one-year decline in the proportion of childhood years spent in poverty will be the same as a decline of 1/18, or 5.556 percent. Applying this to Corcoran and Adams' formula yields roughly 5.556 x 0.00294, or about 0.01633.

33. As explained in the notes to Method 1, CDF calculated lifetime earnings for men and women. For men, the present value of lifetime earnings is estimated to be $721,925 in 1992 dollars, using a 1992 earnings structure, a 3 percent real discount rate, and assuming 1 percent per capita general earnings growth. For women, the present value of lifetime earnings is estimated to be $373,487 in 1992 dollars, using the same assumptions.

For males, an increase of 2.5 percent in these lifetime earnings would be (0.025 x $721,925) = $18,048. For females, an increase of 1.65 percent in lifetime earnings would be (0.0165 x $373,487) = $6,163. Averaging together males and females, the impact on the average American child is estimated to be about $12,105.

34. For example, the proportional impact education on earnings tends to grow

larger as an individual gets older; therefore, the full impact of an inadequate education caused by poverty may not be felt until an individual is in his or her forties or fifties. Similarly, the full impact of a health condition acquired due to child poverty — such as asthma or infection by *Helicobacter pylori,* a bacterium that causes ulcers — may not appear in an individual's labor market performance for decades.

35. For each additional year a child spends growing up in poverty, the likelihood he or she will be behind modal grade by age 18 is between 1.56 percent and 1.59 percent greater, according to estimates published by the Department of Education in 1986. The estimates hold constant single parent families, race, mother's education, region, sex, and parental involvement in schooling. Stephen Chaikind, "The Effects of Short-Term and Long-Term Poverty on Educational Attainment of Children," in Mary M. Kennedy and others, *Poverty, Achievement, and the Distribution of Compensatory Education Services,* Interim Report from the National Assessment of Chapter 1 (Washington, D.C.: U.S. Department of Education, 1986), p. D-10, table 4.

If the chances of falling behind grade level increase by 1.56 percentage points for each of the 14,617,000 children younger than 18 in poverty in 1992, then 228,025 additional children will fall behind in school. If each of them repeats one year of public school at an average cost of $5,131, the cost will equal $1.2 billion. ($5,131 represents the average current cost of a year of public elementary and secondary education for all students in the 1992-1993 school year. National Center for Education Statistics, *The Condition of Education, 1993* (Washington, D.C.: U.S. Department of Education, 1993), p. 399, table 52-5.

In practice, not all of the estimated 228,025 children who fall behind grade level will repeat one year of public school. The data are imprecise for several reasons. First, the data show the number of children who are behind grade level rather than the number who had ever been kept back for one or more years in school; it is likely but not assured that the elevated proportion of poor children behind their modal grade level reflects the elevated proportion kept back. Second, some children will repeat more than one year of public school. Third, some children will drop out and never return to school (some of the costs to society of these individuals' lost years of schooling are included in the estimated impacts on the economy, earlier in the chapter). Fourth, some children will drop out but later receive a GED (their costs — in terms of lower skills, employability, and productivity relative to individuals who complete a regular high school education — are not considered elsewhere). Finally, a small number of individuals may repeat one or more years of private school.

36. Researchers have estimated that poor school-age children in 1988 were 2.4 to 2.7 percentage points more likely than their nonpoor peers to be enrolled in special education, holding constant single parent families, race, parent education, region and rural residence, sex, age, and birth weight. Stephen Chaikind and Hope Corman, "The impact of low birthweight on special education costs," *Journal of Health Economics* 10 (1991): 291-311, p. 300, table 3.

Multiplying 2.4 percent times the number of poor children age six to 15 in 1992 (7,411,000 according to unpublished U.S. Census Bureau data) yields 177,864 added special education students in 1988. The average additional cost of one year of special education in school year 1992-93 was $4,863 (based on figures from Chaikind and Corman and updating for inflation), or approximately $864,952,632 in 1992-93 dollars. Applying the same calculations to 2.7 percent instead of 2.4 percent yields $973,071,711. (For further explanation of these calculations, see Gail D. Pearson, "The Effect of Poverty on Special Education Costs," unpublished technical paper prepared for the Costs of Child Poverty Research Project (Washington, D.C.: Children's Defense Fund, 1994), available from CDF.

It is important to recognize that, while these costs are based on the excess special education enrollment of children who were poor at one point in time, many of these children were also poor in prior years. Therefore these costs may reflect the cumulative impact of several years of poverty, not just poverty experienced in 1988 itself. Eliminating these special education costs may require more than one year of antipoverty investments.

37. Estimated costs during adulthood of poor children's excess disabilities in 1992 were calculated based on the following method. The excess rate of "severe" activity limitation for low-income children younger than 18 was calculated as 0.6 percent (that is, the rate for low-income children was 0.6 percentage points higher than that for non-low-income children), based on National Health Interview Survey data for 1990, 1991, and 1992 (averaged together to improve reliability). The excess rate of activity limitations that were considered "major" but not "severe" was 2.8 percentage points. These excess rates were taken to represent the incidence of se-

vere and moderate childhood disability due to poverty.

These rates were applied to the official Census Bureau tally of 14,617,000 poor children younger than 18 in 1992, to yield estimates of the numbers of severely disabled (87,702) and moderately disabled (409,276) children whose disabilities were due to poverty. Half of severely disabled children were estimated to need institutional care from age 18 through age 44, based on previous research; the average cost for their care was assumed to be $21,226, based on estimates by the U.S. Office of Technology Assessment (adjusted for medical care inflation to 1992 dollars), yielding a total estimated annual cost of $933 million. The other half of severely disabled children, and all moderately disabled children, were estimated to have higher than normal medical expenses from age 18 through age 44; the average amounts of these costs were estimated, based on data from the 1980 National Medical Care Utilization and Expenditure Survey, and yielded to $129 million and $924 million, respectively, in 1992 dollars. All three amounts were added together, to yield $1.99 billion in excess medical costs of adult disability related to childhood poverty. This figure was multiplied by the estimated 26-year adult lifespan of the children from ages 18 to 44, to yield nearly $52 billion. Adjusting for indirect costs (loss of productivity) increased the estimate to nearly $74 billion. The estimates of lifetime costs were discounted to present value and allowance was made for the faster rate of inflation for medical care prices than for prices overall; these two operations balanced each other out and had no net effect on costs.

Detailed information on this estimate is available from Gail D. Pearson,

"Costs in Adulthood of Excess Morbidity Experienced by Poor Children," unpublished technical paper prepared for the Costs of Child Poverty Research Project (Washington, D.C.: Children's Defense Fund, 1994), available from CDF.

38. U.S. Census Bureau, *Statistical Abstract of the United States, 1993* (Washington, D.C.: U.S. Government Printing Office, 1993), p. 202, table 322.

39. "Cost of Crime: $674 Billion," *U.S. News and World Report* (January 17, 1994), p. 40.

40. On the other hand, there are practical limits on how much one can or should increase the minimum wage, enforce child support obligations, or create public sector jobs, and on how many poor children would be reached by these strategies.

41. We assumed the following groups would *not* take jobs: the elderly, those younger than 18, those with work-related disabilities, those who are already earning more per year than they would get in the new jobs, and single parents with children younger than three. (We made some exceptions for individuals who identified themselves as out of work because of a lack of child care: for example, a disabled person who was willing to work given adequate child care was considered a suitable candidate for a job.) All others were assumed to take jobs.

42. Several evaluations of work performed by public assistance recipients as a result of public sector "workfare" assignments, or in private-sector jobs, have found that the work performed is worth the wages paid. In the Supported Work demonstration, for example, evaluators found that the value of work done was worth the wages paid to recipients,
which were close to $7.00 per hour in 1992 dollars. Manpower Demonstration Research Corporation, *Summary and Findings of the National Supported Work Demonstration* (Cambridge, MA: Ballinger, 1980). Calculations by the Children's Defense Fund.

43. Many economists believe that increasing cash benefits for poor families would have work disincentive effects, as would raising taxes to pay for this assistance. However, there is little agreement about the expected size of such effects. Moreover, some economists recently have questioned whether such effects would occur at all, and suggest that in some situations employment levels might even increase as a result of raising revenue for certain antipoverty programs. For an estimate of employment disincentive costs equal to 20 cents per dollar transferred from upper income groups to lower income groups through an earned income tax credit, see Robert K. Triest, "The Efficiency Cost of Increased Progressivity," working paper #4535 (Cambridge, MA: National Bureau of Economic Research, 1993). For a range of estimates, including both net increases and net decreased in employment, see Charles L. Ballard and Don Fullerton, "Distortionary Taxes and the Provision of Public Goods," *Journal of Economic Perspectives* 6, no. 3 (Summer 1992):117-31.

Index

ABC Evening News, 41

Abuse: incidence of, and poverty, xxiv, 29, 35-36, 84-86; by mothers, 82

Accidents, motor vehicle, poverty and, 73

Achievement test scores, 79

Adams, Terry, 102, 112-113

Adolescence: aggressive and violent acts during, 90; preventing teen pregnancy and other problems of, xxvi

After-school programs, xxviii

Aggressive and violent acts, during adolescence, 90

Agriculture, U.S. Department of (USDA), 6, 51

Aid to Families with Dependent Children (AFDC), 3, 6, 51, 52, 68, 100; and future economic output, 109-112

Air conditioning, lack of, 22-23

Alcohol, increase in sales of, during recessions, 38. See also Drinking

Allergies: cockroaches and, 21; cold, dampness, mold, and, 20

American Psychological Association, 92; Violence and Youth, 38

Anemia, 15, 61-63, 64, 74

Anencephaly, 17

Asthma, 20, 23; cockroaches and, 21; hospitalization for, 75, 76; poverty and, 75-76; prevention barriers, 75; rats and mice and, 21

Attention Deficit and Hyperactivity Disorder (ADHD), 115

Ballou, Geneva, 77

Behavior problems, extreme, during childhood, 90-91, 92

Belting, Charles, 76

Birthweight, low, 64; disadvantaged backgrounds and, 56-57; poverty and, 67-69; special education and, 80; undernutrition during pregnancy and, 17

Blindness, partial or complete, 70

Brain damage, 41, 56, 80, 103, 115

Breakfast, effects of missing, on learning, 17

Breastfeeding, value of, 44

Bronfenbrenner, Urie, xxvii, 82

Business Week, xx

Butler, Amy C., 102, 109-112

Cancer, 22, 41, 64

Carnegie Council on Adolescent Development, 46-47

Cash assistance programs, xxviii, 93-96, 116-117

Census Bureau, 3, 4, 7, 67, 106, 116, 117; Marriage and Family Statistics Branch, 37, 83

Centers for Disease Control, 88

Chasnoff, Ira J., 68

Cherlin, Andrew, 83

Chicago, University of, 47-48, 55

Childbearing, unmarried, xxviii, 36-37

Child care, 8; expanding, xxviii; high quality, 54; inferior, 24-25; limited access to, 50

Childhood: deaths during, 65-67 (see also Infant mortality rates, Deaths); extreme behavior problems during, 90-91

Childproofing devices, 46

Children's Bureau, U.S., 64

Child safety seats, 46

Child support, xxviii, 83, 116

Cigarettes, see Smoking

Cleaning and repainting problems, in housing, 22-23

Cocaine, crack, exposure to, in womb, 68

Cockroaches, and allergies, 21

Cold, health problems caused by exposure to, 20

Colitis, 74

College: barriers to, 28-29, 83; completion, four-year, 84; enrolling in four-year, 84; enrolling in postsecondary education, 84; financial aid, 29

Computers, poverty limiting exposure to, 27-28

Conflict, see Stress, depression, and conflict, parental

Conger, Rand D., 33

Corcoran, Mary, 102, 112-113

Costs: of child poverty, xix, 99-101; of ending child poverty, 116-119; comparison of benefits and, 119

Crain, Larry, 8

Crime, 87-88; child abuse and, 35-36; costs of, 114-115; criminal records in adulthood, 92; high residential turnover and poverty leading to, 55; juvenile delinquency and warning signs of adult, 91-92; neighborhoods with high levels of, 39; other warning signs of later, 92-93; parental distress and, 30, 38; poverty and, 38, 55, 88-89; rates in poorer neighborhoods, 88-89; reduced fear of, in suburbs, 40; urban, 90; youth and adult theft rates, 89-90. See also Delinquency; Violence

Crowded housing: and childhood injuries, 55; stress and illness resulting from, 21-22

Cytomegalovirus, 71-72

Dampness: cockroach infestations and, 21; health problems caused by, 20

Deafness, partial or complete, 70

Death(s), 64; during childhood, 65-67; during infancy, 64-65; rate, children's, need for more research on,

96; as subject for school students, 39

Delinquency, 87-88; child abuse and, 35-36; high residential turnover and poverty leading to, 55; juvenile, and warning signs of adult crime, 91-92; parental distress and, 30. *See also* Crime; Violence

Dental health, financial barriers to, 44-45, 76, 77

Dental sealants, 44, 45

Depression, *see* Stress, depression, and conflict, parental

Devine, Joel, 89

Diarrhea, frequent, 74

Disabilities, 70-72; learning, 77; serious physical or mental, limiting daily activities, 70-71

Discipline, harsh and inconsistent, 31-32, 35

Distressed parents, *see* Stress, depression, and conflict, parental

Divorce, 36-37, 83

Drinking, heavy, 38, 46, 48

Dropouts, 26, 40; from high school, 81-83

Drug exposure, prenatal, and poverty, 68

Drug use, by parents, 30

Earned Income Credit, xxviii

Economy Food Plan, 6

Education, poverty's effect on, 78; attending college, 83-84; dropping out of high school, 81-83; falling behind grade level, 80-81; home and work responsibilities compete with, 28; learning disabilities and special education, 79-80; lower test scores, 78-79. *See also* Learning; Lifetime worker output

Education, U.S. Department of, 25, 28-29, 80, 82

Educational materials, poverty limiting, 27

Electrical problems, in housing, 19-20

Electrical safety plugs, 46

Emergency room visits, avoiding, 44

Emergency services, for poor families, xxviii

Externalizing symptoms, 33-34

Failure to thrive: child neglect and, 87; clinical malnutrition and, 15-16

Family support and preservation initiatives, xxviii

Fertility: decline in women's, 6; rates, evidence from randomized experiments on, 95

Financial strain, defined, 31

Fires: likelihood of poor children dying in, 52-53, 73; in mobile homes, 23; from space heaters, 20, 73; utility shut-offs and, 19, 20

Fire safety, smoke detectors and, 45

First aid, financial barriers to, 45

Fluoride, to prevent tooth decay, 44-45, 77

Folic acid, 17

Food, *see* Nutrition, Hunger

Food Research and Action Center, 15

Food stamps, 7, 14, 68, 100, 110; decline in value of, 6; savings from, 3, 118

Foster care, 100

Frank, Deborah A., 68

Gallup polling organization, 4

Garbarino, James, 86

General Accounting Office, U.S., 24, 42, 43, 50

Ginther, Donna, 102, 105

Gortmaker, Steven, 65

Grade level, falling behind, 80-81, 82, 114

Halfon, Neal, 75

Hanger, John, 19

Harvard University, 65

Haveman, Robert, 102, 105, 106

Headaches, 30

Head Start, xvii, xxv, 7, 116; expanding, xxviii; good quality care through, 24; inadequate funding of, 24

Health and Human Services, U.S. Department of, 115

Health care: costs of, for illnesses acquired due to child poverty, 114; financial barriers to, 42-43; lack of routine, 43; limited access to, 50

Health problems, poverty and, 64; deaths, 64-67; disabilities and sensory impairments, 70-72; low birthweight and stunted growth, 67-69; perceived health status and specific diseases, 73-77; school days missed due to illness, 77-78; serious injuries and poisoning, 72-73

Health Services, Department of (Kentucky), 64-65

Health status, perceived, and specific diseases, 73-74

Health supplies, financial barriers to, 45

Heating problems, in housing, 19-20

Helicobacter pylori, 22

Hernandez, Donald J., 37, 83

High school dropouts, 81-83

High school education: and barriers to college, 28; increase in number of mothers completing, 6

Homelessness, 18

Homicide, 88

Hospitalization: for asthma, 75, 76; for injuries, 72-73; for poisoning, 73

Hospitals, lower quality care at, 44

Housing, 18, 101; cleaning and repainting problems, 22-23; cockroaches and allergies, 21; cold, dampness, mold, and allergies, 20; crowded, 21-22, 55; fire-prone mobile homes, 23; heating and electrical problems, 19-20; and homelessness, 18; with leaks, 20; moving from house to house, 19; peeling paint and falling plaster, 21; quality, distractions, and distress, overall, 23; rats and mice, 21; residential turnover, 50; unaffordable and inadequate, 18-19; utility shut-offs and fires, 19, 20

Housing assistance, xxviii, 7, 110

Howard University College of Medicine, 75

Hunger, child, xxvii, 15

Illness, stress and, 38

Immunizations, delayed, 64, 86

Income: effect of lack of adequate, on poor children, xxiv, 11; family, and adolescent success, 84; important things bought by, 11-13

Indiana Youth Institute, 100

Infant mortality rates, 64-65; impact of joblessness/employment on, xxiv, 64, 65; poverty-related low birthweight and, 17

Inflation, failure of wages to keep pace with, 5

Injuries, childhood: crowded housing/limited supervision and, 55; days spent in bed because of, 72; fatal accidental, 73; hospitalization for, 72-73; overall, 72

Iowa, University of, School of Social Work, 109

Ipecac syrup, 44, 45

IQ tests, average, at age five, 78, 82

Iron deficiency, 14-15, 54-55, 61-63, 64, 74

Job Corps, xxv

Jobs: creation of private and public sector, xxviii; limited access to good, 51; opportunities for, in neighborhoods, 39-40

Johns Hopkins University, 64

Johnson, Samuel, 48

Joint Economic Committee of Congress, 89

Kennedy, John F., xv

Kennedy, Robert, xxvii

Lead poisoning, 21, 23, 41, 54-55, 64; brain damage from, 103, 115; as cost of child poverty, 115; legacy of, 80

Learning, poverty's effect on, 23; barriers to college, 28-29; fewer educational materials in home, 27; fewer stimulating activities, 27; greater home responsibilities that compete with school, 28; inferior child care, 24-25; inferior schools, 25; less exposure to computers, 27-28; opportunities for, in neighborhoods, 39-40; parental distress and children's, 34-35; unaffordable textbooks and school fees, 26-27. *See also* Education

Learning disabilities, 79

Learning problems, 23; poor nutrition and, 15

Learning-threatening ailments, 77

Lifetime worker output, child poverty's effect on, 101-105, 113, 119; Method 1, 102, 105-107; Method 2, 102, 107-108; Method 3, 102, 109-112; Method 4, 102, 112-113

Liver cirrhosis, 38

Louisville, Kentucky, *Courier-Journal*, xxv, 8, 78

Lung damage, 41

McLeod, Jane D., 33-34

McLoyd, Vonnie, 31-32

Mallar, Charles, 102

Malnutrition, xxvii, 8; clinical, and failure to thrive, 15-16. *See also* Nutrition

Malveaux, Floyd, 75

Mare, Robert D., 67

Marriage, poverty as threat to stability of, xxii, 36-37

Meals, missed, and interference in learning, 17

Medicaid, 7, 14, 42-43, 44, 50; and asthma, 76; and dental care, 76; and low-birthweight rate, 68; and special education, 80

Medical care, *see* Doctors; Health care; Hospitals

Medicare, xxix

Meningitis, bacterial, 64

Mental disabilities, serious, limiting daily activities, 70-71

Mental health: child, consequences of parental distress for, 31-33; parents', and unemployment and income loss, 30-31

Mental retardation, mild, 71-72

Michigan, University of, 31, 112

Migraines, 30

Minimum wage, raising, xxviii, 116

Mobile homes, fire-prone, 23

Mold and fungi, health problems caused by, 20

Money, *see* Income

Myths, about child poverty, xx-xxiv

National Academy of Sciences, 18, 25, 71, 72, 88; *Losing Generations*, 84, 90

National Fire Prevention Association (NFPA), 45, 73

National Health and Nutrition Examination Survey, 69

National Health Interview Survey (1988), 70, 74, 75, 79

National Incidence Study, 85, 86

National Institute of Justice, 35

National Longitudinal Survey of Youth, 69, 82

Neglect, 35-36, 84-85, 86-87; defined, 86-87

Neighborhoods, 38-39; crime and violence rates in poorer, 39, 88-89; noise levels in, 39; opportunities for learning and work in, 39-40; toxic chemicals and pollution in, 40-42

Newacheck, Paul, 75

New England Journal of Medicine, 63

New Jersey Income Maintenance Experiment data, 102, 107, 108

New York Times, 77

NFPA Journal, 73

Noise levels, in poor neighborhoods, 39

Nutrition, poor children's, 13-14; clinical malnutrition and failure to thrive, 15-16; hunger, xxvii, 15; iron deficiency, 14-15; missed meals, 17; moderate undernutrition, 16-17; stunted growth, 15; undernutrition during pregnancy, 17

Outcomes, pathways from poverty to adverse child, 11-13, 61-63, 103

Paint: dust, lead from old, 23, 115; peeling, dangers of, 21

Panel Study of Income Dynamics (PSID), 82, 102, 105, 107, 109, 112

Parenting education, xxviii

Pathways, from poverty to adverse child outcomes, 11-13, 61-63, 103

Pediatrics magazine, 68

Pell Grants, 7

Philadelphia Daily News, 3

Philadelphia Inquirer, 19

Physical disabilities, serious, limiting daily activities, 70-71

Plaster, falling, dangers of, 21

Pneumonia, 75

Poison control, financial barriers to, 45

Poisoning: hospitalization for, 73; as major poverty-related health problem, 52, 73

Pollitt, Ernesto, 16-17

Pollution, exposure to, in poor neighborhoods, 40-42

Post-traumatic stress syndrome, 39

Poverty: gap between poverty line and actual family income, 117-118; line, 3, 4, 8, 14, 116, 117, 118; official definition of, 3-4, 6-8; thresholds, 3-4

Pregnancy: and Medicaid, 42, 43; and mental retardation, 71-72; and smoking, 44, 48-49; substance abuse during, 38; teen, xxvi, xxviii; undernutrition during, 17

Prothrow-Stith, Deborah, *Deadly Consequences* (with M. Weissman), 88

PSID, *see* Panel Study of Income Dynamics

Racism, 63

Rand Corporation, 42

Randomized experiments, evidence on cash assistance, 93-96, 108

Recommended dietary allowance (RDA), 14

Recreation, 46; fewer recreational facilities, 46-48; limited access to, 50, 55; smoking and heavy drinking, 48-49

Respiratory problems, 20; rats and mice and, 21

Rheumatic fever, 64

Rios, Richard, 41

Roosevelt, Franklin Delano, xv

Rural child poverty, xxi, 5

Safety: devices, financial barriers to, 45; fire, smoke detectors and, 45; plugs, electrical, 46; seats, child, and childproofing devices, 46

Sampson, Robert J., 55

School days missed due to illness, 77-78

School enrollment, evidence from randomized experiments on, 94-95

School failure, defined, 81

School fees: unaffordable, 26-27; waivers for, 27

School performance, child's, financial security and, xxiv, 93-96

School quality, 41-42

Schools, inferior, 25

Seattle/Denver income maintenance experiment (SIME/DIME), 94-95

Senate, U.S., Committee on the Budget, 14

Sensory impairments, 70-72

Separation, marital, 36-37

Shanahan, Michael, 33-34

Shortness in children, *see* Stunted growth

Single-parent families, 51-52; effects of long-term poverty and, on children, 82-83; and rise in child poverty, 5

Smoke detectors, 45

Smoking, 38, 44, 46, 48-49

Social Security, xx, xxvii, xxix, 14

Social support, importance of, 36

Solow, Robert M., xviii

Space heaters, 20; fires from, 20, 73

Special education, 79-80, 114

Spina bifida, 17

Starfield, Barbara, 64

Starvation, 15-16

Steinberg, Laurence, 35

Stores, limited access to low-cost, 51-52

Stress, depression, and conflict, parental, effects on children of, 23, 29-30, 54; and arguments about money, 33; and child abuse and neglect, 35-36, 84-85; and children's learning, 34-35; consequences of, for child mental health, 33; and divorce, separation, and unmarried childbearing, 36-37; and future crime and violence, 38; and illness, 38; and importance of social support, 36; and initial shock of poverty, 33-34; and parents' substance abuse, 38; and unemployment and income loss, 30-31

Stunted growth, 15, 69

Substance abuse, stress and parents', 38, 84-85

Success, adolescent, and family income, 84

Sudden infant death syndrome, 65

Summer programs, xxviii

Supervision, limited, and childhood injuries, 55

Supplemental Security Income (SSI), xx, xxvii

Tamper, Justin, 14

Tamper, Mary, 14

Tamper, William, 14

Tax credit, refundable, xxviii

Telephone, lack of, 52

Temple University, 35

Test scores, lower, 82; achievement scores, 79; average IQ scores at age five, 78, 82; factors not contributing to, 79

Textbooks, unaffordable, 26

Theft rates, youth and adult, 89-90

Thrifty Food Plan, 6-8

Time magazine, 5

Tonsillitis, repeated, 75

Toxic chemicals, exposure to, in poor neighborhoods, 40-42

Transportation, poverty and, 49; lack of car, 49-50; limited access to child care, recreation, health care, and other services, 50; limited access to good jobs, 51; limited access to low-cost stores, 51-52; limited public transportation, 50

Tulane University, 89

Ulcers, 22

Undernutrition, 16; moderate, effects of, 16-17; during pregnancy, 17

Unemployment, 103; and income loss, parents' mental health and, 30-31; rate and crime rate, 89; smoking and, 48

Urban child poverty, xxi, 5

Utility shut-offs, and fires, 19, 20

Victimization, poverty and, 88

Violence, 87-88; acts of, and aggression during adolescence, 90; inequality and, 38; neighborhood, 31; other warning signs of later, 92-93; parents' distress and, 38; rates in poorer neighborhoods, 88-89; study

of intergenerational, 35-36. *See also* Crime; Delinquency

Wages, failure of, to keep pace with inflation, 5

Waivers, for school fees, 27

Washington Post, The, 19, 35, 75

Weissman, Michael, 88

Welfare, xxi, 14; income from work vs., 5; reform, xxi, xxviii. *See also* Aid to Families with Dependent Children

Wells, Sandy, 5

Williams, David, 48

Wisconsin, University of, 105

Wolfe, Barbara, 102, 105, 106

Women, Infants, and Children (WIC), Special Supplemental Food Program for, 14

Work, *see* Jobs

Zuckerman, Barry, 68